Validity and Rhetoric in Philosophical Argument

An Outlook in Transition

Henry W. Johnstone, Jr.

The Dialogue Press of Man & World: Publishers
University Park, Pa.

Published by,
The Dialogue Press of Man & World, Inc.
Offices: 246 Sparks Bldg.
University Park, Pa. 16802

©1978 by The Dialogue Press
All rights reserved
Printed in the United States of America

ISBN:
Library of Congress
Catalog Card Number: 78-17394

```
Johnstone, Henry W.
   Validity and rhetoric in philosophical argument.

   Bibliography: p.
   Includes index.
   1. Reasoning.  2.  Philosophy.  3.  Rhetoric.
I.  Title.
BC177.J63      160               78-17394
```

For
Bill Miller
and
Larry Beals
Colleagues at
Williams College

Acknowledgments

I am grateful to the following publishers for permission to reprint the material indicated. In each case I am the author.

The Journal of Philosophy. "Philosophy and Argumentum ad Hominem." 49 (1952): 489-498.

The Pennsylvania State University Press. "Persuasion and Validity in Philosophy." Chapter 9 of Philosophy, Rhetoric, and Argumentation. 1965.

The Bucknell Review. "Can Philosophical Arguments Be Valid?" 11 (1963): 89-98.

The Monist. "Self-Refutation and Validity." 48 (1964): 467-485.

The Quarterly Journal of Speech. "The Relevance of Rhetoric to Philosophy and of Philosophy to Rhetoric." 52 (1966): 41-46. "Rationality and Rhetoric in Philosophy." 59 (1973): 381-389.

Revue Internationale de Philosophie. "Argumentation and Inconsistency." 15 (1961): 353-365.
" 'Philosophy and Argumentum ad Hominem' Revisited." 24 (1970): 107-116.
"Truth, Communication, and Rhetoric in Philosophy." 23 (1969): 404-409.

State University of New York Press. "Rhetoric and Communication in Philosophy." In Perspectives in Education, Religion, and the Arts, pp. 351-364. 1970.

Philosophy and Phenomenological Research. "A New Theory of Philosophical Argumentation." 15 (1954): 244-252.

The Review of Metaphysics. "New Outlooks on Controversy." 12 (1958): 57-67.

Man and World. Review of The New Rhetoric: A Treatise on Argumentation, by Ch. Perelman and L. Olbrechts-Tyteca. 4 (1971): 224-229.

Logique et Analyse. "Some Reflections on Argumentation." 6 (1963): 30-39.

Kantstudien. "Controversy and the Self." 58 (1967): 22-32.

The final essay in this book, "The Philosophical Basis of Rhetoric," was my contribution to a symposium on rhetoric at Marquette University in June 1967. The essay has never been published in its entirety before, although parts of it appear as Chapter 9 of my book The Problem of the Self (University Park, Pa., The Pennsylvania State University Press, 1970).

CONTENTS

I.
Introduction

This book begins with an attempt to write my way into a certain topic, and ends with several attempts to write my way out of a different but related topic.

Twenty-five years ago I felt that I needed to write something to clarify, for myself at least, the nature of philosophical argument. This feeling had developed as the result of my encounters with those who became my colleagues when I took my first teaching job at Williams College in 1948. I came to Williams from the graduate philosophy program at Harvard. This was at the time a very "tough-minded" program, and as a result of my total immersion in it for several years I was not only deeply committed to empiricism but also under the impression that any philosopher in his right mind would be committed to it. But at Williams I quickly discovered that my colleagues were not empiricists. They were in fact adherents to a position that I thought had long since been decisively refuted; to wit, absolute idealism. They read Hegel long after Hegel — as I had been led to believe — had been consigned to the museum of philosophical aberrations and curiosities. Even worse, they seemed to have no appreciation of the advances that had been made by modern empiricism. They wanted to discuss problems that I thought had long since been solved. In short, my new colleagues seemed to me to be anachronisms and quacks.

So I set about to refute them. As an empiricist, I relied primarily upon the strategy of Hume: I demanded that my interlocutors produce the sense-impressions from which were derived the ideas they claimed to have. I found, however, that instead of retreating in confusion, they began to ask me questions about sense-impressions that I could not readily answer. Once I had declared that sense-impressions were qualities, there was nothing more I seemed to be able to say. A quality implies nothing. Indeed, this very fact is central to Hume's use of the doctrine of impressions to attack the claim that there is causal efficacy. For if an alleged cause is nothing but a quality, it implies nothing. But if a quality implies nothing, there is not even any way to point to it. It is an occult entity. "Qualities tell no stories," my Williams colleagues were fond of saying. When I protested that a quality can at least be characterized as what I am experiencing here and now, they suggested that I read the first section of Hegel's *Phenomenology of Mind*, which, of course, displays "here" and "now" as mere abstractions.

Then they proceeded to tell me how the very notion that there are qualities had arisen. Qualities are markers of difference. Red is the quality that enables us to distinguish this book from that one. Unless there were a need to make distinctions, there would be no qualities. But of course the things that we need to distinguish cannot themselves all be qualities.

In the end, my colleagues showed me that empiricism itself was a historical phenomenon. It had arisen from certain intellectual needs. In turn it had given rise to others, including the need to give a coherent account of qualities, as might well be accomplished in some position superseding empiricism. To say, however, that empiricism is a historical phenomenon is to say that it has a place in history. And this was much more than I had originally been willing to concede with respect to my colleagues' idealism. I had approached that idealism convinced that it had no place in history, certain that it was mere-

1

ly an aberration, a gratuitous step backward into error and bemusedness. My colleagues were exhibiting the plausibility of the claims of my position, while I was repudiating the claims of theirs. They were being generous; I was not.

I have told only part of the story. None of my attempts at refutation was successful. Much more important, however, was my realization, after a painful period during which it was nearly impossible for me to carry forward any intellectual project at all, that I had been caught up in the very idealism that had once seemed so easy to refute.

With this realization came the need to reflect on the etiology of the deep change in my philosophical position. Somehow, my colleagues had argued me into idealism. I wanted to understand the power of their arguments. My reflections took the form of my early writings on philosophical argumentation, including the first few in this book. These writings were not confined to discussions of arguments in favor of idealism; I considered philosophical arguments of all sorts. At the same time, they were necessarily idealistic writings about philosophical argumentation, for it was clear that the very arguments that had persuaded me to become an idealist were idealistic arguments. The thesis, for example, that philosophical positions have a place in history, and that the claims and flaws of such positions can be exhibited as moments in a historical process, is itself an idealistic thesis. It may be contrasted, by way of illustration, with the empiricistic thesis that philosophical positions are meaningful if they can be traced back to Humean impressions, and otherwise are meaningless aberrations. For some reason, however, few readers other than my Williams colleagues seem to have noticed the idealistic character of my writings on philosophical argumentation. They have not seemed to be aware, for example, that when I said that I thought that philosophical arguments were *sui generis* — not to be judged by the standards of argumentation in science and everyday discourse — I was expressing much the same idea that can be expressed by saying that Hegelian dialectic is not to be judged by the standards of argumentation in science and everyday discourse.

That early writing is what I meant by "an attempt to write my way into a topic" — the topic being, of course, that of philosophical argumentation. I turn now to the "attempts to write my way out of a different topic." This topic is rhetoric.

The story of my attempts to extricate myself from rhetoric does not involve the *Angst*, the desperation, of the story I have just told. It begins with the second paper in this book, "Persuasion and Validity in Philosophy." Here, in the course of developing my theory of philosophical argumentation, I depict rhetoric in the worst possible light. This paper appeared in print after I had moved from Williams College to Penn State. Robert T. Oliver, then Chairman of the Speech Department at Penn State, thereupon decided that I must be interested in rhetoric. Perhaps he thought that anyone who could vilify it to the extent to which I had must be interested in it — that if he scratched my hate he could find love. Or maybe he simply wanted to use the venerable and usually successful pedagogical technique that consists in making a pupil aware of the enormity of his prejudices merely by confronting him with them. It has always been difficult, if not impossible, to guess the motives of this wise man. In any event, through the succeeding years Oliver saw to it that there were many occasions on which I had to express myself further on the nature of rhetoric. I spoke several times at meetings of the Speech Association of America, and again to a Symposium on Philosophy and Rhetoric that Oliver had arranged at Penn State. I was involved in collaborative arrangements with visiting professors of Speech and Philosophy. I became editor of the journal *Philosophy and Rhetoric*. Even after Oliver retired, I could sense his continuing presence as a guiding spirit.

I did come to see that my earliest characterization of rhetoric, even though seemingly called for by the view of philosophical argument I took, had been impetuous and unfair. My later utterances on the subject have amounted to a succession of modifications and softenings of that characterization. These changes have by now gone as far as they can go, I think, unless their direction should at some later time be reversed. My present position on the nature of rhetoric and its role in philosophical argumentation is just about the opposite of my earliest one. The process through which I have reached it is what I mean by "attempts to write my way out of a topic." I am by no means certain, however, that I have *succeeded* in writing my way out of rhetoric. Perhaps I shall never complete the task that Oliver assigned me.

It is not only my view of the nature of rhetoric that has undergone change in the past quarter-century. I have also changed my mind about philosophical argumentation viewed apart from the role of rhetoric in it. Some of the changes have come about as efforts to meet a deep and persistent problem present in my position from the beginning, which may conveniently be called "The Consistency Problem." In the Epilogue I will comment on this problem, but readers of the intervening papers, beginning with "Argumentation and Inconsistency," will already be able to see what that name refers to. My responses to the Consistency Problem have included both efforts to solve it and efforts to sidestep it. I do not have the feeling that I have as yet written my way out of that problem.

This book is an attempt to illustrate the remarks I have made about the changes in my outlook over the past quarter of a century. The illustration consists of the papers that follow. They are not in every case in strict chronological sequence, but are arranged with a view to the evolution of themes. Thus there are several series of articles, not altogether distinguishable from one another. One series deals with the idea of validity in philosophical argumentation, another with the place of rhetoric in philosophy and in life in general. A third series treats of the nature of the self as considered from the point of view of argumentation and rhetoric. A fourth discusses views lying exterior to the transitions in my own outlook. One constant, or near-constant, for example, during the period of upheaval in my own theory of philosophical argumentation, has been the steady-state theory of Chaim Perelman and Lucie Olbrechts-Tyteca. In this book I have included some observations of mine made in various decades about their theory. I hope that these observations will serve somehow as benchmarks of my own development.

The Epilogue is an effort of self-analysis. Here I trace the changes in my own theories of argumentation and rhetoric, and try to detect causes and presuppositions that were not evident to me at the time. In this project I am very much indebted to students who have taken the interdisciplinary course on "Philosophy and Rhetoric" that I have given three times in collaboration with Carroll C. Arnold. And naturally I am very much indebted to Arnold himself.

Other friends whose help has been of great value have been Kathy Harbert, Donald Verene, and Boyd Ready.

II.
Philosophy and *Argumentum ad Hominem*

One of the commonest arguments against the naturalistic view of knowledge is that if fails to make its own assertion and defense intelligible. For, as a recent version of this argument points out, "In thus deriving mind and knowledge from nature, as science conceives it," the naturalist

> must assume that his own account of nature is true. But on his premises, the truth of this account, like that of any other bit of knowledge, is merely the function of the adjustment of the organism to its environment, and thus has no more significance than any other adjustment. Its sole value is its survival value. This entire conception of knowledge refutes itself and is, therefore, *widersinnig*.[1]

This criticism characteristically evokes one of two replies. The first is a chuckle. This is the reaction of the naturalist who regards such argumentation as innocent dialectical sport, like the conversations in *Through the Looking-Glass*. The second is a cautionary wag of the finger, intended to remind us of the stratification of types in logical theory.[2] If the statement, "All knowledge, including this, is merely the function of the adjustment of the organism to its environment," is paradoxical, this is surely because the critic has failed to see that "this knowledge" belongs to a higher type than "all knowledge." This obvious proviso is supposed to render the naturalistic theory invulnerable to the criticism in question.

To the chuckle we need not reply. It is the response of the unreflective man when confronted with any reflective analysis, and in fact represents his adjustment to an intellectual environment rather than a responsible argument. The logical admonishment, however, deserves an answer. Let us begin by noting that in general, there are only two reasons for distinguishing among types. One is to avoid logical contradictions, and the other is to represent real differences in scope or abstractness among propositions.

Now the first of these valid motives for citing the theory of types cannot, in the present instance, exist. For the paradox in question — the sense in which the naturalistic position is *widersinnig* — is not logical. The proposition that knowledge of the truth of naturalism has a naturalistic explanation is not formally inconsistent. Indeed, there are occasions when a useful purpose is served by the utterance of such a proposition. To the biographer, for example, it may be of importance to show that a certain naturalistic philosopher adopted his views as a mode of adjustment to his environment.

But this very example suggests the force of the argument we are examining. To explain in naturalistic terms the beliefs of the naturalist, or of the philosopher of any other persuasion, is to discredit those beliefs. It is essential to the philosopher to claim responsibility for his own statements, to come to his own conclusions, to criticize without external constraint, to be governed by ideas rather than by inarticulate forces. Even when he is most aware of the

---

[1]Wilbur Marshall Urban, *Beyond Realism and Idealism* (London: Allen and Unwin, 1949), p. 236.

[2]No one specific version of type-theory is, of course, intended either here or in the sequel. Indeed, the criticism to be developed here would apply, *mutatis mutandis*, to a defense based upon the assumption of a hierarchy of languages as well as of types.

effect of environment upon thought, his expression of this effect must involve a self-control not wholly to be accounted for in terms of environment. No attack upon a philosopher is more devastating than the statement, "Your beliefs are merely the function of your adjustment to your environment," whether his environment be physical, physiological, social, economic, literary, or academic.

Thus the defender of a thoroughgoing naturalistic view of knowledge is, in effect, saying, "I am not responsible for my own statements." This is a paradox. But since it differs only by a personal pronoun from the non-paradoxical statement, "You are not responsible for your own statements," whose importance has just been indicated, this cannot be the type of paradox arising from a confusion of types. What it does arise from is the predicament of the speaker. He cannot express his lack of responsibility while at the same time maintaining the responsibility of his expression. But only he is in this predicament; those who attack him are not.

The type of paradox which besets the thoroughgoing naturalist has been called "pragmatic." In general, a pragmatic paradox is a proposition whose credibility is undercut by the act of uttering it. For the utterance has implications which the proposition itself does not. To utter, "I never use correct English," I must use correct English. But the fact that I must is not implied by the proposition itself. Similarly, the proposition that I am not responsible for my own statements does not in itself imply that I am; only its utterance does. This feature of pragmatic paradoxes serves once again to distinguish them from antinomies engendered by the confusion of types; for the proposition, "The class of all classes which are not members of themselves is not a member of itself," does imply its own contradictory, whether it is uttered or not.[3]

The defender of the naturalistic view of knowledge may agree that the paradox exposed by the argument against naturalism which we are considering is not logical. But he may still insist on the observation of a hierarchy of types. The knowledge that all knowledge is the function of the adjustment of the organism to its environment is not itself such a function, but belongs to a higher type, he may say. The distinction can be indicated by subscripts; I have knowledge$_2$ that all knowledge$_1$ represents adjustment. Phrased in this language, the paradox in question seems to disappear; for I need only assert that I am responsible$_1$ for the statement that I am not responsible$_2$ for my own statements.

[3] I have been helped in coming to conclusions about pragmatic paradoxes by discussions in *Mind* by D. J. O'Connor (Vol. 57, 1948, 358-59, and Vol. 60, 1951, 536-38), and L. J. Cohen (Vol. 59, 1950, 58-87); also by correspondence with Professor C. I. Lewis. Paul Weiss discusses such paradoxical situations in *Man's Freedom* (New Haven: Yale University Press, 1950), p. 212. In "Cosmic Necessities," *The Review of Metaphysics*, IV (1951), Weiss says, "An existential absurdity is not intrinsically impossible. It expresses a conceivable state of affairs. It is not self-contradictory. It can appear; it can be entertained, believed, asserted. It is absurd because its existence or meaning denies what is required in order that it be or have a meaning. It is absurd because it denies the possibility of its own occurrence" (359).

In *The Intelligible World* (London: Allen and Unwin, 1929), Urban gives further reasons why a paradox of this sort is not strictly logical. See especially pp. 45-46.

But can the distinction between knowledge$_1$ and knowledge$_2$ ultimately be maintained? Where knowledge$_1$ is not philosophical, it can; for the two types of knowledge will possess characteristics through which they can be identified and ordered from a point of view neutral to both. Thus, I know$_2$ that my knowledge$_1$ of the land-areas of the continents arises from the latest almanac. In such a case, my knowledge$_2$ is the theory of my knowledge$_1$, and is distinguishable from it by virtue of being more general and of answering to a different procedure of verification.

In the case in question, however, knowledge of the lower type must include philosophical as well as non-philosophical judgments. For surely philosophy is not exempted from the generalization that all knowledge represents the adjustment of the organism to its environment; indeed, the intent of this generalization has usually been specifically to contravene the claim of philosophy to be independent of environment. But here it is difficult to see how the distinction between the two types is meaningful. By what mark can the naturalist distinguish his philosophical knowledge$_1$ from his philosophical knowledge$_2$, other than by his mere wish to withhold from knowledge$_2$ the criticism which he applies to knowledge$_1$? For in principle, there is no difference either in generality or in verifiability between the naturalistic theory of knowledge and the other philosophical theories it "explains."

While non-philosophical knowledge must be distinguished from the theory of that knowledge, there is no corresponding distinction between philosophical knowledge and its theory; for there is no theory of philosophy which is not itself philosophy. So far, only the view that philosophy is a function of adjustment has been considered. Other theories might be cited, on which philosophy is identified as a function of psychology, sociology, logic, language, or world-spirit. But in each case the identification is itself a philosophical point of view, in principle having no characteristics through which it would unerringly be perceived by a neutral observer to belong to a higher type than the philosophies it claims to subsume. Who, for example, can ascertain whether "All philosophy is a function of language" is higher in type than "All philosophy is a function of psychology" without himself being committed to one of these views?[4]

Since philosophical statements cannot essentially be distinguished as to scope or abstractness, the second reason for distinguishing among types does not apply to them.[5] We must conclude that the theory of types has no relevance to arguments such as the attack upon naturalism at present in question.

Our criticism of the naturalistic theory of knowledge was that this did not permit its own responsible utterance. Let us call a philosophy which does permit its own responsible utterance "self-referential." The principle of the polemic we are examining may then be called "refutation by self-reference," or more simply, "self-referential refutation." Many philosophical positions have been attacked by this self-referential criticism. Among them we may in-

[4]Compare Paul Weiss, "The Theory of Types," *Mind,* 37 (1928), 338-48, *passim.*
[5]A clear statement of the view under attack is to be found in Whitehead and Russell, *Principia Mathematica* (Cambridge: University Press, 2d ed., 1925), Vol. I, 38.

stance Scepticism,[6] Behaviorism,[7] Pragmatism,[8] Intuitionism,[9] The Coherence Theory,[10] views which attack Idealism,[11] and views which oppose Utilitarianism.[12] But this represents only a random selection.

A preliminary word may be said in favor of the self-referential type of argument. This is that it is often used by a person to criticize himself.[13] "Do I meet my own standards?" one may ask. And no one thinks that this self-criticism is in any sense "unfair." But if it is not "unfair" for one person, it is difficult to see how the mere introduction of a second party could *make* it unfair.

But the validity of self-referential refutation, and its appeal or force, still require examination. For even those who are willing to admit that this argument violates no canon of type-theory may condemn it as a *non sequitur*. To conclude the falsity of a position merely from the predicament of its advocate is, it will be said, only an *argumentum ad hominem*.

It will not be our purpose to deny that the polemic of self-reference is an *argumentum ad hominem*. Instead, we shall attempt to distinguish a valid employment of this device from its customary invalid uses. We shall try to show not only that self-referential refutation exemplifies this valid use, but also that many other types of philosophical argumentation belong to the same category, and indeed that no genuine *argumentum ad rem* is available for philosophical controversy.[14]

For a good preliminary definition of a fallacy identified by traditional logic, one can do no better than to refer to an older handbook, such as that of Whately. "In the '*argumentum ad hominem*,' " Whately states, "the conclusion which actually is established, is not the absolute and general one in question, but relative and particular; viz., not that 'such and such is the fact,' but that '*this man* is bound to admit it, in conformity to his principles of reasoning, or consistency with his own conduct, situation,' &c."[15]

Now self-referential polemic does seek to establish what a man is bound to admit, in conformity to his principles of reasoning or situation. The naturalistic account of knowledge implies that the philosopher, like all men, is in a situation in which his knowledge is a function of his adjustment to his environment. And the self-referential refutation of that account simply calls attention to that situation. It supposes that the naturalist is now bound to admit that his naturalism is itself a result of adjustment.

---

[6]See Urban, *The Intelligible World,* pp. 45-46.
[7]See Lovejoy, "The Paradox of the Thinking Behaviorist," *Philosophical Review,* 31 (1922), 142-47.
[8]See Royce, "The Eternal and the Practical," Ibid., 13 (1904), especially 128-29.
[9]See Hocking, *Types of Philosophy* (New York: Charles Scribner's Sons, 1939), p. 201.
[10]See Spaulding, *The New Rationalism* (New York: Henry Holt and Company, 1918), pp. 350-51.
[11]See Royce, *Lectures on Modern Idealism* (New Haven: Yale University Press, 1919), pp. 237-40.
[12]See Bentham, *An Introduction to the Principles of Morals and Legislation* (Oxford: Clarendon Press, 1876), chap. I, secs. 13-14.
[13]Compare Max Black, *Critical Thinking* (New York: Prentice-Hall, 1946), p. 216.
[14]I find my opinion corroborated in general in the two books by Urban which I have already cited, and by F. B. Fitch in "Self-Reference in Philosophy," *Mind,* 55 (1946), 64-73.
[15]Richard Whately, *Elements of Logic* (New York: William Jackson, 1838), p. 196.

Let us compare this use of *argumentum ad hominem* with an obviously fallacious application of it. To an opponent who defends suicide, says Schopenhauer in *The Art of Controversy*,[16] "you may at once exclaim, 'Why don't you hang yourself?' Should he maintain that Berlin is an unpleasant place to live, you may say, 'Why don't you leave by the first train?' Some such claptrap is always possible."

Why is this "claptrap"? Only because the principle of reasoning or situation to which the refuter calls attention is one in which his opponent has no essential stake. The distaste for Berlin may be only an idiosyncrasy. Or if it is a consistent motive, it may not be an ultimate one. Most men identify themselves with a purpose which takes precedence over geographical considerations; perhaps such a purpose irresistibly detains this man in a Berlin which he nevertheless finds unpleasant. Similarly, he who argues for suicide is not likely to feel an undeniable urge for self-destruction; he will represent it as contingent upon conditions, like sacrifice or *Weltschmerz*, which he may not regard as at all relevant to himself.

Suppose, however, that one's respondent does in fact feel an unconditional obligation to leave Berlin or to do away with himself. The force of the argumentation ironically suggested by Schopenhauer can only be to confirm such a feeling. And the man who asserts that he is essentially bound to leave Berlin, and yet fails to leave it, is in a position of fundamental confusion. No logical canon is violated by a critic insofar as he merely points out this confusion.

Borrowing the terminology of Kant, but not necessarily his conclusions, we may say that *argumentum ad hominem* is invalid when the principle to which it calls attention is intended only as a hypothetical imperative. The resident of Berlin who says "Leave Berlin!" cannot properly be accused of confusion if what he really means is "Leave Berlin if you want to preserve your health." For he may be prepared to take the consequences of continued residence. The only valid method of attacking such a principle is *argumentum ad rem:* one might, for example, adduce evidence that living in Berlin is not necessarily injurious to health.

But where a principle proposed as a *categorical* imperative is violated or disregarded by its proponent, it can only be circumspect to point this out. If a deliberate liar should say, "Never tell lies," then at the very minimum this would mean that the command has come from a confused mind — one unable to identify an act as falling under a rule it has itself proposed. In addition, suspicion may properly fall upon the command itself. For there would appear to be a viewpoint from which it both ought to apply to all cases and need not apply to them. But to point out such confusion it is only necessary to show what "*this man* is bound to admit, . . . in conformity to his principles of reasoning or consistency with his own conduct [or] situation." *Argumentum ad hominem* is therefore valid in exposing confusion with respect to a categorical imperative. Nor is any *argumentum ad rem* available for attacking an imperative of this sort. For if an obligation is truly unconditional, it is conditional upon no fact. "Even if it should happen that, owing . . . to the niggardly

---

[16]Trans. Bailey Saunders (London: Swan Sonnenschein & Co., 1896), p. 28.

provision of a step-motherly nature [a good] will should wholly lack power to accomplish its purpose," Kant asserted, ". . . like a jewel, it would still shine by its own light. . . ."

Now if there is any respect in which the philosopher has a fundamental stake in his viewpoint, or in which he intends that viewpoint as a categorical imperative, *argumentum ad hominem* will in that respect be a valid polemical device. And the following considerations should make clear what fundamental stake the philosopher does have in his own philosophy.

Any genuinely philosophical view is perfectly general. To restrict it to statements about any specifiable class of individuals or entities is to reduce it to the special theory of that class. Thus the study of man is philosophy, and so is the study of time. But the study of man in America is sociology or anthropology, and the study of the seventeenth century is history.

To the extent, therefore, that the philosopher characterizes human nature and the categories of human thought, he must be characterizing his own nature and thought. On pain of exclusion from the philosophical enterprise altogether, he must suppose that his assertions reveal what is essential to him as well as to other men. In proposing that his view be adopted he is in effect stating a categorical imperative ("Interpret the world in this particular way!"). Not only is this a rule from which he cannot make himself an exception, as he would if he thought he could interpret *himself* in some privileged way, but also he may accept this rule for no ulterior reason. For such a reason, if authoritative, would suggest that some men are fundamentally motivated in ways not envisaged by the philosophy in question. The philosopher who asserts that all men are basically motivated by a need for adjustment takes an incoherent position if he supposes that *he* can be basically motivated by a need for truth.

Yet philosophers have frequently attempted to exempt themselves from their own outlooks. A case in point would be the naturalist to whom we have referred as an example. His viewpoint represents a fundamental confusion. And the propriety of arguing *ad hominem* in order to call attention to such confusion has already been indicated. We can only conclude that this is a context in which the use of *argumentum ad hominem* to attack philosophy is valid.

Having established that *argumentum ad hominem* is formally valid in certain restricted contexts, let us consider its appeal or persuasive force within these contexts. For while the naturalist may confess that his position is confused, he may deny that he is under any obligation to mitigate the confusion. Perhaps he will aver that it is just because such confusion seems characteristic of metaphysics that he prefers to speak only the language of science.

In this case we can remind him that the confusion is still there, and that his argumentation, like any, is cogent only in a universe of discourse free from confusion; the price of confusion is failure to maintain the conditions of controversy. This is in itself an *argumentum ad hominem*; it elicits the secondary confusion of supposing that a primary confusion can be intelligibly admitted. More fundamentally, we can point out that when the confused mind is pitted against the clear one, the presumption is with the latter and the burden of proof is on the former. Indeed, only the latter can prove anything.

Not only ought confusion to be shunned in itself, but also the confused mind can make no appeal to the clear one. On the other hand, the clear mind can exploit the inconsistencies of the confused one. The force of this exploitation is to invite the latter to abandon ambiguity and incoherence. But it is likely to be objected that the occasions of this valid use of *argumentum ad hominem* are far too restricted for this type of argument to serve as a general device of philosophical polemic. One may perhaps in this manner impugn the qualifications of an occasional slipshod philosopher. But philosophical controversy does not concern the qualifications of particular philosophers; it has to do rather with the merits of philosophical points of view, considered without regard for their authors.

The reply here hinges on the intelligibility of the proposition that a philosophy might be true even though all of its proponents had been refuted. For if one proponent can be refuted by *argumentum ad hominem,* all can. While this does have a purely personal force, the ingredient of personality to which it appeals in the attack we are now considering is precisely that identified with the philosophical point of view in question. And even though each proponent staunchly maintains that he is not affected by the polemic addressed to his principles, yet there is an obvious sense, just now clarified, in which he *ought* to admit defeat. The obligation is simply that of the confused mind confronted by the clear one.

To all intents and purposes, then, *argumentum ad hominem* operates as an objective argument against a philosophy, as well as a means of discrediting its witnesses. So the polemic of self-reference is not invalidated by the use of this argument. And since it is not, any philosophy not permitting its own responsible utterance can be refuted. From this there follows a general desideratum of philosophy, as well as a first principle of polemic. The desideratum is to be self-referential. The principle is to attempt to attack alien philosophies by showing that on their own principles they are unintelligible.

The question suggests itself whether there can be any genuine *argumentum ad rem* against a philosophical point of view. Three considerations, perhaps not independent of one another, but brought out at different points of this essay, have the force of a negative reply. In the first place, to the extent that a philosophy functions as a categorical imperative, it is conditional upon no fact. In the second place, philosophical views cannot be arranged according to any unquestionable order of types. Propositions asserting facts or hypotheses, on the other hand, can be so arranged; indeed, they must be, if logical paradoxes are to be avoided. A philosophy does not, therefore, assert a fact or hypothesis, and so cannot be supported by any appeal *ad rem.* Finally, the significance of asserting that a philosophy ought to be *self*-referential is to imply that its validity depends on no reference to a fact or situation *external* to it.

In the absence of any valid *argumentum ad rem* we must suppose that all philosophical polemic, not just that of self-reference, is, in essence, addressed *ad hominem.* And, in fact, the one feature common and peculiar to effective argumentation in philosophy is that it takes seriously the point of view it sets out to overthrow. In the scope of this essay, however, it would be hopeless to attempt to document this thesis. Perhaps we can do no better than to refer in conclusion to some of the more common principles, other than the one we have examined, which govern effective philosophical argumentation. A close relative of self-referential refutation is the *tu quoque* argument, which consists in pointing out that one's opponent has committed an error of which he ac-cuses others. And another argument belonging to the same family is the charge that in applying a certain term to the whole of a region, the philosopher under attack has undercut the very distinction between the term and its contraries which makes its application significant. (If all men are basical-ly selfish, how can we distinguish selfish from unselfish behavior in the first place?) Self-reference and these two related polemical principles are of fun-damental importance in attacking monisms.

One may attack a dualism, on the other hand, by showing that its proponent cannot, in his own terms, maintain the distinction regarded as fun-damental. And in general, one may refute principles by pointing out that they are arbitrary, or occult. That this is not an *argumentum ad rem* is indicated by the consideration that while it is no criticism of astronomy to assert that nine is an arbitrary number of planets or of electronics to point out that electrons are occult, to bring these charges against the seven deadly sins and material sub-stance, respectively, seems relevant. Above all, a philosophical position may be refuted by showing that it is inconsistent. This, like all the other principles just mentioned, is purely and simply an *argumentum ad hominem*. "In the game of disputation," says Joseph, "we may be held to score a victory if we force an op-ponent to an admission inconsistent with the thesis he propounded. But in the search for truth, to convict any one of inconsistency is irrelevant; we have to determine what is true."[17] Instead, we are content to let our criticism dwell only upon the *statement* of a point of view. Even the realist, who of all philosophers will feel most shocked and affronted by this repudiation of *argumentum ad rem*, possesses much paraphernalia for detecting fallacies,[18] but no instruments for observing facts. It is in this respect that philosophy in general parts ways with descriptive discourse.

---

[17]H.W.B. Joseph, *An Introduction to Logic* (Oxford: Clarendon Press, 1916), p. 591, n. 2.

[18]See, for example, Holt et al., *The New Realism* (New York: The Macmillan Com-pany, 1912), pp. 11-21.

III.
Persuasion and Validity in Philosophy

It has often been asserted that philosophical statements are non-cognitive — that they do not convey genuine knowledge. With this assertion I am inclined, for various reasons, to agree. But I do not agree with a conclusion that is sometimes drawn from the assertion that philosophical statements are noncognitive. This is the conclusion that there can be no valid arguments supporting philosophical statements. It is certainly not obvious, I admit, that valid argumentation could yield a noncognitive conclusion. Of course, a formally valid argument with at least one noncognitive premise could have a noncognitive conclusion; this is shown, for example, by recent work on the Logic of Imperatives.[1] But this observation is not to the point. Those who deny that noncognitive philosophical statements can be the conclusions of valid arguments are not thinking of validity in a purely formal sense. What they have in mind is rather the notion of a valid argument as one leading to a necessary conclusion — a conclusion, in other words, which, in view of the argument, it is obligatory to accept. Now the existence of an obligation to accept a statement seems to create a presumption that what the statement expresses is an item of knowledge. There has been a strong tendency to suppose that the conclusion of any argument valid in this sense must be cognitive, from which it would follow that no noncognitive statement could be the conclusion of a valid argument.

But the contention that all the arguments employed by philosophers to reach noncognitive conclusions are invalid seems to require some further explanation. Is it through sheer naïveté that the philosopher uses invalid arguments? While this interpretation may hold in certain cases, it fails to do justice to the fact that some philosophers obviously capable of distinguishing valid from invalid arguments have argued for conclusions that would surely be noncognitive if any philosophical statements are. Leibniz, for example, who stated that "All is for the best in this best of possible worlds," was one of the keenest logicians of all times. Perhaps, then, the philosopher uses invalid arguments for the same reason that the scientist does; namely, because philosophical arguments to noncognitive conclusions are inductive, and no inductive argument could be, strictly speaking, valid. A moment's reflection, however, serves to show that the arguments in question are not inductive. For inductive arguments must surely have cognitive conclusions. There is finally the possibility that the philosopher deliberately uses invalid arguments in the effort to persuade — that his ulterior motives for seeing to it that certain noncognitive philosophical statements are accepted are sufficiently strong, in other words, to drive him to provide rationalizations for these statements, genuine reasons being unavailable. This explanation is itself persuasive, and needs to be reviewed with considerable care.

The view that the philosopher who argues to a noncognitive conclusion is aiming to persuade his audience to accept it, even though he may know perfectly well that the argument is invalid, might seem to raise questions about the candor of such a philosopher. Yet if there are no valid arguments to

---

[1] See R.M. Hare, *The Language of Morals.*

noncognitive conclusions, he is surely not attempting to do dishonestly what other people are capable of doing honestly. In resorting to persuasion, furthermore, he may be performing a function vital to the maintenance of society, since it is not valid but persuasive arguments, whether valid or not, that evoke action. The choice that faces the philosopher is not between valid and invalid argumentation, but between argumentation that serves a social purpose and argumentation that does not. Under these circumstances, it is altogether unrealistic to accuse the philosopher of failing to be candid.

One may be tempted to dismiss this view by simply saying that not all philosophical arguments leading to noncognitive conclusions are intended to evoke action. But this reply might well invite the retort that the philosopher who is not concerned with action is not attending to his proper business. It is perhaps better to answer in terms of a closer examination of the actual properties of philosophical arguments in general, in the hope that this will serve not only to distinguish the use of such arguments from the use of arguments intended to persuade but also to contribute to a positive account of validity in the case of the former.

I shall begin by remarking that it is commonly supposed that anyone who makes a philosophical statement is under some obligation to respond to the criticisms of those to whom the statement is addressed. The philosopher unwilling to discuss his own explicit philosophical statements with others inevitably invites questions regarding his right to be considered a philosopher. He need not, of course, reply to all criticisms or questions. But associated with any philosophical statement is a class of criticisms and questions more or less relevant to the statement, and with these he must deal. His critic is naturally under a similar obligation.

The obligation that I am pointing to here is no more than an aspect of the disorientation produced by a philosophical statement or question uttered out of any argumentative context. What appears to an observer as the phenomenological incompleteness of such a statement appears both to its propounder and to its critics as an ethical incompleteness — as a promise that he must now attempt to fulfill. The discussion to which this promise commits him has, within his point of view, the same function as the genetic story that the observer wants to be told: both are required in order to mitigate what is essentially the same incompleteness. The argument for a philosophical statement — that is, the attempt to support it — is to the résumé of events leading to the statement — the argument for it in another sense — as inner is to outer.

The situation described so far, however, might not appear to differ essentially from the conditions that give rise to argumentation primarily intended to persuade. The man who wishes to persuade usually cannot hope to do so merely by making a statement. He, too, must fulfill whatever promise is implicit in his having made the statement. Unless he is regarded as a prophet, he must be willing to discuss it with others and defend it against their objections. Not every objection will be relevant, but there will be a class of possible relevant objections.

It is important to notice, however, that in discussing his position, the philosopher is not satisfying a requirement of exactly the same sort as the requirement that is satisfied when the man who intends to persuade is willing to discuss what he has to say. The latter must support his views because if he does not, he is not likely to be very effective in persuading, owing to the fact that statements ordinarily have less persuasive impact in isolation than they do in an argumentative context. In addition, his audience may be disappointed by his failure to keep the promise that his utterance seemed to imply. The philosopher, on the other hand, must discuss *his* position, not in order to achieve effectiveness, but simply because he has accepted the obligation to undertake the discussion promised by his initial statement, regardless of the consequences of this discussion.

But even if the persuasive speaker — I use the word "speaker" as an obvious abbreviation for "speaker or writer" — were obligated to discuss his assertions for the same reasons that account for the philosopher's obligation, there would remain essential differences between the persuasive speaker's *method* of discussion and the philosopher's method. The aim of the merely persuasive speaker is to secure adherence to his point of view. This aim is difficult to achieve in the measure that his audience is aware that he is trying to achieve it. To the extent that the rhetorical techniques used by a speaker are recognized by his audience, that audience is alienated or left unmoved rather than persuaded. There are no doubt many individuals who enjoy surrendering themselves to a powerful speaker. But once the technical sources of the speaker's power become evident, this surrender loses its enchantment. Such sources of power are, of course, capable of being appreciated as techniques. But to appreciate the artistry of a rhetorical technique and to be persuaded by that technique are two different things. The point is not merely that people want, or think that they want, to be told the truth rather than to be managed. As a psychological generalization, this observation is in fact open to serious doubts. The point is rather that it is impossible to be persuaded by a technical device at the same time that one sees it as merely a device. This is true even if on occasion a persuasive speaker may explicitly avow his intention to persuade his audience, and even call the attention of the latter to the rhetorical devices that he uses. For such a performance could itself be an effective technique of persuasion, provided that it were not recognized as a technique. Rhetoric is perfect only when it perfectly conceals its own use. To be assured of effectiveness, a speaker must operate unilaterally upon his audience, and at the same time prevent it from seeing that he is operating unilaterally.

None of these considerations, however, would seem to affect the way in which the philosopher must conduct the defense or clarification of his position. No philosopher worthy of the name would wish to secure assent to his position through techniques concealed from his audience. One reason for this is that it would be impossible for him to evaluate such assent philosophically. Did his interlocutor really understand his position or not? In the situation in which the use of rhetoric is in order, this question is, of course, pointless; so long as the interlocutor *acts* in the required fashion, the rhetorical argument has been effective. But it is philosophically important to know whether one's interlocutor did understand one's position or not, if only because the problem of comparing the implicit content of two explicitly similar avowals is always relevant to a philosophical discussion.

It is not only for this reason that the philosopher attempts to avoid the use of unilateral techniques of argumentation. Another reason is that he wishes to test his assertions against the criticism of his colleagues. He naturally wants his point of view to prevail. But no philosophical purpose is served when a point of view prevails only because its author has silenced criticism of it through the use of techniques that are effective because they are concealed from the critics.

It is perhaps tempting to suppose that the whole point might be put much more briefly by simply saying that the philosopher is obligated to tell the truth. Yet while this is perhaps suggestive of the distinction I am trying to draw between the philosopher and the persuasive speaker, it is not sufficient. For the latter may intend to do no more than to carry out the obligation to tell the truth. But the kind of truth that he wishes to tell requires him to consider various ways of telling it, some more persuasive than others. The kind of truth the philosopher wishes to tell, on the other hand, is rendered less rather than more acceptable when persuasive ways of telling it are deliberately chosen. It is acceptable only to the extent that telling it is tantamount to putting it to the test critically.

The philosopher's method of discussion is thus one that avoids the use of unilateral techniques. It is, in fact, essentially a bilateral method, in the sense that the philosopher is obligated not only not to conceal from his audience any of the techniques he uses in arguing, but also to make available to it all the techniques that he does use. For if he is unwilling to submit to the very arguments he uses against others, he thereby shows that it is not criticism but persuasion that interests him. In itself, of course, this consideration is not sufficient to distinguish philosophical from rhetorical argumentation. For a unilateral appeal to emotions, to authority, to laughter, or to force does not become a philosophical discussion merely as the result of becoming bilateral, as, for example, when A, who has been ridiculed by B, ridicules B in return. Such a discussion is at best an alternation of assaults which each participant would like the exclusive right to indulge in, because he sees that his own advantage is diminished by his opponent's use of the same technique. The philosopher, on the other hand, sees that there is an advantage in the adoption of his techniques by others, because that adoption constitutes an authorization of his use of them. Conversely, each new mode of criticism to which he is willing to submit increases the arsenal of criticisms that he can in turn make use of.

Having drawn a number of distinctions between philosophical arguments and arguments intended to persuade, I want to return to the topic of validity. Let us recall that those who deny that a philosophical argument can be valid if its conclusion is noncognitive are not denying that such an argument could be *formally* valid. What they are denying is rather that it could ever be obligatory to accept the conclusion of such an argument, in view of the argument. Now I have already tried to show that the philosopher is obligated to discuss his views. But the obligation to discuss could scarcely exist unless the philosopher were also obligated to accept the *results* of the discussion. One cannot at one and the same time suppose both that the parties to a discussion are obligated to be parties thereto, and that they are also free at any time to ignore what has been said during the course of the discussion. From this I conclude that it can be obligatory for someone to accept the conclusion of a philosophical argument, in view of the argument; and thus not only that a valid philosophical argument is possible, but also that this possibility exists whether the conclusion of such an argument is regarded as cognitive or noncognitive.

Although it is my view that the philosopher is under a general obligation to embark upon discussion, I do not wish to suggest that there are any specific conclusions that he is obligated to accept. Any discussion that he pursues will surely depend, at least partly, upon the point of view that he is defending and upon his interlocutors' criticisms of it. The obligation to accept one conclusion rather than another will arise from the discussion itself.

There may still be something puzzling about the idea of a valid argument to a noncognitive conclusion. When an argument establishes the obligation to accept its conclusion, how can that conclusion fail to be cognitive? But the notion of a valid argument as one leading to a conclusion which, in view of the argument, it is obligatory to accept does not specify whether the obligation to accept the latter is imposed on everyone or just on certain individuals. If the obligation is imposed on everyone, the conclusion is clearly cognitive, which is equivalent to saying that if the conclusion is noncognitive, the obligation is not imposed on everyone.[2] In particular, if, as I have attempted to show on in-dependent grounds, all philosophical conclusions are noncognitive, then not everyone can be obligated to accept any such conclusion. Whenever a philosophical argument is valid, some individuals, but not all, are obligated to accept its conclusion.

If there is any residual difficulty, it lies in the idea of a conclusion that some, but not all, are obligated to accept. But there should be no mystery about this. Few indeed are the obligations that are imposed on everyone. Most obligations arise from commitments made by specific individuals, or by groups of them, and are not imposed upon those who have not made the relevant commitments. A promise is a common example of such a commitment. If in uttering a philosophical statement an individual has implicitly made a promise, then he, but not necessarily everyone, is obligated to keep that promise. He will find that as a result of his initial commitment, he must accept conclusions that not everyone need accept.

An example of what I am trying to say — one of a great many that might equally well have been chosen — is the discussion between Socrates and Thrasymachus in Plato's *Republic*. Having asserted that justice is the interest of the stronger, Thrasymachus asks why his audience does not praise him. Now such applause might indeed have been appropriate if this assertion had been regarded as the utterance of a somewhat prophetic orator. But it is not so regarded, at least by Socrates. Before praising Thrasymachus, he must first un-derstand him. The questions he begins forthwith to raise serve to remind Thrasymachus that he must now fulfill the obligation of clarifying and defending his assertion. Nor is Thrasymachus unwilling to be reminded. Once

---

[2]The converse of this statement is sometimes assumed: to wit, "If not everyone is obligated to accept a certain conclusion, the latter must be noncognitive." Thus ex-amples putatively showing that the obligation to accept certain statements (e.g., "Killing is wrong.") is effective only for certain cultures or at certain periods of history may be ad-duced in the effort to show that such statements are noncognitive. This reasoning, however, seems inconclusive, because there are many cognitive statements that no one is obligated to accept; namely, those whose truth has not yet been established.

Socrates' queries begin, Thrasymachus is no longer an orator seeking praise but a philosopher trying to keep a promise. There are times when he attempts to revert to a rhetorical role — accusing Socrates, for instance, of being a slanderer. But further references to his obligation to maintain his end of the discussion are sufficient to force him back to a philosophical level. Having undertaken the discussion, he has no right to abandon it. He must, furthermore, accept the results of the discussion, including, for example, the distinction between the strict and the popular sense of the word "ruler." Also, the obligation to accept this conclusion and certain others is imposed not on everyone, but on Thrasymachus and perhaps on some others who take a position similar to his. It is not, for example, imposed on those who participate in discussions in which it would be entirely pointless to introduce this distinction. Nor is it imposed on anyone who departs from the premise or assumption that it makes no sense to talk about the ideal practitioner of an art, as opposed to the actual practitioner. Socrates and Thrasymachus, on the other hand, hold in common the view that this kind of talk does make sense, and since it is a kind of talk directly related to the thesis that justice is the interest of the stronger, the distinction in question is far from pointless for them. This may be put positively by saying that they are under an obligation to consider the distinction, thus that the argument through which they are led to it is valid. But the question whether this argument is *formally* valid simply does not arise. The fact that Thrasymachus, having asserted that justice is the interest of the stronger, must, in view of his assumption that it makes sense to talk about the ideal practitioner of an art, go on to distinguish between the strict and the popular sense of the word "ruler" (an obligation surely not imposed on everyone) has nothing to do with the *form* of the argument here employed. To analyze this form would be beside the point.

One other idea that receives especially solid exemplification in the same passage is that philosophical discussions are bilateral. It is only because Socrates has compared the ruler to a shepherd that Thrasymachus is entitled to do so. Thrasymachus leaves no doubt that he is gratified by this unexpected authorization to use what he considers to be a devastating analogy.

The view that a valid philosophical argument obligates some individuals, but not all, to accept its conclusion serves as a reminder of the existence of genuine philosophical disagreement. It implies that any philosophical statement must be a source of disagreement between those obligated to accept it and those not so obligated. Such disagreement is radical, in the sense that it cannot be overcome through compromise. When two or more arguments lead to incompatible conclusions, compromise can be achieved only by correcting at least some of the arguments in such a way as to remove the incompatibility. But when all the arguments in question are valid, they are not subject to correction at all, so that no compromise is forthcoming.

The character of philosophical disagreement is further suggested by some remarks regarding the role of disagreement in rhetoric. Persuasive argumentation is pointless unless there is an initial disagreement that it aims to overcome. But it is impossible unless it can make use of beliefs, attitudes, prejudices, or explicit premises adopted by its audience. These constitute an initial area of agreement, in the sense that if the speaker appeals to them, the audience will not protest. There is no reason, however, why the speaker

himself need espouse such beliefs, attitudes, prejudices, or premises; it is sufficient for him to be able to rely on his audience's espousal of them. Regardless
of whether the speaker shares the preconceptions of his audience, and
regardless of whether he actually believes in the conclusion he is attempting to
promote, it is always possible, in principle, to regard him as uncommitted; for
the actual commitments of the speaker do not enter into the analysis of his
rhetorical success. (Of course, if his audience thinks that his actual commitments are incompatible with the conclusion he is advocating, his success
will be diminished; but we can still analyze this situation without referring to
the speaker's actual commitments as such.) From the point of view of the
analysis of persuasion, the role of the speaker is to treat his audience as an object. He must begin by assessing as accurately as possible the initial area of
agreement. He must then consider how best to exploit this preliminary
situation in order to persuade his audience to accept the statements he wants it
to accept — statements with which it is not yet in agreement. His task is to
manipulate his audience so as to secure agreement. All relevant disagreements
must be overcome. Furthermore, the attempt to overcome disagreement must
itself be concealed. For the audience will wish to reserve the right to disagree
with the speaker and is likely to react in an adverse fashion if it feels that he is
ignoring this right. This phenomenon is probably closely related to the impossibility of persuading through a technique that is seen as a mere technique.

   The wish of an audience to reserve the right to disagree with the speaker
addressing it may be viewed as a desire on its part to come to its own conclusions. It is just such spontaneity, however, that the speaker must suppress,
or at least restrict, if he is to perform his role of manipulating his audience. Yet
he must always create the illusion that he is inviting the latter to come to its
own conclusions; for if he does not, it will exercise a residual spontaneity of
judgment, lying inevitably beyond his control, to reach the conclusion that its
right to reach its own conclusions is being threatened. One may think of this
reaction as a process through which an audience in turn comes to regard the
speaker addressing it as an object whose harmful properties are well known
but can be rendered ineffective by means of equally well-known precautions.
This seems an appropriate fate for the speaker who has too bluntly attempted
to deal with his audience as an object.

   In the rhetorical situation, then, disagreement exists only to be overcome
through the exploitation of an initial agreement, and the desire of an audience
to reach its own conclusions must be circumvented. In philosophical discussions, on the other hand, whether there is an initial agreement or not, it
cannot be exploited to overcome disagreement, since the latter is radical, permitting no compromise. What must be exploited is just the desire of each participant to reach his own conclusions. A conclusion has no philosophical use if
it is not reached freely. To be philosophically useful, it must represent the unconstrained attempt on the part of its advocate to fulfill his obligation to
defend and clarify his position. Thus philosophical discussion is, in effect, a
collaborative effort to maintain the conditions under which disagreement is
possible. If it has arisen from an initial disagreement engendered by valid
arguments to incompatible conclusions, it can proceed only by inviting further
valid arguments from its participants, because it is precisely by employing valid
arguments that each participant achieves the perfect exercise of his right to

reach his own conclusions. This account may suggest a kind of monadism of philosophical positions — a plurality of positions, each obeying its own inner law of development but wholly incapable of interacting with the others. In fact, however, it contains the germ of what I want to say about the ways in which philosophical positions do interact. Interaction of this type, which is appropriately referred to as "philosophical controversy," is possible only because philosophical discussion, in order to maintain itself, must *exploit* the desire of each participant to reach his own conclusions, and must *invite* him to argue validly. When the motive to maintain the discussion is lacking, philosophical positions do, in fact, tend to become monadistically isolated from each other; and this isolation owes itself to the radical nature of their disagreements with each other. When this motive is present, on the other hand, the disagreements are no less radical, but it is possible for the partisan of one position to invite a partisan of another to develop through unconstrained argument the consequences of a statement the latter has made. Since such consequences may prove to be an unexpected source of embarrassment to the individual who develops them, it is an effective technique of philosophical controversy to invite one's opponent to come to his own conclusions. Indeed, in the absence of the possibility of compromise, it is the only effective technique.

The success of the rhetorical speaker will depend upon the extent to which there are beliefs, attitudes, prejudices, or premises constituting an initial area of agreement on the part of his audience. Thus the speaker whose audience is most uniform in membership is likely to have the greatest chance of success. The audience of rhetoric is therefore essentially limited. It is unlikely that there are any statements that mankind as a whole could be persuaded to accept, because it is unlikely that there is any area of agreement to which all men would subscribe. The view has been taken, however, that there are arguments addressed to mankind as a whole; to wit, the ones employed by the philosopher.[3] Such a view has the same source as the view of philosophical argumentation that I have been taking in this chapter: both arise from the feeling that the arguments employed by the philosopher are somehow different from those the persuasive speaker employs. But here, I think, the similarity ends. There are, in my opinion, two basic difficulties with the view that philosophical arguments are addressed to mankind as a whole. First, it has not been made clear how mankind as a whole could constitute an audience or what the philosopher could be intending to accomplish by addressing such an audience. According to the authors who take the view in question, the audience that the philosopher addresses has, in the last analysis, only an ideal existence: "We invent a model of man — the incarnation of reason . . . which we seek to convince, and which varies with our knowledge of other men, or other civilizations, or other systems of thought, with what we take to be incontrovertible facts or objective truths."[4] If certain individuals remain unmoved by his solicitations, the philosopher's only recourse is to regard them as

---

[3] See Ch. Perelman and L. Olbrechts-Tyteca, *Rhétorique et philosophie* and *Traité de l'Argumentation.*
[4] *Rhétorique et philosophie*, p. 22.

irrational and thus as excluded from the ideal audience that he supposes himself to be addressing. In so doing, he substitutes the idea of an elite audience for that of a universal one. We seem to be left with the tautology that the philosopher addresses the audience that he addresses. But this has no tendency to show that the audience which the philosopher does address is mankind as a whole. Nor does it clearly indicate what transaction the philosopher is undertaking with his audience. What does it mean to "convince" a model that one has invented?

The second difficulty is that the radical nature of philosophical disagreement seems to diminish the force of the contention that the arguments of philosophers are addressed to a universal audience. If disagreement plays a fundamental role in philosophical argument, as I think it does, then the audience of such argument, like the audience of rhetorical argument, must be limited. What distinguishes one limited audience of philosophical argumentation from another is the impossibility of resolving the issues between the two audiences by compromise. In this situation, the arguments effective against one audience would seem pointless to the other. It would appear that no philosophical arguments addressed to mankind as a whole could be effective. This again raises a question about the point of saying that they are so addressed.

It has been objected that my characterization of philosophical argumentation emphasizes criticism or polemic, and that if I had paid proper attention to arguments of a constructive type, my results would have been compatible with the contention that the latter are addressed to a universal audience.[5] Now I admit the importance of the distinction between critical and constructive philosophical argumentation. Nevertheless, throughout this chapter what I have been attempting to characterize is philosophical discussion in general, whether critical or constructive in intent. I have tried to exhibit such discussion as the response to an obligation to amplify and defend. I see no reason why such a response would necessarily be confined either to criticism or to constructive elaboration. Both activities are appropriate to an obligation of the sort that I have in mind. Nor is there any reason why constructive arguments should, any less than critical arguments, constitute an effort to maintain the conditions of disagreement — an effort, that is, to invite the audience to reach its own conclusions. A constructive conclusion to which an audience acquiesces merely because it has been persuaded to do so is as philosophically useless as a critical conclusion reached under the same circumstances.

There is, nonetheless, an appealing quality in the idea that philosophical arguments are addressed to a universal audience. For this is a way of recapitulating the agelong theme that philosophy is fundamentally an exercise of reason. I do not take exception to this theme. I want only to raise the question whether reason must involve universality in the way it has usually been supposed to. There may be truths reached by reasoning that are equally acceptable to all rational beings. But if such truths exist, they are entirely without content. My view, however, is that the results of philosophical reasoning have content. Hence reason in its philosophical use cannot be universal.

[5]See Ch. Perelman, "Reply to Henry W. Johnstone, Jr.," *Philosophy and Phenomenological Research*, 16 (1955), 245-47.

IV.
Can Philosophical Arguments Be Valid?

Because Friedrich Waismann's position on philosophical argument is now fairly common, I shall launch my discussion from it. In "How I See Philosophy,"[1] Waismann argues that there are no proofs in philosophy, since, as he says, "Proofs require premises. Whenever such premises have been set up in the past, even tentatively, the discussion at once challenged them and shifted to a deeper level."[2] The so-called "teleological proof" is one of a myriad of illustrations that Waismann might have used. The premises of this "proof" raise doubts as soon as they are explicitly stated. In a seductive metaphor Waismann says that ordinary language, which he takes to be the medium of philosophy, "simply has not got the 'hardness,' the logical hardness, to cut axioms in it. It needs something like a metallic substance to carve a deductive system out of it such as Euclid's. But common speech? If you begin to draw inferences, it soon begins to go 'soft' and fluffs up somewhere. You may as well carve cameos on a cheese soufflé."[3]

Later I am going to contend that the difference between philosophy and mathematics is not, in fact, one of the hardness of the medium. For the moment, however, I want to indicate what Waismann thinks the philosopher gains by arguing, if his arguments prove nothing. What the philosopher does instead of proving, he says, is to *build up a case.* "First, he makes you see all the weaknesses, disadvantages, shortcomings of a position; he brings to light inconsistencies in it or points out how unnatural some of the ideas underlying the whole theory are by pushing them to their furthest consequences; and this he does with the strongest weapons in his arsenal, reduction to absurdity and infinite regress. On the other hand, he offers you a new way of looking at things not exposed to those objections. In other words, he submits to you, like a barrister, all the facts of his case, and you are in the position of the judge. You go over them carefully, go into the details, weigh the pros and cons and arrive at a verdict."[4] Even though such a procedure is not deductive, Waismann argues that it can still be rational.

No doubt the activity of building up a case or choosing on the basis of a case that has been built up can be rational. Certainly the barrister and the judge engage in reasoning. But when we call philosophy a rational activity, we have something more in mind than reasoning of this kind. The crucial difference between case-building and philosophy is that although the rightness of the choice of anything for which a case has been built up can be analyzed in independence of the considerations in terms of which the choice was made, the rightness of the choice of a philosophical position cannot be so analyzed. Let me develop this difference.

1

Not only the barrister but also the salesman and the politician must build

---

[1] "How I See Philosophy," in *Contemporary British Philosophy*, 3d. sers., ed. H.D. Lewis (London, 1956), reprinted in *Logical Positivism*, ed. A.J. Ayer (Glencoe, Illinois, 1959), pp. 345-80.
[2] Ibid., p. 346.
[3] Ibid., p. 366.
[4] Ibid., pp. 372-73.

up a case. The politician brings out inconsistencies in the point of view of his opponent and offers the audience a new way of looking at things; the audience then decides. Similarly, the prospective buyer weighs the pros and cons and then buys. But it is conceivable that the buyer or voter could make the right decision on the basis of fallacious arguments addressed to him. The product might have the merits ascribed to it, and competing products might have the disadvantages imputed to them, even though the arguments used by the salesman were altogether deceptive. The program advocated by the politician might turn out to be the most fruitful even though irresponsibly advocated. In both cases, what would be meant by calling the choice right could be explained without referring to the considerations in terms of which the choice was made.

The rightness of the choice of a philosophical position, on the other hand, cannot be analyzed in independence of the considerations in terms of which the choice was made. The person whom the philosopher addresses can make the right choice only if he makes it for the right reasons. It does not make sense to speak of stumbling onto the right philosophical choice by accident or through a misunderstanding of the arguments in favor of the position. A position chosen in such a way might be said to have been adopted on faith, but it would then no longer count as a philosophical position. Of course I am using the term "arguments" broadly. Any responsible discourse aimed at justifying a philosophical position would be an argument in my sense.

When the arguments in favor of a philosophical position or against its rivals are shown to be invalid, all that the philosopher advocating the position can do is to cast about for better arguments. He cannot, like the salesman in whom we lack confidence, be content to wait for vindication until the merit of the product appears in its own right, for the merit of the position he advocates never will appear except as the conclusion of an argument. Once the merit of a product appears in its own right, of course, the statement that it does appear will constitute a further argument for it, and a valid one. But there is no way in which the merit of a philosophical position can appear except as already explicitly supported by an argument.

My point is that when we are confronted with a choice of philosophical positions, the choice could not be right unless the arguments bringing about the choice were valid, whereas choices of other kinds can be right even when the arguments are invalid. My objection to Waismann's description of the philosopher as a man who builds up a case is that this description does not seem to take account of the difference I have in mind. Indeed, it seems clear that Waismann does not suppose that, except in rare instances,[5] philosophical arguments can be valid at all.

The temptation to ask what Waismann thinks he is doing in his entire essay is irresistible. Is he just building up a case? Or is he trying to tell us something about the nature of philosophy? If the former, will he be satisfied merely to win our assent to his account, regardless of our reasons for assenting, as the barrister is content to win the assent of the judge?

Indeed, the very notion of a man's setting out to win assent to a philosophical position regardless of his audience's reasons for assenting is odd.

[5] Ibid., p. 374.

Assent to the solicitations of a salesman or a political orator has a specific kind of action as its correlate, and it is to secure the action, not merely the assent, that the persuader persuades. The defense lawyer who has just succeeded in getting his client acquitted does not ordinarily pause to consider whether the jury reached the verdict for the right reasons. Even the evangelical preacher aims at securing action rather than assent as such, and so is not unduly worried about the validity of the considerations that have brought the assent about. But the only action correlative in this sense to philosophical assent is that which marks a genuine understanding of the position assented to; e.g., the action of making comments which are genuinely appropriate to the position. Assent accompanied by inappropriate remarks just would not be assent at all. Thus if Waismann is really trying to get us to see philosophy as he sees it, he must be using arguments that he regards as valid.

In addition to philosophical discourse, there are undoubtedly kinds of nonphilosophical discourse in which the right choice cannot be made except for the right reasons. These are the kinds of discourse which aim to secure no action except that of continuing the discourse in an appropriate way. Critical talk is an example. Another example is the discourse that takes place in a classroom, for most subjects are taught on the assumption that the right answers are not enough. Subjects of which this is true, including philosophy, are rational in a sense in which deliberation is not rational when, although the right choice is essential, the right reason is non-essential. Such deliberation may, of course, as Waismann says, be rational in another sense.

2

People often say that the only valid arguments occur in mathematics and other formal disciplines, since it is only here that terms can be so unambiguously defined that genuine inferences can occur. In Waismann's metaphor, it is only here that the language is sufficiently hard. Philosophical arguments are lumped with all others in non-formal discourse as using a language too soft to carry genuine inferences. Since they cannot be valid, the point of using them is accounted for by saying that they are forceful or persuasive.

The people who say this sort of thing are, of course, overlooking a perfectly good sense in which a philosophical argument can be valid. This is the sense in which valid arguments cast in ordinary language appear in the pages of elementary logic textbooks. Indeed, it is precisely when philosophical arguments are given this logical form that their premises are challenged and the discussion shifts to a deeper level. Thus once the teleological argument is presented as a formally valid proof, doubts arise regarding such premises as "The Universe exhibits design." That such a regression of the discussion is not due to the softness of the language is shown by the formal validity of the argument. A language hard enough to cut formally valid arguments in it is as hard as ever could be desired. The difficulty is not that the terms are ambiguous; it is rather that the premises are so clear in meaning that they immediately raise doubts.

Formally valid arguments may be constructed within any field, and when they are constructed, their premises are often subject to doubt. The technique of taking a valid dilemma by the horns or escaping between the horns makes use of such doubts. But the doubts in this case arise neither because the premise is not clearly stated nor because it is clearly stated. They arise simply because a situation is envisaged of which the premise does not hold. Sometimes, of course, no such situation can be envisioned, and there is thus no reasonable basis for doubting the premise. "If I swallow this cyanide, I will be dead within 500 years; if I do not, I will be dead within 500 years" is a case in point. It is a common feature of philosophical premises, however, that doubts arise once they are clearly stated — this is, in fact, precisely the regressive phenomenon noted by Waismann. The very process of clearly stating a philosophical premise seems to raise the question of its warrant, and this question is always reasonable in a philosophical context.

Outside philosophy, then, it is possible to construct formally valid arguments, the truth of the premises of which it would not be appropriate for anyone to doubt. The best examples of such arguments occur in mathematics, although what represses doubt in mathematics is unlike what represses it in the dilemma about taking cyanide. There are mathematical arguments the premises of which no one could appropriately doubt because it is just not to the point to doubt such premises. Anyone who rejects a geometrical theorem on the ground that he doubts the axioms on which it is based, for example, just does not see the point of the demonstration. As Aristotle pointed out, such a person is not concerned with geometry but with some other inquiry; perhaps he is interested in the structure of empirical space. A mathematical axiom need not be true; it need only imply, in conjunction with the other axioms, the requisite theorems. For this reason, rigorous proofs are possible in mathematics.

These remarks may seem to confirm Waismann's thesis that rigorous proofs are not possible in philosophy. Certainly premises that *no one* could appropriately doubt are unavailable in philosophy. But there may be premises that *someone* could not appropriately doubt. If there are formally valid arguments in which all of the premises are of this nature, then those people who cannot appropriately doubt the premises will not be able appropriately to doubt the conclusions either. Consider the infinite regress argument. Aristotle asserts that those who insist that every principle be proved are vulnerable to this argument, for principle P_1 can be proved only in terms of principles $P_2 \ldots$, P_n, which require further principles for their proof, and so on, supposing we have succeeded in avoiding circularity. One step of the argument may be put as follows:

A principle is acceptable only if there are acceptable principles that imply it. Therefore, a principle that implies an acceptable principle is acceptable only if there are acceptable principles that imply it.

This step, which may be repeated *ad infinitum,* and hence is the basis of the regress, is a formally valid argument, and so is the readily constructed demonstration that it may be repeated *ad infinitum.*[6] But why not evade the conclusion reached in this step by denying the premise? While this maneuver is available to most people concerned with the argument in question, it is not

---

[6] Let $(P_1, P_2, \ldots)$ be a set of distinct principles. For each i, let S_i be the statement that principle P_i is acceptable only if principles $P_{i+1}, \ldots, P_{i+n}$ are acceptable and together imply P_i. It immediately follows that for each S_i there is at least one P_j, where $j > i$. If we now assume, with Aristotle's opponent, that for every P_i there is an S_i, it immediately follows that there is no last S_i; and hence no last step.

available to all. The man who holds that a principle is acceptable only if there are acceptable principles that imply it cannot appropriately doubt this premise at the moment he is holding it to be true. Here, then, is the case of a premise that *someone* could not appropriately doubt, which can be compared with the case in which, as in mathematics, *no one* could relevantly doubt the premises. The two cases point up the existence of two different conditions under which it is inappropriate to doubt a premise. Let us say that when to doubt the premise is to miss the whole point of a valid argument, the argument is rigorous, while when the doubt is impossible because the premise is exactly what the doubter is holding, the argument is *cogent*. Mathematical proofs, then, are rigorous; and some philosophical arguments are cogent.

Philosophical arguments can have the same appearance of formal necessity as mathematical arguments. Many cogent philosophical arguments, for example, resemble cases of *reductio ad absurdum* in mathematics. In both cases, a proposition is rejected on the grounds that it has absurd consequences. But there are differences. The *reductio* is one of the devices through which new mathematical truths are established. But can we say that new philosophical truths are established through the use of infinite regresses and similar arguments? It would seem that nothing is ever established in philosophy in the way in which propositions can be established in mathematics; once anyone makes the claim to have established a philosophical proposition there are bound to be cogent arguments attacking this claim, just as alleged philosophical axioms may always be attacked. Consider whether the infinite regress cited above *establishes* that some principles must be accepted without proof. Many philosophers are sure to deny that any such thing is established or that it is of philosophical significance. They will seek to widen the concept of proof so that all principles can again be proved, or they will deny that any principles need be accepted at all. When it is pointed out that in the original sense of "proof" and of "principle" it remains true that some principles must be accepted without proof, they will stigmatize this assertion as utterly uninteresting and trivial. Nothing that philosophers would consider non-trivial could be established as mathematical theorems are established.

Again, a mathematical *reductio* depends on axioms, but no cogent philosophical argument can do this, since any supposititious axioms brought into an argument of this kind would immediately be subject to an appropriate doubt. Finally, there is point to a mathematical *reductio* whether or not anyone has ever asserted the proposition whose absurd consequences are exhibited. There is, however, no point to a cogent philosophical argument unless someone has held the position we are attacking; otherwise the attack is upon a "straw man." In other words, while in a mathematical *reductio* we may make the assumption "for the sake of the argument," in the cogent philosophical argument, we assume nothing for the sake of the argument; instead, we simply take an interlocutor at his word and assume what he assumes.

Cogent philosophical arguments are formally valid, and no formally invalid philosophical argument could be cogent. Even a formally valid philosophical argument *could* be invalid in the sense that Waismann and others have in mind when they say that all philosophical arguments are invalid; i.e., uncogent. I have cited the teleological argument as an example. More important cases are those in which uncogent arguments superficially appear to be cogent. Suppose, borrowing a formula from Passmore,[7] I say, "I never fully understand a principle until I have seen its proof." From this it follows that I never fully understand the proof of a principle unless I have seen the proofs of the principles appealed to in its proof — and so on, *ad infinitum*. But this infinite series of steps does not refute me. It only shows that there will be some principles that I do not fully understand. The argument would, however, be cogent if it were also my position that a partial understanding is no understanding at all. If I do not maintain this additional thesis, then the argument misses the point. An uncogent philosophical argument always does miss the point; since it assumes what those to whom it is addressed do not assume, and thus begs the question, its premises are always subject to an appropriate doubt. Even the cogent philosophical argument is not, of course, absolutely cogent; it is cogent only relatively to interlocutors who maintain the premises on which it depends. An argument cogent against one interlocutor may be uncogent against another. And *vice versa;* the premises of the teleological argument could conceivably constitute a cogent attack on a man who accepted them, showing him that he must likewise accept the conclusion.

Even a cogent philosophical argument does not force our assent; its conclusion can always be evaded if we are willing to forego one premise or another. This is a point which Waismann misinterprets to mean that philosophy is defective in lacking a "logical stick"; [8] and it is a point which Passmore clearly makes in an early chapter of his book [9] but forgets in later ones.[10] To take a simple example: Aristotle's interlocutor can claim — as Aristotle himself did — a privileged status for certain principles, thus stopping the regress. When this happens, the defendant has actually taken a new position, abandoning the old one. Thus he has, in effect, acknowledged the cogency of a cogent argument. But it is not a cogency so strong that it paralyzes him. It does not deprive him of his power to change his mind, any more than a logical dilemma deprives him whom it attacks of the power to take it by the horns or escape between the horns. He is not, therefore, stuck with the conclusion of the argument, any more than the person against whom the dilemma is addressed is stuck with the conclusion of that. If there is no logical stick in philosophy, it is only because there is no logical stick anywhere. To be sure, when all the premises of a formally valid argument are true, the conclusion is true. But this is a factual stick, not a logical stick.

One reason why Waismann and others have unfavorably compared philosophical arguments with mathematical proofs is that the latter do seem coercive in a sense in which the former do not. No one, confronted with a mathematical proof, is likely to change his mind about the axioms he accepts. But this is only because no one has his mind "made up" in the first place. Mathematicians do not decide in favor of the commutative law or the distributive law as philosophers may on occasion decide in favor of the law of

---

[7] John Passmore, *Philosophical Reasoning* (New York, 1961), esp. pp. 28-31.
[8] See Waismann, p. 372.
[9] See Passmore, p. 36.
[10] See, for example, Passmore, p. 80.

causality or the principle of utility. They just use the laws. There would be as little point in evading the conclusion of a mathematical proof as there is in doubting its premises. Precisely because there would be no point in the evasion, mathematical proofs can be rigorous. But they do not have a coercive force that philosophical arguments lack, because they do not have a coercive force at all. No one can be made to accept a mathematical theorem against his will. For coercion of this kind, we must rely on the hypnotist, not the mathematician.

It may be objected that although Waismann primarily has constructive philosophical arguments in mind, speaking, as he does, of "building up a case," my answer to him has appealed exclusively to features of destructive or polemical arguments such as the infinite regress. But in the first place, "building up a case" involves "bringing to light inconsistencies" in rival views as well as "offer[ing] a new way of looking at things." More basically, the distinction between constructive and polemical arguments in philosophy does not seem to me to be fundamental. The philosopher who aims to establish a position intends at the same time to deny its rivals, and the philosophical critic is only a carper unless he has some constructive point in mind, or at least some axe to grind. Furthermore, the definition of cogency for constructive argumentation is precisely that for polemic. In both cases, there must be a formally valid argument the premises of which someone cannot appropriately doubt. In the case of the constructive argument, the person for whom doubt is inappropriate may well be the arguer himself. Perhaps his argument is just an attempt to get clear with respect to the consequences of his own presuppositions. If so, it will be cogent only for those who share those presuppositions. But similarly, the cogency of the cogent polemical argument is limited to those who accept the presuppositions whose consequences it exhibits. In neither case is there absolute cogency. But this is just another way of saying that there is no philosophically neutral point of view from which the cogency of all philosophical arguments may be assessed. This is perhaps the decisive difference between philosophy and other fields.

V.
Self-Refutation and Validity

It has often been argued that since all sound arguments are either inductive or deductive, and philosophical arguments are neither, no philosophical arguments are sound. In his recent book, *Philosophical Reasoning,*[1] Passmore attempts to show that sound philosophical arguments are possible. He does this not by attacking the premise that all sound arguments are either inductive or deductive, but rather by attacking the premise that philosophical arguments are neither deductive nor inductive. In fact, he asserts, "Philosophical reasoning, if it is to be valid at all, must be deductive in its formal structure."[2] Passmore's point is that deductive arguments are by no means confined to mathematical reasoning. Mathematics uses deductive inference in one way, and philosophy in another. Passmore does not attempt to define this alleged difference between the way mathematics uses deductive inference and the way philosophy uses it. Instead he gives examples of kinds of argument that are used often in philosophy and seldom elsewhere. One such kind of argument consists in pointing out that one's opponent has begged the question. Another is the so-called "infinite regress" argument. Again, the kind of argument that a philosopher is using when he "reminds" his interlocutor of a principle that he has presumably forgotten or overlooked in the process of formulating his philosophical position is fairly common in philosophy although not frequently used in other fields. Other sorts of argument cited by Passmore as basically philosophical are "verbal analysis" and "self-refutation." The considerations that Passmore has in mind in characterizing all of these arguments as philosophical are stylometric. By this I mean that what motivates him to classify an argument as philosophical is not any property attaching to the argument itself, but rather the fact that it occurs for the most part in philosophical contexts. He explicitly states that other kinds of arguments, including those mainly used in mathematical contexts, can occur in philosophy, and that the arguments which he classifies as philosophical can occur in non-philosophical contexts.

Although Passmore holds that all valid philosophical arguments must be deductive in formal structure, he scarcely makes any attempt to exhibit the formal structure of the arguments he considers in the book. Nor is it obvious what the formal structure of most of the arguments he considers is; indeed, in many cases, it is not obvious that the arguments have formal structures at all. But the validity of a valid deductive argument can be established only by means of an examination of its formal structure. In consequence, there are many cases in which we cannot be sure what Passmore means when he says that a certain philosophical argument is valid.

One of the kinds of philosophical argument to which Passmore directs especial attention is the "Self-Refutation." An example is the argument against the view expressed by the sentence, "No sentence conveys anything." The argument is obvious: if no sentence conveys anything, then *this* one does not convey anything. This example is trivial because no one has ever maintained

---

[1]John Passmore, *Philosophical Reasoning* (New York: Charles Scribner's Sons, 1961).
[2]Ibid., p. 6.

29

the view in question; but Passmore is right in supposing that a great many important arguments in philosophy, attacking views which have in fact been maintained, derive their force from features they share with this trivial example. One may instance familiar arguments against pragmatism, empiricism, relativism, and scepticism, to name just a few. If the true is the useful, then it is not true, but only useful, to say that the true is useful. If we assert that all knowledge arises from sensation, then we are led to the absurdity that the knowledge that all knowledge arises from sensation arises itself from sensation. And so on.

A self-refuting proposition in philosophy is not merely an inconsistent one. In expressing his view, a philosopher may find himself denying at one place what he has asserted at another. This is inconsistency. But in the self-refuting proposition, the two places converge, so that what the philosopher says at a certain place both asserts and denies itself.

Passmore distinguishes absolutely self-refuting propositions in philosophy from ones which, in his opinion, while self-refuting, are not absolutely self-refuting. "Formally," he says, "the proposition p is absolutely self-refuting, if to assert p is equivalent to asserting both p and not-p."[3] Thus it is, strictly speaking, only an absolutely self-refuting proposition which both asserts and denies itself all in one place in a philosophical context.

Before considering the types of self-refutation that Passmore wishes to distinguish from absolute self-refutation, I would like to pause for a moment to ask what it means to say of a refutation that it is absolute. A refutation is absolute when it proves beyond any question that the proposition it attacks is false. The propounder of a proposition that has been absolutely refuted cannot claim that there is any sense in which the proposition is still true. As Passmore says, "No evasion is possible."[4] Now the only area in which propositions are conclusively shown to be false and no evasions are possible is that of formal deductive reasoning. Here evasions are not possible because evasions are not to the point. When the falsity of a proposition has been deduced from unquestioned axioms or assumptions, to claim that there is still a sense in which the proposition is true is implicitly to bring the axioms or assumptions into question, and this kind of doubt is never relevant to the procedure whereby the falsity of the proposition has been deduced. But conclusions in nonformal reasoning can always be evaded, and nonformal premises can always be questioned. As Strawson,[5] Crawshay-Williams,[6] and other recent authors have shown, man has an unlimited capacity for sophistry. Hence if there is any absolute self-refutation, it must occur within a system of formal deductive reasoning.

According to Passmore, the forms of self-refutation other than absolute self-refutation are those that permit evasion. One of these forms is the pragmatic self-refutation, addressed against the person who has uttered a sentence allegedly inconsistent with its own utterance. An example is "I can-

[3]Ibid., p. 60.
[4]Ibid., p. 80.
[5]*Introduction to Logical Theory* (London: Methuen and Co., Ltd., 1952), pp. 6-7.
[6]*Methods and Criteria of Reasoning. An Inquiry into the Structure of Controversy* (New York: The Humanities Press Inc., 1957), passim.

not pronounce 'breakfast.' " "It is always logically possible," says Passmore, "for the person accused of a pragmatic self-refutation to deny that the alleged counterexample is a counterexample. 'That noise I just made' [the person accused of a pragmatic self-refutation] might reply, 'that's not pronouncing "b-ɾ e-a-k-f-a-s-t." That I *cannot* do.' "[7]

The other form of self-refutation which, in Passmore's eyes, is not absolute, is the *ad hominem* self-refutation. Here "a person's *admission* that he is speaking or thinking — as distinct from the fact that he is speaking or thinking — is used as an argument to show that what he is speaking or thinking cannot in fact be the case."[8] If Descartes' *cogito* can be paraphrased as a refutation of "I sometimes think that I do not think" (Passmore thinks it cannot), then the *cogito* has the form of an *ad hominem* refutation. Another example is Socrates' attack upon Protagoras, who claims to teach people that no one can inform anybody of anything. As is always the case with *ad hominem* refutations, there is a way of evading the attack. Protagoras can say that teaching people is not informing them, but merely advising them; and that the possibility of such advice is not inconsistent with the impossibility of actually giving anyone information.

Absolute self-refutation depends not upon the fact that the defendant is thinking or speaking, or that he is admitting something, but upon the fact that he is making an assertion that denies the very possibility of making an assertion. Thus, "No sentence conveys anything" denies that discourse has a fundamental function — that of conveying something — in the absence of which there seems no longer to be any point in using any sentence at all. A similar account could be given of "All propositions are false." That sentences convey something, that the distinction can be made between truth and falsity, that names are not radically ambiguous — such, for Passmore, are "invariant conditions of discourse," and "a view is absolutely self-refuting only if it is incompatible with [such] invariant conditions of discourse."[9] We begin to have an intimation here of the system of formal deductive reasoning which, in Passmore's view, may underlie the possibility of absolute self-refutation. It is a philosophically neutral system in which the invariant conditions of discourse are formalized. We still have to see, however, whether the self-refutations that Passmore regards as absolute can actually make use of such a system.

I wish to challenge Passmore's distinction between self-refutations that are absolute and those, including *ad hominem* self-refutations, that are not. There are three reasons for which I believe that this distinction cannot be maintained. In the first place, I do not believe that absolute refutations can be reduced to the assertion of *both p and not-p*; or, alternatively, if they can, so can the refutations that Passmore regards as not being absolute. In the second place, I do not believe that the conclusions of absolute self-refutations are immune to evasion in the way Passmore thinks they are. In the third place, Passmore's distinction cannot be made on the supposition that absolute self-refutations are valid and other self-refutations invalid; for if certain other arguments cited as valid by Passmore are in fact valid, these non-absolute self-refutations must also be valid.

I turn to the first point. I begin by observing that Passmore nowhere actually carries out the reduction of an absolute self-refutation to *both p and not-p*. On the face of it, furthermore, a sentence such as "No sentence conveys anything" does not imply a contradiction. If we place no restrictions upon the range of our quantificational variables, we may derive "The sentence 'No sentence conveys anything' does not convey anything" from the sentence "No sentence conveys anything." But "The sentence 'No sentence conveys anything' does not convey anything" is not a contradiction; it does not in the least have the form *both p and not-p*. Yet it is all that we can logically derive from "No sentence conveys anything" that will be of the slightest use to us. If we want a *contradiction* of the form *both p and not-p*, we must attempt to derive "Both 'No sentence conveys anything' conveys something and 'No sentence conveys anything' does not convey anything." But it is only the second conjunct that we have derived from "No sentence conveys anything." We must still account for the first conjunct, " 'No sentence conveys anything' conveys something." But this is not a particularly perplexing problem. If it is assumed as an invariant condition of discourse that *every sentence conveys something*, then, if we continue being liberal in our quantification, we can derive that "No sentence conveys anything" conveys something.

Clearly "Every sentence conveys something" is an assumption from which " 'No sentence conveys anything' conveys something" might be derived. And certainly if there are "invariant conditions of discourse" in Passmore's sense, this is one of them. Yet once one explicitly states "Every sentence conveys something," doubts about its truth immediately arise. What, for example, of "Quadruplicity drinks procrastination"? What does this sentence convey? I do not need to press this point. I only note that doubts regarding the truth of an alleged invariant condition of discourse seem relevant; they cannot be immediately dismissed as missing the point. But doubts regarding formal axioms can always be dismissed as missing the point. And if doubts are possible with regard to allegedly "absolute" self-refutation, then the self-refutations are not absolute in the sense intended by Passmore. The question arises whether what Passmore calls the invariant conditions of discourse do indeed have the role in philosophical reasoning that he thinks they have.

The point may be put in another way. The sentence "No sentence conveys anything" is equivalent with *both p and not-p* only when a further assumption is made; for example, the assumption that every sentence conveys something. We might say, more simply, that "No sentence conveys anything" is inconsistent with "Every sentence conveys something," since sentences exist. Why, then, can we not treat this as a case in which a philosopher has been inconsistent? The reason we cannot is that he has not simply asserted *p* at one place and *not-p* at another. In particular, "Every sentence conveys something" is not something that the philosopher is inclined to assert in spite of the fact that he has already asserted "No sentence conveys anything." But if the contradiction were formal, it ought to be possible to treat it in this way. It should be possible to say of a proposition stated at one place that it is inconsistent with a theorem or axiom (or set of theorems and axioms) stated elsewhere. But it is clear that Passmore wants to distinguish the self-refuting proposition from any such set of inconsistent propositions. In the self-refuting proposition, the inconsistency occurs all at one place. Thus we cannot hope to analyze the inconsistency of "No sentence conveys anything" by setting that sentence up against another sentence alleged to occur at another place. Self-refutation is *self-refutation*; i.e., not refutation by something else; and Passmore has this in mind when he distinguishes self-refutation from ordinary inconsistency.

How, then, does "No sentence conveys anything" refute itself? We have seen that from it, " 'No sentence conveys anything' does not convey anything" can be derived. But if we are to exhibit a contradiction, we must also have " 'No sentence conveys anything' conveys something," and we are not permitted to derive this from any assumption we have made at another place; for then we would have just an ordinary inconsistency. Thus " 'No sentence conveys anything' conveys something" must somehow be evident on the basis of "No sentence conveys anything," even though it is not logically derivable from it.

Certainly something can be evident on the basis of a sentence even when it is not logically derivable from it. A sentence not only has logical consequences but also a use. One of the possible uses of sentences is to convey something. If it is evident that "No sentence conveys anything" is used to convey something then we can say that "No sentence conveys anything" conveys something, and thus exhibit the contradiction we have in mind.

As I have said, there is no contradiction in the sentence "No sentence conveys anything" taken simply by itself. The sentence is seen to refute itself only when its use is taken into account. "No sentence conveys anything" might have been used to illustrate the grammatical structure of an English sentence. In this case, it would be a sentence, but it should not be necessary for it to convey anything. Or again, "No sentence conveys anything" might have been used to suggest something but not to convey anything. It is only when "No sentence conveys anything" is used to convey something that a contradiction develops.

But how do we know in what manner a sentence is being used? We cannot know this simply by inspecting the sentence. We must be aware of the intentions of the user. We must be sure, for instance, that he is using the sentence to convey something and not just to illustrate the grammatical structure of an English sentence or to suggest something. In other words, we must ascertain to our own satisfaction that he is *asserting* the sentence; for to assert is to intend to convey something.

Let us review the defining features of the forms of self-refutation other than absolute self-refutation. The pragmatic self-refutation pivots upon a *fact* about the speaker; the fact, for example, that he is speaking, thinking, or writing. The *ad hominem* self-refutation depends upon an *admission* that the speaker has made in the process of speaking. (I obviously intend the word "speaker" to be understood in a very broad sense.) We can now add that the so-called "absolute" self-refutation depends upon the *intention* of the speaker, for example, his intention to convey something. And having juxtaposed this last statement with the others, we can see that the difference between the "absolute" form and the *ad hominem* form of refutation is certainly no greater in principle than the difference between the *ad hominem* form and the pragmatic form. The difference is one of degree, not of kind. In the pragmatic self-refutation, the attacker exploits a less fundamental feature of the speaker's utterance; in the so-called "absolute" self-refutation, he exploits a more fundamental feature. But none of these features is absolutely fundamental, in the sense that it belongs to the utterance itself regardless of who the speaker may be or what his intentions are. No proposition could be absolutely self-refuting, because no proposition could refute *itself* without the intervention of a speaker.

In summary, I would argue that Passmore has not succeeded in reducing "No sentence conveys anything," or, for that matter, any other so-called "absolute" self-refutation, to the form *"both p and not-p"* unless some assertion is available over and above the self-refuting proposition itself. Nor can the required supplementary assertion be the assertion of an "invariant condition of discourse." It must rather pertain to the intended use of the proposition in question. But surely if an assertion about the intended use of an allegedly "absolutely" self-refuting proposition can be appended to a logical consequence of the proposition to form *"both p and not-p,"* we may similarly derive *"both p and not-p"* in the case of an *ad hominem* refutation. Consider my attempt to inform you that no one can inform anyone of anything. From "No one can inform anyone of anything" it follows that I cannot inform you of anything. This is one-half of the required contradiction. The other half, to the effect that I can inform you of something, is evinced by my use of the sentence "No one can inform anyone of anything" to inform you. Passmore is quite right, of course, to point out that I *may* be using the sentence to advise you rather than to inform you. But similarly, I *may* be using the sentence "No sentence conveys anything" to illustrate the grammatical structure of an English sentence or to suggest something, rather than to convey something. The appropriateness of the reduction to *"both p and not-p"* is thus precisely the same in both cases.

I may be giving the impression that I do not suppose invariant conditions of discourse to have any bearing upon self-refutations, or, worse still, that I deny their existence. In fact, I am perfectly willing to agree that they exist and have a bearing. I only insist that we think of such invariant conditions as being hypothetical rather than categorical in form. While I am suspicious of "Every sentence conveys something," and doubt that it has a role in self-refutation, I would be perfectly happy with "If a sentence is used as an assertion, it must convey something." For I am willing to see the consequent of this conditional apply to every sentence to which the antecedent applies. It is only the cases in which the antecedent does not apply that cause me to reject the categorical version.

This leads me to the second way in which I would like to challenge Passmore's distinction between self-refutations that are absolute and those that are not. I have just argued that an allegedly *absolutely* self-refuting sentence can in fact be refuted only by means of an appeal to the intention of the person who uses the sentence. Thus "No sentence conveys anything" is self-refuting only if it is the intention of the speaker to convey something. Therefore, a speaker accused of having uttered a self-refuting sentence can reply that the accusation involves a misinterpretation of his intentions. He can say, for example, "I did not intend to *assert* 'No sentence conveys anything.' I was merely using that as an example of the grammatical structure of an English sentence." As Passmore himself remarks in connection with the pragmatic self-refutation, some such reply is always in principle possible, even if it sometimes requires "almost inconceivable hardihood."[10] The point is that a philosopher can waive the conclusion of an "absolute" self-refutation in exactly the way in which he can waive the conclusion of a pragmatic or *ad hominem* self-refutation. The function of saying "I was merely using that sentence as an example of the grammatical structure of an English sentence" or "I was only trying to suggest the radical impossibility of communication" is precisely the same as the function of saying "I was not pronouncing 'b-r-e-a-k-f-a-s-t'; that I cannot do." In each case, the attack is shown to have been misconceived.

These replies are fairly trivial, and of little philosophical concern. But having now made the point that the invariant conditions of discourse may not be so invariant after all, we can perhaps invent better replies, not concerned with this point. Why not, for example, invoke a theory of types in order to evade the attack upon "No sentence conveys anything"? Let us claim that we are using this sentence in a second-order way to refer to the first-order uses of sentences. The question immediately arises, of course, whether such a stratification is defensible. But that question is not the same as the attack upon "No sentence conveys anything." That attack has been successfully evaded, because we can now no longer exhibit the relevant contradiction.

Have we succeeded, then, in showing that "No sentence conveys anything" does *not* refute itself — that the attack was invalid? There are places where Passmore seems to be suggesting that when an argument is valid, its conclusion cannot be evaded.[11] If this is true, I have succeeded in showing that a self-refutation supposed by Passmore to be valid is in fact invalid. But this is not the claim I am going to make. I want instead to assert, as Passmore himself does elsewhere in the book,[12] that the conclusion of a valid argument can always be waived. This is, in fact, a perfectly familiar logical point. The dilemma, for example, is a formally valid argument. But we can still take it by the horns or escape between the horns. Similarly, we can waive the conclusion of a valid self-refutation if we are willing to pay the price. The price I have in mind is that of making a distinction, or stating a reservation, which did not appear in the original formulation of the view. The philosopher who sees the untenability of holding that he can inform others that no one can inform anyone of anything is led to distinguish between informing and advising, and "No sentence conveys anything" could be maintained as a philosophical thesis by one willing to pay the price of stratification or prepared to urge the radical impossibility of communication. The issue can, of course, be joined once more over such new developments — "Can advising and informing really be distinguished?" "Is not stratification arbitrary and *ad hoc?*" — but the valid argument that occasioned any such development now no longer applies; it has been successfully evaded.

The main difference between a valid argument and an invalid one in philosophy is that while the valid one forces the defendant either to complicate his position or else to abandon it, the invalid argument calls only for explanation, not complication. Thus the self-refutation is inappropriate, and

[10]Ibid., p. 63.
[11]E.g., p. 80.
[12]Ibid., p. 36.

hence invalid, against the person who was merely using "No sentence conveys anything" to illustrate the grammatical structure of an English sentence. It is valid, on the other hand, against the man who is forced by it to stratify his uses of sentences. An argument, then, may be valid against one position and invalid against another. But there is no mystery in this; a valid criticism of one play is not necessarily a valid criticism of another, and a valid reason for doing one thing is not necessarily a valid reason for doing another.

An invalid argument, when it is at all plausible, often arises from a misunderstanding, as is the case when a man whom I thought was stating a philosophical thesis was in fact only illustrating a point in English grammar. A valid argument, on the other hand, presupposes that the arguer has correctly understood the thesis he attacks, both in the sense of seeing its logical consequences and in that of knowing how the sentences expressing it are used. But what the arguer understands about the defendant's position as actually articulated does not enable him to foretell how the defendant will modify it so as to pursue its defense in the future; his arguments cannot encompass every possible turn of the discussion. To put the point more directly, there is no argument, valid or not, that can altogether silence a philosopher if he wishes to continue the discussion. However devastating the attack upon him, there is always something more that he can say.

I shall return at the end of this paper to the general question of the validity of philosophical arguments. For the moment, my point is only that one cannot distinguish absolute self-refutations from others on the ground that their conclusions cannot be evaded. The conclusions of all arguments can be evaded.

I turn to my third reason for doubting the distinction that Passmore tries to make between absolute and non-absolute self-refutations. I think that it is wrong to attempt to make the distinction by suggesting that absolute self-refutations are the only valid self-refutations; for there are many arguments, the validity of which Passmore never questions, which are of such a nature that if they are valid, then certain non-absolute refutations must also be valid. An example is the argument in which we accuse our interlocutor of begging the question. Passmore cites with approval the following argument from Hume:

> We have said that all arguments concerning existence are founded on the relation of cause and effect; that our knowledge of that relation is derived entirely from experience; and that our experimental conclusions proceed upon the supposition that the future will be conformable to the past. To endeavour, therefore [to construct] the proof of this last supposition by probable arguments, or arguments regarding existence, must be evidently going in a circle, and taking that for granted, which is the very point in question.[13]

I agree with Passmore that this is a powerful argument. Nor do I find any fault with his analysis of its power. Passmore points out that a circular piece of reasoning, such as that against which Hume is arguing, does not constitute a proof. All that I feel constrained to add is that in this argument, and in other powerful philosophical arguments accusing someone of begging the question, the circularity exposed is not absolute. It is circularity only from the point of

---

[13]*Enquiry*, par. IV, pt. II, quoted in Passmore, p. 3.

view of the arguer. Suppose someone wished to justify induction by appealing to experience. He might begin by supposing, as Whitehead did, that experience is directly revelatory of natural regularities. There would be nothing circular about the attempt to reason from experience so construed to the principle of induction — although, of course, this piece of reasoning might contain flaws of some other sort. Circularity would exist only if someone were to reason this way *in the presence of Hume*. For it is Hume who has said — and the passage quoted by Passmore begins "We have said" — that "our experimental conclusions proceed on the supposition that the future will be conformable to the past." The piece of reasoning is circular, then, not because it assumes what it had set out to prove, but because it assumes what Hume has explicitly denied. It "[takes] that for granted, which is the very point in question." But the point is in question only because Hume has put it in question. Hume is asking only that his interlocutor take him seriously. Those of us who adjudge his argument as valid are admitting that Hume has every right to insist on this.

The *ad hominem* refutation seems to me to involve nothing but an extension of the analysis I have just given of Hume's argument. If a philosopher has a right to insist on being taken seriously, his interlocutor has a duty to take him seriously. But it is just by carrying out his duty that a philosopher's interlocutor is able to attack him. Consider "No one can inform anyone of anything." One might be tempted to reject this statement on the grounds that there are exceptions to it. It might be supposed that one could point to cases in which people have actually succeeded in passing information to one another. But any attempt to argue in terms of such supposititious counterexamples fails to appreciate the significance of the original statement. If literally no one can inform anyone of anything, then anything that seems like an example of the transmission of information will in reality be something else; it will be, perhaps, a case in which opinion has been transmitted but not information — or perhaps again a case of pre-established harmony. Thus, anyone who cites such an example is begging the question; he is assuming precisely what has been denied by the philosopher who has claimed that no one can inform anyone of anything. How, then, can one attack the man who makes this claim? Only by taking him seriously. Instead of looking for a counterexample one must suppose that the man means exactly what he says. If he does, then he himself cannot inform anyone of anything. Thus if his statement has issued from a desire to inform people, he refutes himself. But no thinker refutes himself unless we help him to do so by taking him seriously.

I have tried to show that if we suppose that an argument that exposes a *petitio* is valid, similar considerations should lead us to suppose that an *ad hominem* refutation is likewise valid. Thus we find the *ad hominem* refutation buttressed on all sides. Not only are we incapable of making any important distinction between it and the so-called "absolute" self-refutation, but also it seems to bear a strong kinship to arguments the validity of which has seldom, if ever, been questioned. If an *ad hominem* refutation is possible, it is difficult to see what more could be demanded. The *ad hominem* argument establishes its conclusion as absolutely as any other.

The final point I wish to discuss is the nature of the validity that the valid philosophical arguments I have dealt with in this paper share. It does not seem to be a sufficient condition for the validity of a philosophical argument that it be formally valid, although this is probably a necessary condition. In addition to being formally valid, the valid philosophical argument must strike home. Faced with a valid argument against his position, a philosopher must either abandon it or revise it. An invalid argument, on the other hand, does not impose this necessity. It calls for explanation, but not revision. As long as invalid arguments are used, the discussion does not progress. There is simply a reiteration of existing positions. This situation is likely to characterize fundamental philosophical oppositions. When the linguistic analyst faces the existentialist there is little that either can do except to beg the question. The wheels of argument spin idly, and the encounter reduces to a statuesque confrontation. Discussion degenerates into repetition relieved from time to time by name-calling.

The view of the nature of validity that seems to be presupposed by my treatment of philosophical arguments throughout this paper, then, is that the valid argument is the one that maintains philosophical discussion as a distinctive mode of inquiry. Bridging the gap between interlocutors, it forces each to elaborate his position rather than just to repeat it. The discussion takes a decisive turn even when someone is compelled to abandon his position altogether, for the abandonment commits him to the quest for a more satisfactory substitute.

Yet we have no way of knowing *in advance* that a given philosophical argument will be of such a nature as to maintain the discussion, even though in retrospect we may be able to see that it has maintained it. There is no effective criterion for the validity of a philosophical argument. It is no doubt this fact that accounts for the open, free, and reflective character of philosophical inquiry.

VI.
The Relevance of Rhetoric to Philosophy and of Philosophy to Rhetoric

My title is intended to suggest not that there is a *mutual* relevance between philosophy and rhetoric — a single relation that each bears to the other — but that each of these disciplines is relevant to the other in a distinctive way. I turn first to the relevance of rhetoric to philosophy. It is tempting to suppose that this consists in what rhetoric has to teach philosophy about the art of persuading. Now of course philosophical arguments are to various degrees persuasive, and no one can object to studying their persuasive qualities. Similarly, no one can object to making a "stylometric" study of Euclid's *Elements* — an analysis in which Euclid's sound combinations, choice of words, use of alliteration, and the like, are examined. But just as the stylometric analysis would be altogether irrelevant to the *point* of the *Elements,* so the analysis of the persuasive force of a philosophical argument would be an entirely irrelevant to the *point* of the argument. The *point* of Euclid's *Elements* is its concern to prove theorems. Sound combinations, choice of words, and alliteration, have nothing whatever to do with the cogency of the proofs that Euclid attempts to carry out. Similarly, the *point* of a philosophical argument is the claim to establish some conclusion. The argument can establish the conclusion persuasively or unpersuasively. But the question whether a philosophical argument establishes its conclusion persuasively or unpersuasively must be distinguished from the question whether it establishes its conclusion or not. Of course, a wholly unpersuasive argument is not likely to establish anything. Similarly, a Euclidean passage in which the text is badly garbled cannot properly be called the proof of a theorem. But once the words are clear enough for us to see what they mean, our decision as to whether they constitute a proof will take no account of their stylometric analysis. And once the point of a philosophical argument is clear enough for us to see what the arguer is driving at, we can evaluate it without taking account of its persuasiveness.

It is true that philosophers have often attempted to persuade and edify. Plato no doubt wrote the *Republic* as a proposal which he hoped somebody would adopt. Augustine, Pascal, and Kierkegaard sermonized. Fichte addressed the German nation. Bentham and Mill sought to bring about political reforms. But in each case what is philosophical about the appeal is distinct from its persuasive quality, and can be evaluated wholly apart from that. Perhaps it will be retorted that in this respect philosophy is just like other fields to which rhetoric can be applied. We can distinguish the value of a political proposal from the persuasiveness of the oratory in its favor, and the value of a commercial product from the effectiveness of the accompanying advertising campaign. Doesn't that mean that philosophy uses rhetoric in exactly the same way as do politics and commerce? I think not. Politics and commerce use rhetoric to produce action, and the need to produce this action is essential to them. A political proposal which required no action would be a contradiction in terms, as would an item on the market which required neither seller nor buyer. But a philosophical conclusion calls for no action whatsoever. One cannot even say that it requires the action of assenting; for unless this action is performed for the right reason by an interlocutor who has understood the entire course of the argument leading to the conclusion, it is altogether irrelevant. Thus philosophy literally has no need for rhetoric. If Plato, Augustine, Pascal, Kierkegaard, Fichte, Bentham, and Mill used rhetoric, it is because over and above the philosophical conclusions they reached, there were programs that they advocated; and these programs were practical rather than philosophical.

If we reflect on the relevance of art, science, and morals to philosophy we shall see why it is unreasonable to expect philosophy to depend on rhetoric primarily as a means to persuasion. Art is relevant to philosophy, but not to render it artistic or beautiful. Science is relevant to philosophy, but philosophy does not as a result become scientific. Morals enter into philosophical investigation, but they do not make the investigation or the investigator either more or less moral. The relevance of each of these fields to philosophy is that instead of serving as an instrument each serves as an object. There is a philosophy *of* art, a philosophy *of* science, and a philosophy *of* morals (better known as ethics). This relationship is preserved in the case of each mode of human experience; not only art, science, and morals, but also politics, history — and rhetoric. In each case philosophy examines the mode of experience but is not itself characterized by it except incidentally. Doubts will perhaps arise with regard to logic as a mode of experience. If the philosopher argues in order to establish conclusions, must he not *use* logic as well as examining it? Now I hasten to admit that in my view logic is relevant to philosophy in a way in which the other modes of experience that I have mentioned are not. If by logic is meant the use of reason, then logic animates philosophy; for philosophy is just the use of reason to examine each mode of human experience. This is, of course, an extremely broad sense of the word "logic." In a narrower sense logic in the form of an explicit system may itself be the object of philosophical study, just as art, science, and rhetoric can be. But no explicit system of logic is identical with the implicit logic that animates philosophy. To render a system of logic explicit is to formalize it; but behind the formalization there is always an informal and intuitive logic that is presupposed by our very grasp of the formalization.

What I have been calling the relevance of rhetoric to philosophy may sound more like a relevance of philosophy to rhetoric. Indeed, if rhetoric exists in its own right and philosophy does it the service of examining it (in a fashion which I have not yet suggested), then it is just the relevance of philosophy to rhetoric that has been established. But the situation is more complicated than that. The philosopher does not examine rhetoric as the assayer examines a rock or as the journal editor examines an incoming manuscript. For the assayer could, without compromising his qualifications as assayer, refuse to examine some particular rock. The structure of the art that he practices does not require him to examine it. Similarly, the policies and procedures of the editor do not imply that he must examine any particular manuscript; for no one manuscript is a necessary part of the definition of the art that he practices. But the art that the philosopher practices is defined in part by his willingness or refusal to regard rhetoric as a necessary mode of human experience. For a philosophy which takes account of the existence of rhetoric as a necessary mode of experience will necessarily differ from one which does not. Hence a philosopher who refuses to examine rhetoric, on the ground that he does not regard it as necessary, is practicing an art different from the art practiced by the philosopher who chooses to examine it as a necessary mode of experience. I am not saying, of course, that rhetoric must be an explicit object of attention in every piece of philosophical writing issuing from the pen of the latter; only that each piece of writing must be compatible with its necessity.

How does a philosophy that acknowledges rhetoric as necessary differ from one that does not? Let us be clear what it means for philosophy to acknowledge something as necessary. I have just pointed out that the philosopher does not acknowledge the necessity of a mode of experience in the way that the assayer acknowledges the existence of a rock. The rock might or might not exist. It is just one of an altogether arbitrary batch. But the modes of human experience that the philosopher examines are necessary modes in that they must exist wherever man exists. For they are definitive of man. To be a man is to be a scientific animal, a political animal, a moral animal, an animal capable of responding to art. It makes a considerable difference whether we add to this list "a persuading and persuaded animal." If we leave this last phrase off, the implication is that we do not regard rhetoric as a necessary mode of human experience. It follows that we think that persuasion is in principle eliminable from experience. Perhaps it is merely an expedient in situations in which we lack sufficient information to make a rational decision. Then if we had the information we would no longer need to persuade or be persuaded. This is a familiar philosophical thesis. According to it, man is fundamentally a communicating animal rather than a persuading and persuaded one. And the difference between these two theses is radical. If man is fundamentally a communicating animal, certain conclusions logically follow regarding the nature of language, the nature of rational decision, and the significance of poetry and politics; and these conclusions are inconsistent with the corresponding conclusions reached when it is assumed that rhetoric is indispensable to human experience. Since an entire philosophical point of view is defined by the willingness to admit the necessity of rhetoric and to examine it in its own terms, it is neither an exaggeration nor a distortion to say that rhetoric is relevant — highly relevant — to philosophy.

I want also to maintain that philosophy is relevant to rhetoric; and I have already indicated in broad terms what I think this relevance is. Philosophy is relevant to rhetoric precisely because it examines rhetoric. Of course further evidence is also required. I must show that the examination is not a mere act of voyeurism — that rhetoric needs to be examined and benefits from the examination. why does rhetoric need examination? The problem really is, "Why does any subject need philosophical examination?" My answer is that such examination. Why does rhetoric need examination? The problem really is, "Why pose a problem. Thus it becomes necessary to study ethics primarily at times when private and public morals seem to be on the verge of collapse; and we become philosophically occupied with the nature of knowledge mainly in those historical periods when the criteria in terms of which we have been distinguishing knowledge from mere belief seem to be systematically threatened. Similarly, the need for a philosophical examination of rhetoric is most acute and the examination most welcome when the orderly processes through which people are normally able to persuade one another suddenly go awry and can no longer be counted on. Aristotle's examination of rhetoric was carried out in just such a period of reversal. Individuals claiming to be able for a fee to persuade anyone of anything were making a mockery of the art of persuading. In so doing, they unwittingly called attention to the need for a philosophical scrutiny of the foundations of rhetoric. Aristotle supplied such a scrutiny, disengaging persuasiveness from dialectical shenanigans and associating it firmly with virtue.

Our contemporary interest in rhetoric betokens a similar uneasiness regarding the process of persuasion, but our uneasiness does not arise primarily from the threat of sophistry. It arises partly because Aristotle's association of persuasion and virtue has come unstuck. We see awesome persuasive powers in the hands of those who could not by any reckoning be counted as virtuous. But this fact has been known and commented on throughout the modern era, and does not in itself account for the severity of the problem that rhetoric faces in the middle of the twentieth century. The other constituent of the problem is that we live in an age in which persuasion has been radically dissociated from communication. One way of conveying the distinction we make between the two processes is in terms of what we think it means to succeed at each. We suppose that action is the measure of successful persuasion; that if as the result of a speaker's urgings those whom he has been addressing do what he wants them to do, the speaker has succeeded in *persuading* his audience regardless what beliefs he may have *communicated* to it. Conversely, if A claims he has persuaded B to accept proposition *p*, but B acts as if *p* were false or he had never heard of *p*, we are not impressed by A's claim, even if B himself claims that A has persuaded him to accept *p*. The measure of success of communication, on the other hand, is the degree to which information has been transmitted. The exemplar of such transmission is the feeding of a punch-card to a computer or the receipt of some signal from it. It may be tempting to suppose that in feeding information to the computer we are trying to get it to act in a certain way, and thus trying to persuade it. But if this were the case, there would have to be some specific pattern of action, describable in advance, such that we would not be reluctant to feed the computer whatever information it took to produce this action, or even to tinker with its circuits in order to produce it. Obviously this is not to the point.

The implication is that such manipulation is to the point when we are persuading. Most of us, of course, disapprove of unlimited manipulation of this kind. We do not feel that it is decent to treat human beings as if they were mere objects we were trying to stimulate to action. We would like to draw the line between responsible and irresponsible persuasion. But how are we to draw this line? The ancients drew it by insisting that the persuader be virtuous. Having abandoned this requirement, can we look to the act itself as the locus of responsibility? The difficulty is that whatever the act, there can be circumstances under which it is immoral to persuade a person to perform it. Chief among these circumstances is the agent's ignorance of what he is doing. Can we draw the line, then, by insisting that persuasion is never permissible unless the agent is fully aware of all the relevant details of his prospective act? In this case, the significance of succeeding in getting the person to act tends to vanish; what becomes important instead is success in imparting information to him regardless of how he acts. In other words, we are no longer concerned at all with persuasion; we are concerned with communication. If we try to regain a foothold for persuasion by claiming some respect in which it is proper to procure action in the absence of complete information, the foothold becomes total occupation, because information is never in principle complete. Once again we bump up against the problem of determining how persuasion can be responsible without either totally displacing communication or being altogether swallowed up by it.

It is just this sort of problem that makes a philosophical examination of rhetoric imperative in our time. It is just in this way that philosophy is relevant to rhetoric. Let me sketch out some possible results of the examination. The philosopher might begin by taking the position that man is in fact a persuading and persuaded animal, and that whenever he steps outside the forum in which rhetoric holds sway, he is in danger of losing his human dignity. If I push another around with a pistol at his back, I am obviously not treating him as a man. But if I refuse to talk to him except to communicate information, am I doing greater justice to his humanity than I am if I treat him violently? It may seem that in this case I am treating him as a computer rather than as a man. In fact, in circles in which information is regarded as important, men are being replaced by computers, and the threat of automation is beginning to loom in our time as large as the threat of violence. But we must be careful not to oversimplify. To deal with another at pistol-point is still treating him as a person; the threat is a form of persuasion, albeit a degenerate form, and could not be applied to a mere animal. Perhaps it can be plausibly argued that communication is likewise a degenerate form of persuasion — a form in which we report not in order to incite people to action but merely for the sake of reporting. In this case, information is an essentially human concern, although derivative from the more fundamental concern to persuade. In any event, we can't tell that a computer is concerned with information merely by looking at it; for no matter how hard we look, all that we shall see is not units of information but impulses of electricity. Can information be defined at all except in terms of human concerns more like persuasion than like data-processing?

If threatening and informing are both degenerate forms of persuading, perhaps we have the basis for a new criterion of responsible persuasion; to wit, persuasion is responsible when it does not tend to degenerate. One must persuade only in such a way as to maintain the possibility of persuasion. This maxim can be further illustrated in obvious ways. When a person becomes aware of an attempt to manipulate him through persuasion, he is likely to stop listening. The most responsible forms of persuasion are those that a speaker can freely place at the disposal of his audience, to be used by both sides alike. This bilateral attempt to persuade, in which no rhetorical device is concealed, comes close to being what most people mean by reasoning. It is even close to what I mean by the use of reason in philosophy, except that I would still maintain that a philosophical argument is not an inducement to act.

Since I am not attempting here to assert any particular philosophical thesis, but only to exemplify how philosophy might relevantly examine rhetoric, I shall not develop the thesis I have adumbrated. I will be content if I have succeeded in showing that rhetoric needs philosophy because it faces a systematic problem. The problem is systematic in that it is not a problem within rhetoric. It is not a problem concerning some particular rhetorical situation or technique. Hence it is not a problem that can be solved by rhetoric. In order to solve it we must turn to philosophy as the discipline primarily concerned with systematic problems.

In sum, rhetoric is relevant to philosophy not as an organ of persuasion but as a condition of human existence. Philosophy is relevant to rhetoric as a means of clarifying that condition.

VII.
Argumentation and Inconsistency

I wish to discuss a serious problem that is raised by my own position concerning philosophical arguments. My position is that all philosophical arguments are *ad hominem*. By this, I mean that a valid argument against a philosophical thesis must exhibit that thesis as inconsistent with its own assertion or defense, or with principles that must necessarily be accepted by anyone who maintains the thesis. I regard any valid argument *in favor of* a philosophical thesis as fundamentally reducible to arguments *against* theses held by the limited audience to which the argument is addressed, so that the polemical argument is, in my opinion, the basic type.[1]

The problem that I now face concerns the inconsistency which, on my view, any philosophical critic must exhibit between his opponent's thesis and what that thesis presupposes, if his criticism is to be valid. What the critic must do is not only to exhibit explicit assertion X and presupposition Y, but also to call attention to the *inconsistency* between X and Y. The difficulty here is in showing why the defendant need *acknowledge* the inconsistency. If he is under no obligation to acknowledge it, then clearly the criticism could not have been valid. Indeed, many a philosophical argument has missed its mark for just this reason, and unless there are cases in which there is an obligation to acknowledge an inconsistency, there are no valid philosophical arguments at all. But it seems unlikely to me that every rational being would be under an obligation to acknowledge such an inconsistency, regardless of his philosophical orientation. My own orientation in philosophy leads me to this doubt, for two reasons. In the first place, the very notion of inconsistency is itself subject to philosophical interpretation. Later on in this paper, I shall discuss three possible philosophical views with regard to the conditions under which a set of statements is inconsistent. Thus whether a person is under an obligation to acknowledge an alleged inconsistency may depend upon whether it *is* an inconsistency in his terms. In the second place, if every rational being is under obligation to acknowledge an inconsistency, then the inconsistency must be subject to verification by every rational being — as, for example, "68 x 31 = 2,108" is subject to verification. But cases of inconsistency subject to verification by every rational being can occur only in formal systems, in which the axioms and rules of inference are unambiguously stated and it is irrelevant to consider the meanings of the symbols. But clearly the assertion of a philosophical thesis or point of view is not like this, for the meanings of the symbols in terms of which the assertion is made are clearly essential to the enterprise of making the assertion.

Yet are we to conclude that there are *no* valid arguments outside formal logic? If so, argumentation is no more than an instrument of suggestion — albeit a more civilized and subtle one than hypnosis. There are types of argument for which this characterization is not at all improper. But philosophy is supposed to be an affair of reason. This can be maintained only if valid arguments can occur in philosophy. So we must try to make sense of the kind of inconsistency which such arguments would have to exhibit.

---

[1]For a fuller account of my view, see *Philosophy and Argument,* The Pennsylvania State University Press, 1959.

This essay is an attempt to illustrate and clarify the problem I have just been spelling out, and to take a tentative step toward its solution. First, I want to consider a concrete case of philosophical conflict, consisting of arguments and counter-arguments that could not be properly analyzed except in terms of the notion of inconsistency. Then I shall make some suggestions as to how this notion might be construed without treating it either as independent of philosophical orientation or as a purely formal notion.

I want to discuss the relationship between two contrasting philosophical interpretations of the laws of logic. The first of these, which I shall call functionalism, asserts that the significance of the laws of logic is exhausted by the role of those laws in mathematics and other areas where deductive proofs occur. If there are versions of deductive proof calling for alternatives to the usual laws, then alternative logics can exist side by side, none with more right than the others. For in order to establish the propriety of any kind of logic, it is sufficient to show that it has a use in deduction.

Functionalism in this sense would be opposed by what I shall call realism, according to which no law of logic is ultimately acceptable unless it is intrinsically connected with the structure of the world. Generally, realism lends its support to the so-called "classical" version of logic, although as I shall point out later, it is by no means necessary that it should. Classical logic is characterized by its inclusion of certain laws such as the law of the excluded middle, and when realism espouses this version, it may show its interest in the structure of the world by expressing the law of the excluded middle, and other laws that it regards as fundamental, in ontological terms. It may assert, for example, that to be is, *inter alia,* either to have a given property or not to have it — what violates the law of the excluded middle cannot exist. According to realism, the alleged alternative logics lacking the law of the excluded middle are actually only incomplete versions of classical logic, which indeed is presupposed by the very act of interpreting these alleged alternatives. Realism, it will be seen, inclines toward monism, while functionalism is hospitable to a plurality of logics.

I have chosen functionalism and realism in logic as examples because their opposition seems to me to have a structure shared by many other pairs of opposing philosophical positions. According to one member of each pair, the meaning of any experience of a certain type reduces to its form. Thus, we have behaviorism, on which behavior has no meaning over and above its form, ethical formalism, according to which the rightness of an act is uniquely determined by its form, and formalism in aesthetics, as well as the logical theory that I have called "functionalism." The other member of each pair asserts that meaning resides in something over and above form; the meaning of behavior, for instance, must be sought in the conscious or unconscious mental activity of which the behavior is merely the expression. What I shall have to say about functionalism and realism in logic, then, would apply *mutatis mutandis* to many other examples of philosophical disagreement.

Let us consider the arguments for functionalism and for realism. The functionalist may point to various types of deduction in which, in his view, various logics are involved. The considerations leading to the development of modal logics are a case in point. The relation between the premises and conclusion of a valid argument is pointed to as a situation in which the classical treatment of conditional or hypothetical propositions falls short. For we do not say that an argument is valid merely because not all the premises are true or the conclusion is true. We say that it is valid only when it is *impossible* for all the premises to be true while the conclusion is false. There is, then, a logic of impossibility, possibility, and necessity, which contrasts with the classical logic of truth and falsity. To say that there "is" such a logic, however, is not to say that such a logic reflects the structure of what exists; it is only to say that there is a domain of deduction that requires it.

Modal logic is an alternative to classical logic in the sense that it involves a supplementation of the classical laws. Intuitionistic logic, on the other hand, represents a weakening of classical logic. Yet the functionalistic argument can be used to defend intuitionism as easily as it can be used on behalf of modal logic; for there "is" a logic without the laws of double negation or excluded middle only to the extent that there are areas of mathematics demanding this logic. No doubt, a non-functionalistic defense of logics that deny the laws of double negation or excluded middle is also possible. The Marxist defense is a case in point; in a world of dialectical flux, the negation of the negation is an emergent. This is actually what I have called realism; for it sees logic as the mirror of reality. Modal logic can undoubtedly also be defended on the basis of cosmic necessities and possibilities. For that matter, classical logic has a functionalistic defense; witness the formalism of Hilbert. What these variants show is just that one should not confuse types of logic with interpretations of logic. It is with interpretations that I am now concerned; for it is interpretations of logic, not types of logic, that can collide philosophically.

I have spoken of the functionalistic arguments for various types of logic. The evidence on which such arguments rest is simply the existence of various domains of deduction, each alleged to require the type of logic in question. I turn now to the realistic argument for a logic based on ontology. The evidence here is the world. But it might be objected, for example, that the world does not constitute clear-cut evidence of the law of double negation. What is *solid* is *not-liquid,* but what is *not-liquid* is not necessarily *solid.* So the denial of the denial of *solid* is not necessarily *solid.* Supposing that the realist wishes to defend classical logic, he will reply that this objection rests upon a misunderstanding of what it means to deny a term. Once this point is cleared up, the formula "For any property P, P = non-non-P" expresses without distortion an aspect of the structure of the world.

But there is something unsatisfactory about both the functionalistic and the realistic arguments that I have outlined. They seem to sidestep issues that one thinks ought to be met head-on. They certainly do not meet each other head-on. The outlines I have given are, in fact, incomplete; and what is missing will soon be obvious enough. As matters now stand, both functionalism and realism constitute excellent documentation for the statement that every philosopher has reason on his side and none can, accordingly be refuted. The elaboration and defense of each doctrine is clearly a rational activity. For the functionalist, it is the activity of examining various domains in which deductions occur to see what logics are required. For the realist, it is the activity of correcting language, so that the ontologically warranted logic can appear without distortion. But no functionalist will be much impressed by the report that there is ontological evidence for the ultimacy of a certain type of logic;

the "evidence" shown him is simply not evidence for him at all. Nor does his own report that, for example, certain areas of discourse require a modal logic impress the realist, who is busily occupied in correcting those areas of discourse to make modal logic unnecessary. Each of the two conflicting positions begs the question in attempting to refute the other, for each argues on the basis of premises explicitly denied by the other. It would seem then that neither position can touch the other at all.

Yet I have characterized functionalism and realism as *conflicting*. Functionalism is not merely *non*-realism; it is *anti*-realism, and the logic of "anti-" is different from the logic of "non-." Non-objective art, for instance, is not necessarily anti-objective art. In a treatise on art, objective and non-objective art can be discussed side-by-side, and the contrasts between them made clear. But this is just what could not adequately be done in the case of functionalism and realism. For there is no universe of discourse in which their contrasts can be made clear. Each position claims possession of the only universe of discourse in which comparison can be made at all. Each compares itself to its rival from its own point of view. To ignore this claim is to disqualify oneself from making any comparisons except ones that both of the conflicting positions must disown.

But I still have not shown how positions related in the way that I have maintained that functionalism and realism are related could conflict with each other at all. How can two positions conflict, if neither is capable of regarding the other as a challenge? What I have said about the logic of "anti-" needs supplementation. Let me return to a previous point. The relation between objective and non-objective art is one that it might conceivably be instructive to consider. In other words, a person uncommitted to either type of art could be instructed as to the difference. But it could never be very instructive to consider the difference between functionalism and antifunctionalism in logical theory. For on the face of it, both views are equally arbitrary in a way in which we would not say that objective and non-objective art are arbitrary. Functionalism and realism, to the extent that I have so far described them, seem arbitrary because the sketches I have given contain no clue as to the *point* of either position. Why on earth should any sane person adopt either one of them? One does not see the *point* of a philosophical position until he grasps the motivation underlying the position. The descriptions of positions in dictionaries of philosophy are usually inadequate because they omit reference to motivation. But, of course, it is insufficient merely to describe the motives from which a philosophical position is taken, since such motives will themselves seem arbitrary. Suppose we are told that functionalism stems from a concern with deduction, and realism from a concern with ontology. We are tempted to ask "What on earth is the point of such odd concerns?" The only way to answer this question is to become involved in the differences between functionalism and realism, instead of being content merely to describe these differences. Being involved in the differences, we shall have to be polemical instead of instructive; we shall have to win over minds committed to an alien position, rather than merely supplying the truth to those who lack it. The unsatisfactoriness of the functionalistic and realistic arguments, as I have outlined them so far, arises from the failure of these outlines to suggest the polemical orientation of the arguments. So oriented, the arguments do not sidestep the issues, but meet them and each other head-on. ·

Realism cannot refute functionalism by pointing to evidence, for the "evidence" it points to is not such as functionalism can even admit to exist. But the realistic *polemic* against functionalism has little in common with the attempted refutation based on alleged evidence. Polemic, rather than making a point that the position under attack must on its own principles ignore, makes a point that the position under attack cannot on its own principles ignore. Thus the full realistic argument against the functionalistic waiver of the law of double negation would *not* appeal to the structure of what is. It would appeal instead to the principles of functionalism itself. But it is necessary to make only a minor change in the wording of the argument in order to implement this major shift in strategy. According to the argument I outlined before, the realist wished to specify precisely what it means to deny a term so that symbols might express reality without distortion. Instead, the realist might wish to specify the precise meaning of denial in order to make explicit a hitherto implicit presupposition of functionalism. The argument might then run as follows: "Let us grant the functionalist his deviant notions of negation and the queer logics that he develops from these notions. But he will find that he cannot even state these queer logics without making use of normal logic with its customary law of double negation. For if a formula in a queer logic is *not* *un*provable, it is provable; if a queer system is *not* *in*consistent, it is consistent; and so on; and these are relationships that the functionalist continually relies on in developing his logic."

The realist can also observe that the functionalist is not interested in *all* deductions; he is interested only in *valid* deductions. Thus the functionalist's investigations do not in fact concern deduction wherever it occurs; they concern deduction only to the extent that it possesses a certain property over and above the mere stepwise movement from premises to conclusion. But the fact that this property itself remains invariant as it applies or fails to apply to every deduction in every domain suggests that the functionalist is actually guided by an ontological consideration over and above all of the peculiar deductive patterns that he investigates. The distinction between a valid and an invalid deduction is, after all, that a valid deduction is a real deduction, while an invalid one is only an apparent one.

Similarly, the functionalist must take the realist seriously if he is to meet the issue. For example, he may try to show that each of the queer logics he recommends is implicit in the realistic defense of an ontologically warranted logic. Validity, invalidity, and inconsistency can, after all, easily be construed as modal properties. The categories of "theorem" and "non-theorem" are not necessarily exhaustive, since in addition to statements that are theorems and statements that are non-theorems there may be formulas that are not statements at all. Indeed, what of statements whose status as theorems or non-theorems cannot be determined? Of course the realist whose reply consists merely in citing the law of the excluded middle begs the question.

The functionalist can also challenge the realist's intentions in correcting and purifying language. The realist claims that he does this so that the structure of reality can be expressed without distortion. But where does "the structure of reality" really come into the picture at all? If one *defines* "non-P" as

"everything but P," then non-non-P is naturally the same as P; but this is certified by the results of deduction, not by ontological insight. It looks as if the
real reason why the realist wants to refine language is just that he is interested
in deduction.

This much will perhaps suffice as an example of the logic of "anti-." I
should like to generalize as follows. Suppose there are two philosophical
positions A and B such that A is anti-B and B is anti-A. Then there are
arguments for A, the propriety of whose premises an advocate of B could not
acknowledge; and there are arguments for B, the propriety of whose premises
an advocate of A could not acknowledge. Both sets of arguments thus beg the
question, and to the extent that the positions rely upon the arguments, they
are solipsistically isolated one from the other. Each has reason on its side. But
in this situation, not only would it be hopeless for an advocate of A to attempt
to convert an advocate of B, or vice versa, but also not even the "anti-" would
make sense. If A is committed to ignoring all "evidence" for B, and vice versa,
then there is no genuine opposition. In fact, however, A and B will both be
supported by additional arguments, in terms of which there is genuine opposition. The additional arguments for A will consist in attempts to show that B
in fact presupposes A; in other words, that implicit in the very formulation of B
are presuppositions acceptable to A but inconsistent with the formulation of B.
Similarly, among the arguments for B will be found ones claiming to show that
A presupposes what is inconsistent with its very formulation as a philosophical
position.

The question arises, however, whether these additional arguments can
really overcome the solipsistic impasse that seemed to preclude genuine opposition. Suppose an advocate of A produces a presupposition involved in B
that is, in his opinion, inconsistent with the formulation of B. What reason is
there to suppose any advocate of B must agree that there is an inconsistency? If
he need not agree, the impasse remains.

Of course, the attacker may be mistaken; perhaps what he takes to be an
inconsistency between the formulation of B and the presuppositions of B is not
really an inconsistency. The question I am now raising is just whether such an
attacker must always be mistaken. Is it possible for an inconsistency to develop
within a position that "has reason on its side"? If it is possible, that will be sufficient to overcome the impasse.

Let me turn the matter the other way round. In point of fact, there will be
criticisms of realism to which the realist must reply. It is difficult to see, for example, how he could avoid being obligated to make some sort of reply to the
functionalistic objection I have outlined above. To shed light on the necessity
of this reply, let us see what the reply is that is necessitated. Consider the functionalist's criticism that modal logics are involved in the development and exposition of classical logic, so that if classical logic is to be the standard of exposition, the realist has failed to meet his own standard. The realist could
counter that the development and exposition of classical logic is far different
from classical logic itself. While classical logic is, or reflects, the structure of
what is, its expositor is thrown upon his inadequate human resources in
attempting to express this structure. Who can say but what modal logic simply
represents the failure of a finite mind to come to grips with the truth? Perhaps

it is just the best we humans can do. Perhaps an omniscient being could do without modal logic.

In replying, the realist has made a distinction. He has been forced to do this by his own failure to meet his own standards of exposition. Thus the distinction he has made was already implicit in his original position, because it was presupposed by the very act of articulating that position. All that the functionalist has done is to have called this fact to the realist's attention. He has not sought to impose anything on the realist. He has merely invited him to overcome disequilibrium by revising his own critical basis. This example, then, shows how an inconsistency can develop within a position that "has reason on its side," and how the very reason it has on its side may be forced to undergo revision in the effort to overcome the inconsistency.

The problem of this essay can now be stated more specifically than at first. I have said that the position of the realist, at least before he distinguishes classical logic from human thought, is inconsistent and that the functionalist calls this inconsistency to the attention of the realist. Does this not presuppose that the realist and the functionalist both accept the same criterion of inconsistency? If they do, and if the relation between realism and functionalism is really typical of opposed philosophical points of view, then this criterion of inconsistency must be universal, i.e., it must be the same for all philosophers regardless of their philosophical orientations. For any philosopher who wishes to engage in effective criticism of an alien position will have to appeal to this criterion in order to make his criticism clear. But if there were such a universally accepted criterion, philosophical arguments would be subject to non-philosophical criticism — a consequence certainly out of keeping with the view that all philosophical arguments are *ad hominem*. On the other hand, consider the alternative. Suppose there were no criterion of consistency common to two philosophical positions. Then neither could criticize the other. The functionalist, for instance, who thought that he saw an inconsistency in the realist's original position would be met by the reply, "But that is *not* an inconsistency in my terms! If you call it an inconsistency, you are just begging the question!"

In dealing with this problem, I first want to point out that even if conflicting points of view must share a criterion of consistency, it does not follow that any such criterion is universal. All that does follow is that for every pair of conflicting points of view, there is some or other criterion of consistency — not necesssarily the same in all cases of conflict.

Also, it is obvious that different criteria of consistency are operative in different conflicts. Sometimes, for example, positions are condemned as inconsistent when contradictory consequences can be drawn from them. Sometimes the alleged inconsistency is felt to lie in the impossibility of exemplifying a position. Neither of these criteria, however, seems particularly relevant to the issue between the functionalist and the realist. The criterion to which appeal seems to be made here is a pragmatic one: no view is consistent if the truth of the view would imply the impossibility of stating the view. I call this criterion pragmatic because of its obvious relationship to what is called the pragmatic paradox; i.e., the paradox of a proposition whose utterance by certain speakers would be self-refuting.

Indeed, the very notion of a universal criterion of consistency immediately destroys itself, because universal criteria of consistency are among the very things that philosophers argue about. Aristotle attempts to defend the law of non-contradiction as a universal criterion of consistency in Book Gamma of the *Metaphysics*. It is highly significant that Aristotle's defense pivots upon precisely the pragmatic considerations adduced in the last paragraph; when someone ignores or denies the law of non-contradiction, his inconsistency must then consist in a systematic incapacity to state his own position. For such a person cannot legitimately say anything, and so a *fortiori* cannot give articulate expression to any particular point of view.

I do not wish to imply, however, that I regard this pragmatic criterion of consistency as having any more of a role in philosophical criticism than does any other criterion. Let us consider the role of the criterion of exemplifiability. By this, I mean the principle that a philosophical position is inconsistent if the contents of the world cannot be interpreted in such a way as to exemplify the position. The use of such a criterion obviously hinges upon an agreement between critic and defendant to the effect that certain interpretations of the contents of the world are precluded. Consider the realistic polemic against the functionalist claim that all deductions are equally worthy of attention. What the realist claims is that this generalization is too inclusive to have any model. It says too much, and therefore says nothing. The most that one could properly say is that all *valid* deductions are equally worthy of attention. This implies that on any possible interpretation, the world contains invalid deductions as well as valid ones; it is impossible to interpret the world as containing valid deductions only. So the issue between the functionalist and the realist presupposes a common ontological commitment. But from this it does not follow that there is any ontological commitment that is presupposed by all philosophical issues. The fact that there is not is immediately proved by the occurrence of arguments over ontological commitments of all kinds. Even the point on which the functionalist and his realistic critic agree has been denied; e.g., by the philosopher for whom all talk is rhetoric and the distinction between valid and invalid talk is an illusion.

What I am proposing then is to deal with the problem of inconsistency by asserting that there are a number of criteria of inconsistency no one of which would be appropriate to all philosophical arguments. Any one valid philosophical argument, then, will exhibit an inconsistency determined by the appropriate criteria, i.e., criteria that are or ought to be acknowledged by the partisans of the position under attack. Thus, I have shown how the functionalist attacks the realist in terms of a pragmatic criterion, which it is somehow obligatory for the latter to accept; and when the realist attacks the functionalist, he employs an ontological criterion which is somehow implicit in the functionalist's own position. I do not at the moment know how to describe the mechanism which I have indicated by "somehow." In fact, it seems odd, on the face of it, that the realist should be committed to a pragmatic criterion, and the functionalist to an ontological one; one might have supposed that it would be the other way around. But on second thoughts, dialectical mechanisms do often operate in this way. In any event, this seems to me to be a way of defending the purely *ad hominem* character of philosophical argument against the objection that inconsistency is a matter of fact.

VIII.
"Philosophy and *Argumentum ad Hominem*" Revisited

My article "Philosophy and *Argumentum ad Hominem*,"[1] which became a pivotal section of my book *Philosophy and Argument*,[2] first appeared eighteen years ago. Although I am no longer satisfied with the way I expressed the thesis I was trying to develop in that article, it is a thesis which in principle I still maintain. Let me try to recapitulate it. I began by assuming a distinction between *argumentum ad rem* and *argumentum ad hominem*. One thing I did not see in 1952 is that while the latter is a specific form of argument, the former is not. *Argumentum ad rem* is a purely negative phrase. It denotes the entire spectrum of arguments other than *argumentum ad hominem*, or at least all those which are not obviously fallacious. Perhaps *argumentum ad populum*, *argumentum ad misericordium*, and the like, are not examples of either *argumentum ad hominem* or *argumentum ad rem;* but the vast majority of arguments whose premises are relevant to their conclusions are *ad rem*. If I asked someone to classify a certain argument, I might accept any of Aristotle's *topoi* as an answer, and *argumentum ad hominem* would be among the possible answers. But it would hardly be helpful to classify the argument as *ad rem*. Similarly, if I asked a jeweler to identify a stone I brought in, it would hardly be helpful to be told merely "It is a valuable stone"; for what I should want to know is whether it was an agate, an opal, or an onyx.

So many arguments, then, are *ad rem* that it would be difficult either to enumerate them or to find a positive common property running through them. The best way to define the class is in fact by contrast with *argumentum ad hominem*. The definition of *argumentum ad hominem* given by Bishop Whately in 1832, which I quoted with approval in my article and later in my book, still seems to me to be acceptable:

> In the *argumentum ad hominem*, the conclusion which actually is established, is not the absolute and general one in question, but relative and particular; viz., not that "such and such is the fact," but that "*this* man is bound to admit it, in conformity to his principles of reasoning, or consistency with his own conduct, situation," etc.

Argumentum ad rem, then, is any sort of argument, or at least any sort of not obviously invalid argument, that exhibits these properties which, according to Whately, *argumentum ad hominem* does not exhibit. Thus it establishes, or at least aims or claims to establish, an absolute and general conclusion, of the form "such and such is the fact." Its cogency does not depend on its audience. Whether it establishes its conclusion or not depends in no way upon the principles of those to whom it is addressed.

The thesis I have been trying to defend, on and off for eighteen years, is that a philosophical argument cannot be valid unless it is addressed *ad hominem*. Let me give an example. In 1942, in an essay on G. E. Moore, Norman Malcolm wrote "Ordinary language is correct language."[3] Notice that

[1] *Journal of Philosophy*, 49 (1952), 489-98.
[2] University Park: The Pennsylvania State University Press, 1959. See the critical study of this book by Ch. Perelman in *Revue internationale de philosophie*, 51 (1960), 96-100.
[3] "Moore and Ordinary Language," *The Philosophy of G.E. Moore*, ed. P.A. Schilpp (Northwestern University, 1942), p. 357.

in making this statement Malcolm actually intended to state a somewhat stronger position than the one explicitly expressed by the sentence. He meant to be declaring that ordinary language is the *only* correct language, at least in philosophy. But with this understanding, the statement became the motto of many philosophers who identified themselves as linguistic analysts or ordinary language philosophers. The analysts tried to dismiss a host of philosophical problems by showing that some departure from ordinary language was required in order to state the problems. Since such departures could not constitute a correct use of language, they argued, the problems did not exist. For example, we are not using the word "beginning" in an ordinary way in asking whether the world has a beginning. We can ask in ordinary language whether a process has a beginning only when the process occurs *within* the world; e.g., "Was Mr. X born blind, or did his blindness begin at a certain age?" But if we ask whether the *world* had a beginning, this question makes no more sense than the question "What is the square root of green?"

How can one attack the thesis that ordinary language is the only correct language? One might begin by pointing out to Malcolm and the other members of his school a myriad of uses of extraordinary language in the literature of philosophy. From Plato's technical use of *eidos* through Kant's *Ding*, to Sartre's *projet* and Whitehead's "actual occasion," philosophers have been violating ordinary language. Must not linguistic analysis retreat before such massive evidence? Hardly. The alleged "evidence" is precisely grist for the analysts' mill — it is no more than a record of 2400 years of linguistic aberration resulting in the squandering of untold energy on problems that did not exist.

There is, however, a more hopeful way of attacking the thesis. To start with, one might express some reservations about the very motto "Ordinary language is correct language." Viewed from a certain angle, this does not seem like a very ordinary thing to say. Ordinary language, in the sense intended here, is itself rarely if ever a topic in ordinary language. One might say, of a distinguished orator whom one has interviewed in private, "He used only the most ordinary language when I talked to him," but in this sentence the phrase "ordinary language" does not function as it does in Malcolm's motto. For Malcolm it denotes the exalted public utterances of the orator as well as his prosaic private pronouncements. It denotes the technical statements of the scientist as well as the deliverances of the layman. But it does not denote *all* speech. Philosophical talk, as far as Malcolm is concerned, is extraordinary language. But the motto "Ordinary language is correct language" is clearly philosophical talk. Hence it seems to impugn its own correctness.

Like Norman Malcolm (and like G. E. Moore, on whom Malcolm was commenting when he formulated his motto), Ludwig Wittgenstein regarded ordinary language as the touchstone of correctness. Wittgenstein's own motto, "The meaning is the use," implies that if an expression has no use in ordinary language it has no meaning. Yet it is clear that in presenting this thesis Wittgenstein moves beyond ordinary language, and so do his followers. I quote from E. A. Burtt's recent book *In Search of Philosophic Understanding*:

> When one turns from Wittgenstein's teaching about ordinary language to his practice as a pioneering philosopher it becomes obvious that he departed rather drastically from established ways of speaking — and some of the extraordinary

ways he introduced have already become current coin in philosophical discussion. In certain cases the words themselves are new; notice the tendency among philosophers to talk about a significant step in an argument as a "move," thus reflecting the Wittgensteinian view of language as a game. Other key terms are "family of meanings" and "paradigm." . . . Traditional words are retained while their meanings are transformed. Consider the crucial words "logic," "rule," and even "philosophy" itself. Thinkers who were trained in an earlier era did not learn to use these words in the novel senses they have now acquired, except largely through Wittgenstein's influence (p. 66).[4]

What I have tried to illustrate in terms of the contrast between an ineffective argument against ordinary language philosophy and a relatively effective one is the difference between the use of *argumentum ad rem* in philosophy and the use of *argumentum ad hominem*. To tell Malcolm that *eidos, Ding, projet,* and "actual occasion" constitute uses of extraordinary but perfectly correct language is to engage in an *argumentum ad rem*, since the argument does not depend on or refer to Malcolm's own principles, but seeks to establish the absolute and general conclusion that some extraordinary language is correct. Instead of appealing to Malcolm's principles, it appeals to alleged facts. But this is precisely why it is ineffective. For what the arguer takes to be facts are not at all facts so far as Malcolm is concerned. From Malcolm's point of view, it is simply not true that when Plato used the word *eidos,* he was using language correctly, or that Kant's use of "Ding" is a correct use of language. Indeed, that is the very point at issue. The motto "Ordinary language is correct language" is precisely a declaration concerning the range of possible facts. To attack it by adducing alleged facts that it specifically rejects is just to beg the question; it is to argue on the basis of a premise which Malcolm expressly denies.

It seemed to me in 1952, and it still does, that any philosophical argument based on alleged facts or evidence is doomed, because a philosophical position always is, or implies, a decision as to what is to count as facts or evidence. I am not saying that an appeal to the ordinary use of a word or sentence could never serve as the basis of an effective argument concerning the correctness of the use. Clearly, there are cases in which the Merriam-Webster *Third International Dictionary* can be used to determine whether a given usage is ordinary and hence whether it is correct. If a colleague begins to spout archaic words, I can show him that they are marked as archaic in the *Third,* hence that they are not ordinary, and thus that they are not correct by present-day standards. Notice, though, that this is not Malcolm's appeal to ordinary language. For the words he is concerned about are in the dictionary, and are *not* marked as archaic or as departing in any other way from standard usage. Thus Plato's use of *eidos* can be found in Liddell and Scott, Kant's use of *Ding* in the Brockhaus, etc. The issue over philosophical words and sentences is not whether they are in some *objective* sense ordinary. The critic who has adduced the extraordinary Platonic and Kantian usages in order to combat the motto that ordinary language is correct language is, for that matter, perfectly willing to admit that the usages are in the dictionary. What he means by "ordinary," and what Malcolm means by it, is simply a property not to be defined

---

[4]New York: New American Library, 1967.

in objective terms. Not that there is anything arbitrary about the process of identifying it; Malcolm and his critic can presumably agree that *eidos* and *Ding* are not examples of ordinary language. Their disagreement concerns the correctness of language that is extraordinary in this non-objective way. Such a disagreement cannot be resolved by any appeal to facts.

What I have said so far is no more than a review of my reasons for regarding *argumentum ad rem* as a generally invalid argument in philosophy, and thus for seeing *argumentum ad hominem* as the only hope for valid philosophical argumentation. Notice that I do not mean "valid" in the sense of "formally valid." The formal validity of an argument can be assessed only when the premises can be clearly distinguished from the conclusion. But once the premises of a philosophical argument are distinctly set forth, they become the locus of doubts that vitiate the argument. While a formally valid argument can thus be vitiated, the sense of "valid" I have in mind is one in which a valid argument cannot be vitiated. It forces the person to whom it is addressed to revise or abandon his point of view. It seems to me, for example, that the *argumentum ad hominem* that I have proposed as an attack on Malcolm's motto "Ordinary language is correct language" necessitates at the very least that the motto be revised. Perhaps the required revision is "Ordinary language is correct language, and pronouncements about ordinary language can also be correct."

In a recent Ph.D. thesis,[5] Warren J. Hockenos scrutinizes what I mean when I say that only the *argumentum ad hominem* can be valid in philosophy. It is criticisms of the kind that Hockenos makes, whether actually expressed by others or myself, that have caused me, over the years, gradually to modify my conception of the nature and purpose of philosophical argumentation. One of Hockenos's main questions is whether my account of the validity of *argumentum ad hominem* does not in fact presuppose the validity of *argumentum ad rem*. He raises this question in two ways. In the first place, he makes the point that the success of *argumentum ad hominem* depends on logical considerations. Unless there is in fact a contradiction between the principles of the philosopher it attacks and some overt statement or act on the part of the philosopher, the argument does not force him to revise or abandon his position, and hence is not, by my own standards, valid. But how do we show that such a contradiction exists? We argue "Any proposition of the form '*p* and not-*p*' is a contradiction; this proposition is of that form; therefore, this proposition is a contradiction." This is an absolute and general conclusion, which, while it may *concern* the principles of the man to whom it is addressed, does not in any way *depend* on those principles. The argument, it would seem, is *ad rem*.

There is a difference, however, between this argument and the *ad rem* arguments which seem to me to fail in philosophy. Let us recall the ineffective *ad rem* argument that might have been used against Malcolm's thesis that ordinary language is correct language. This consisted in pointing out cases of extraordinary language that is still correct. The argument is ineffective because

---

[5]"An Examination of *Reductio ad Absurdum* and *Argumentum ad Hominem* Arguments in the Philosophies of Gilbert Ryle and Henry W. Johnstone, Jr." (Boston University, Ph.D. diss., 1968).

Malcolm need only reply that he does not regard the extraordinary uses as correct. In other words, he refuses to accept as evidence the alleged evidence that his critic has offered. His refusal is grounded in the fact that his very thesis defines the range of possible evidence, and what the critic has brought forward falls outside this range. The range of possible evidence concerning correct language, so far as Malcolm is concerned, falls within ordinary language; to say this is just to restate his thesis. To attempt to attack this thesis by appealing to alleged evidence specifically excluded by the thesis is just to beg the question.

Now to criticize a statement as inconsistent with the principles of the philosopher who has made the statement is no doubt to appeal to alleged evidence of some sort. But it does not necessarily fall beyond the range of possible evidence as explicitly stated by the philosopher under attack. If I argue, for example, that there is an inconsistency between the *position* that ordinary language is the only correct language and the *statement* "Ordinary language is the only correct language," what I am declaring to be a contradiction does not necessarily fall beyond the range of possible contradictions as defined by Malcolm. Indeed, in taking the position he does, Malcolm is not the least concerned to define the range of possible contradictions. Such a thesis might, of course, be adopted; it would be a thesis about logic. But not all philosophical theses concern logic in this way.

These remarks can be generalized to cover logical criticisms of many kinds. Not only can a critic find a contradiction not specifically disavowed by the philosopher accused of it, but also cases of *non sequitur* can be pointed to in the utterances of philosophers whose explicit pronouncements afford them no defense against the charge of *non sequitur.*

Thus it seems to me that Hockenos is right to suppose that an appeal to logic can have special force in philosophical argumentation. Whether this force can be accounted for only by regarding the appeal to logic as an *argumentum ad rem* remains to be seen. There are in fact several ways in which one might consider handling the existence of these seemingly *ad rem* arguments which are efficacious in philosophy. One might hold that, among not obviously fallacious arguments, *argumentum ad hominem* and *argumentum ad rem,* contrary to the position I have taken, are not exhaustive. Or one might equivalently assert that if they are exhaustive, there are two kinds of *argumentum ad rem,* one valid and the other invalid. A valid philosophical argument appealing to logic might then be classified either as a valid *argumentum ad rem* or as neither *ad rem* nor *ad hominem,* but some third form. However neither of these ways of accounting for the efficacy of logical criticism in philosophical argumentation seems to me to be ultimately satisfactory. For logical criticism can be *invalid* in several ways. A critic can claim, for example, to have found a contradiction where there is none. If all invalid logical criticisms could be subsumed under this paradigm, there would be no problem; it would be sufficient to characterize the valid criticisms as *ad rem* and the invalid ones as unsuccessful attempts at *ad rem.* But there is another way in which a logical criticism can be invalid, and this cannot be explained as an unsuccessful attempt at *ad rem* — or at least as being unsuccessful in the same way as the previous example. If the thesis criticized is explicitly a thesis about logic, but the criticism fails to take the thesis into account, the critic has begged the question precisely as one would beg the question in appealing to evidence specifically rejected by the position one attacked. A thinker might, for example, take some definite position concerning the nature of contradictions; he might declare that only statements of a certain form are contradictions. If a critic attempted to attack this thesis by pointing to contradictions in it not of this form, he would be begging the question in just the way that Malcolm's critic has begged the question in citing Plato and Kant as users of extraordinary but correct language, and this begging of the question is an error of a different order from the act of seeing a logical error where there is none. I do not actually *know* any relevant philosophical theses about the nature of contradictions that are sufficiently plausible to be appealed to here. But in the history of logic some very plausible philosophical theses concerning the nature of such logical concepts as the excluded middle, implication, and sets have been vigorously advocated. To criticize such theses as violating standards that they explicitly reject is clearly to engage in *ad rem* argumentation exactly similar to the argumentation of this type that I have so far considered. Such argumentation is invalid just because it is *ad rem;* it should be contrasted with unsuccessful attempts to use *ad rem.*

So far, then, there is no need to allow for *valid argumenta ad rem* in philosophy. But what of valid logical criticisms of theses not explicitly concerned with the nature of logic? It seems to me that no great violence would be done to our understanding of the meaning of the phrase *"argumentum ad hominem"* if we were to classify such criticisms under the *ad hominem* heading. Long ago Aristotle remarked that the last resort in getting a man to admit that his view is inconsistent is an *argumentum ad hominem.* More generally, the function of logic is to maintain the possibility of discourse. A man who expresses his position presupposes the availability of discursive forms of language. If his very expression threatens to destroy these forms which he presupposes, the logical criticism that points this difficulty out to him can properly be called a valid *argumentum ad hominem.*

Malcolm, for example, implicitly but quite clearly endorses the principle of noncontradiction. His very appeal to ordinary language shows this. For speakers of ordinary language have always taken this principle for granted. Any locution seeming to violate the principle is immediately felt to be of extraordinary import. If you tell me that it is raining, I take your statement at face value, but if you tell me that it is raining and not raining, I automatically attempt to read between the lines. It follows that if we criticize Malcolm on the ground that he contradicts himself in saying "Ordinary language is correct language," we are very properly appealing to his own principles; i.e., arguing *ad hominem.*

I want now to consider Hockenos's second attempt to show that the validity of *argumentum ad hominem* presupposes that of *argumentum ad rem.* I have said that a valid philosophical argument against a position is one that vitiates the position. This is to say that in view of the argument the enunciator of the position must either revise or withdraw it. Hockenos objects, however, that there is a limit to what will be acceptable as a revised version of an original position. If, for example, the thesis at issue is one that presumes to define the range of correct language, we cannot accept a revision on which the sentence "Quadruplicity drinks procrastination" comes out to be a correct sentence.

There must be a neutral criterion of correctness which, in Hockenos's words, "provides the real source of force for the *argumentum ad hominem*."[6] And similarly for any other thesis put forward as a definition of reality, knowledge, the good, the beautiful, or any other term of this sort.

I am willing to admit both the need for and the effectiveness of such neutral criteria, provided that neutrality be regarded as a relative term. The rules of sentence formation in English, for example, are neutral relatively to the proposal that ordinary language is correct language. If this proposal is attacked *ad hominem*, no revision made in response to the attack can be satisfactory if it requires the violation of these rules. But the rules themselves are not beyond argumentation. They define the conditions under which discourse of a certain kind is possible. But surely there is no binding obligation to engage in discourse of this kind. Poetry takes liberties with the rules of sentence formation. The rhetoric of the New Left attempts to suppress discourse altogether in favor of action. Who is so prosaic as not to be able to visualize "Quadruplicity drinks procrastination" as a line in a poem or as a shout from a student protestor trying to reduce all talk to rubble?

Thus if someone revises his stand on ordinary language by saying "Quadruplicity drinks procrastination," and we attack this revision by calling attention to the rules of sentence formation, our attack is relevant only insofar as our interlocutor has not intended to abandon philosophical discourse altogether. Of course, if this has been his intention, it is somewhat inappropriate to say that he has "revised" his position. But the point is that by appealing to the rules in question we cannot get him to reconsider the change he wishes to make *unless* he subscribes to the rules; and he need not subscribe to them. Hence our appeal is *ad hominem*, not *ad rem*. Similarly for other appeals one might make to the allegedly neutral criteria that "provide the real source of force for the *argumentum ad hominem*" by providing limits, as Hockenos sees the matter, to what is acceptable as a revision in response to the *argumentum ad hominem*. Among the allegedly neutral criteria that fall within this class are the logical rules in terms of which *non sequitur* and inconsistency can be identified. I have already spoken of the *ad hominem* status of appeals to these rules. Hockenos adds to the list when he says, "It is surely a philosopher's right to point out to another that his position is inadequate with respect to common sense or science or history."[7] Clearly, such criticism is *ad hominem*, since it is valid only if the position under attack endorses the common sense, science, or history it is alleged to conflict with. Notice that it is unlikely to endorse all three; the conflict between science and common sense has often been commented on.

It might be asked whether I have not at this point reduced all argumentation to that of an *ad hominem* kind. Are there any genuine *argumenta ad rem* to which I can point? The example of trying to attack "Ordinary language is correct language" by adducing Plato, Kant, and Whitehead is, to my way of thinking, still relevant. A person attempting to silence the advocate of ordinary language by confronting him with these *loci classici* of extraordinary language is appealing to facts regarded as beyond the range of the ordinary language

---

[6] p. 260.
[7] p. 260.

philosopher's position. But of course the critic misses the point. What he fails to see is that to his opponent these utterances are incorrect precisely because extraordinary.

Any use of *argumentum ad rem* in philosophy is similarly marked by this question-begging character. We cannot tell in the last analysis whether an argument is *ad hominem* or *ad rem* unless we know whether it has begged the question. If someone says "Quadruplicity drinks procrastination," and I point to the rules of sentence formation, I am arguing *ad rem* if my interlocutor intends to be reciting poetry.

I do not mean to be suggesting that by any means *all* uses of *argumentum ad hominem* in philosophy are valid. There are other fallacies beside begging the question. An *argumentum ad hominem* can, for example, simply be a *non sequitur;* that is how the argument got its bad name. If I attempt to criticize Malcolm's thesis that ordinary language is correct language by pointing out that Malcolm was born in Selden, Kansas, where the language is, after all, pretty ordinary, this is just a mudslinging attack that has no relevance to the issue.

There is a problem about the use of *argumentum ad hominem* in philosophy, a problem to which Hockenos does not refer but which has bothered me considerably during the past eighteen years. In order to get someone else to admit a contradiction you must be sure that it is a contradiction in precisely *his* sense of the term — that the contradiction he has fallen into contradicts precisely what *his* principles require him to say in order to make sense. But there is the general problem of explaining how it is that we could ever be aquainted with another's principles in the first place. For it might seem that one's principles condemn one to purblindness. If I accept the principle that ordinary language is correct language, I cannot see the language of Plato or Kant as constituting an exception. A person's philosophical principles rule out the possibility of exceptions. How, then, is one ever in a position to appreciate the principles of another? Since the valid *argumentum ad hominem* depends upon this appreciation, it is essential that the question be answered.

The answer I want to propose in bringing this discussion to a conclusion is one that is only dimly prefigured in *Philosophy and Argument.* That book ended with a chapter on "Argumentation and Selfhood," in which it was rather oracularly maintained that the self is the pivot of philosophical argumentation. In the eleven years that have elapsed since making that statement, I have been trying to understand what it means. What I now think it means is something like the following. To occupy a philosophical position is to interpret the whole world in a certain way. An optimist, for example, sees everything in the world as an eventual good. Everything is grist for his mill. If you point a catastrophe out to him — an earthquake or a war — he will just use it as evidence for his thesis; he will show you the eventual good in it. You can't argue *ad rem* against an optimist. But at the same time, optimism as a philosophical thesis is a radical denial. It is a denial of pessimism. The optimist sees pessimism as a threat to his own position. Even though the only possible world for him is one in which everything is an eventual good, he must somehow be able to visualize the pessimist's world, in which everything is an eventual evil. He must treat this anti-world as not only impossible in his own terms but also possible in the sense of existing as a negation or threat. In other words, the optimist must be both totally enclosed by his own view and not totally enclosed by it.

Here, I think, is where the concept of the self is called for. As a locus of tension, or, if one will, of contradiction, the self is the point of view from which the optimist can see himself as both surrounded by the only possible world and threatened by another possible world. The contradiction evokes his self, and his self brings together under a single perspective the inconsistent propositions, and asserts them simultaneously.

How do these considerations apply to the *argumentum ad hominem?* Any valid use of this argument requires an understanding of alien principles on the part of one who attacks them. The attacker is both inside and outside the view he attacks. The argument against Malcolm, for example, succeeds only because the attacker has understood Malcolm's thesis in Malcolm's own terms. He has, in fact, understood it better than Malcolm himself. But to *understand* it and at the same time to *attack* it requires him both to *espouse* and *reject* it. Here the self is evoked as the fulcrum from which this feat can be accomplished.

In this paper I have spoken of changes in my view of *argumentum ad hominem.* These changes have been accompanied by a shift in my attitude toward the role of rhetoric in philosophical argumentation. From the position that philosophical argumentation must be sharply distinguished from rhetoric, I have moved to the position that all philosophical arguments have a neccessary and proper rhetorical vector. This new view is explained in several recent or forthcoming papers, to which I refer the curious reader.[8]

---

[8] See "Rhetoric and Communication in Philosophy," *Contemporary Philosophic Thought,* Vol. III (Albany: State University of New York Press, 1970), and "Truth, Communication and Rhetoric in Philosophy," *Revue Internationale de Philosophie,* 90 (1969), 404-409.

IX.
Rhetoric and Communication in Philosophy

In this essay I want to focus on rhetoric and communication, and consider what they are in themselves and how they are involved in philosophical activity. How one construes the concepts depends upon the overt or covert philosophical position one takes. In investigating the role of rhetoric and communication in philosophy, I cannot help taking a stand on the philosophy *of* rhetoric and communication. To the extent that developing the philosophy *of* anything is an activity in which rhetoric and communication have necessary roles to play, rhetoric and communication are required by the very activity that seeks to define them. I do not believe that the circularity here is vicious; the phenomenon is simply an example of the often noted reflexivity of philosophical activity.

One reason why determining the roles of rhetoric and communication in philosophy is a problem is that undue emphasis on one to the exclusion of the other in the pursuit of the philosophical enterprise has usually resulted in a caricature of that enterprise. The belief that the function of philosophy is to communicate and not to persuade is characteristic of at least the extreme forms of positivism. Persuasion is here dismissed as merely a function of emotive language. What positivism has found par excellence communicable, however, has been scientific fact and theory rather than philosophical doctrine. Once the sciences have been identified as the chief locus of communication, there is not much left for philosophy as such to do, except perhaps to formulate the principles of scientific communication. An example of such principles is the Verifiability Criterion, according to which only empirical statements and tautologies can be communicated — everything else is meaningless. But even the ultrapositivist is willing to concede that the principles formulated in his philosophy, including the Verifiability Criterion itself, are neither empirical statements nor tautologies; they are rather conventions. Clearly, conventions are not formulated merely to be ignored. The positivist attaches considerable importance, for example, to a scrupulous observance of the Verifiability Criterion. He insists on this observance as a necessary condition for meaningful discourse. Since such insistence is not grounded in fact or logic, it can have only the status of urgent persuasion. Rhetoric has thus made its uninvited appearance. That the positivist tacitly recognizes its presence is indicated by his vague and apologetic explanation that the Verifiability Criterion has a pragmatic if not a logical or empirical justification. For what has only a pragmatic justification can only be contended for as a means of facilitating action. But a belief that facilitates action is itself an action or a program of action; and it is precisely the function of rhetoric to incite actions and programs.

Philosophies in which rhetoric is given an exaggerated role to play and communication none at all are not likely to have much professional standing because professionals must communicate; "Publish or perish" is merely a corollary of "If you can't tell us what you're doing, how do we know that you're doing anything at all?" But clearly there are hyperrhetorical positions whether or not they are mentioned in academic circles. One symptom of such a position is its use of the idea of philistinism. The philistine is the obtuse individual who demands to be told what no one can hope to learn merely by being told. Only by being open to rhetoric can one hope to be sensitized to the doctrine in question, but the philistine is closed to rhetoric. Implicit in such a hyperrhetoricism is the principle that one cannot understand a doctrine unless one has been persuaded to believe it. This principle is to rhetoric as the Verifiability Criterion is to communication. As the latter defines the limits of communication without itself being communicated, so the former defines the limits of rhetoric without itself being the object of rhetorical activity. If it were itself the object of rhetorical activity, we would be plunged into an infinite regress, for we would then have to argue that the meta-philistine who cannot understand why to understand is to believe would understand this principle if he believed it. The principle is the inverse of a convention — whatever that is. It is the one principle that the hyperrhetoricist must communicate, and is thus his Achilles' heel. Of course, if he saw no one as a philistine, he would have no use for this principle. But it is precisely the beliefs, platitudinous and thoughtless though they are, of those whom the hyperrhetoricist identifies as philistines that define the content and point of his own position. Without philistines to deplore there would be no occasion for exhortations to the faithful. Similarly, without nonsense to attack, the positivist would have nothing philosophical to communicate.

We may note in passing that even though hyperrhetorical positions have little standing in professional circles, the professional himself may have hyperrhetorical tendencies. Although he can comfortably communicate with his colleagues, he may regard those who are not his colleagues as philistines. When asked by someone outside the field to describe his concerns, he may find that there is nothing he can communicate which would be of the slightest use, and that all he can say is "If you really want to know, you'd better take my course." To be sure, professional philosophers are by no means alone in this aloofness; professional economists and physicists are inclined to give the same answer, and the aloofness itself can be interpreted as no more than despair over the task of attempting to communicate briefly what can only be communicated at length. Yet there are few professional philosophers who suppose that all they have to convey to their students is information, even of a difficult and involved kind. Most of us have the feeling that the student who merely has the information is still a philistine, and that some turning, some acquiescence of the will to concerns that must be first accepted if they are to be understood, is required if the student is to be set on the road to becoming a professional philosopher. Since I myself unabashedly share in this feeling, it would be ludicrous of me to condemn it; I cite it only in order to show that hyperrhetoricism is more common than it may at first appear to be.

But the sketches I have drawn of positions in which the roles of communication and rhetoric are exaggerated are themselves exaggerated. Perhaps all that can be safely gleaned from them is just a preliminary understanding of the concepts of communication and rhetoric. Communication, as the positivist embraces it and the hyperrhetoricist rejects it, is a transaction concerned with propositions. A proposition, as I am using the term, must be either true or false, but need not be true. The same proposition, furthermore, can be expressed in a variety of ways. Communication, in the weakest sense of the word, occurs when one person expresses a proposition and, as a result, another person understands the same proposition. If there are no linguistic or intellectual considerations that prevent a recipient of a message from understanding it — if he can read the language in which the message is couched, and the message is not too complex for him to follow — then the Verifiability Criterion can be thought of as an attempt to define what can be communicated in this sense. Nothing meaningless can be communicated; i.e., nothing which is neither a tautology nor empirically testable. It is communication in this weakest sense that the hyperrhetoricist finds ineffectual in reaching the philistine; for no amount of it will make the philistine understand the doctrine he has, in his oafish good nature, inquired about. A stronger sense of the word is that in which A communicates proposition P to B if and only if as the result of A's efforts B believes P. This is the way in which I will use the word unless I give special notice to the contrary. The strongest sense of "communication" is that in which only true propositions can be communicated; that is, B believes P, and P is true. It is in this sense of "communicate" that what one communicates is information.

Rhetoric emerges from our discussion up to this point as concerned with attitudes rather than propositions. To the extent that it is occupied with linguistic forms, it will focus not on propositions as such but upon the sentences that most effectively present them to others. Propositions need not be believed in order to be understood, and communication, in the weakest sense, solicits only the understanding of propositions; but rhetoric solicits belief first in the expectation that understanding will follow. Communication in the strongest sense essentially conveys information, but rhetoric essentially seeks to stimulate action, including the action of adopting a recommended belief. It is thus the art of persuasion. Its success or failure is not to be measured by the truth or falsity of the beliefs it recommends, but by the extent to which others have by its agency been persuaded to accept these beliefs.

I have spoken of the dialectical reversals that await both the ultra-positivist seeking to avoid using rhetoric and the hyperrhetoricist seeking to avoid using communication. What I have just said in the attempt to define communication and rhetoric suggests that even if we do not attempt to erect these concepts into doctrines, as the ultrapositivists and the hyperrhetoricists do, a powerful dialectic is at work that prevents more than a provisional distinction between the concepts themselves. When communication is defined in the intermediate and standard way as getting someone else to believe what one believes, it is obviously difficult to see why such an evocation of belief should not be considered a rhetorical transaction as well as a communicative one. In a perhaps somewhat less obvious way, furthermore, the weakest form of communication is saturated with rhetoric. If I want to get you to understand a proposition that I understand, I may proceed, as the positivist wants me to do, by first making sure that what I have to communicate is actually a proposition; i.e., is empirically testable or logically true. I may then carefully formulate it with your linguistic and intellectual requirements in mind. But surely it is a mistake to suppose that all that I would now have to do is to enunciate the proposition as I have now formulated it. What I would also have to do is to get your attention. The art of getting another person's attention, however, clearly falls within the province of rhetoric rather than communication, and there is no genuine act of communication that does not require the use of this art. No doubt we can count on having the computer's full attention when we feed it a stack of punched cards, but when we talk of having communicated something to it via these cards we are using "communication" in a borrowed and anthropomorphic way. As the result of having been fed the cards, the computer stores certain values and instructions, but we cannot make sense of the assertion that it has come to understand a proposition. Understanding is an achievement; whatever one understands, one could have failed to understand. But being primed with certain data is no achievement for the machine; it is at best an achievement for its maker or operator. The machine could have stored the wrong values, but we would describe such a situation as a malfunction, not as a failure on the part of the machine to understand what someone had tried to communicate to it.

The concept of rhetoric is similarly not dissociable from that of communication. Having gotten someone to listen to you, you must then proceed to say something. While it is action that rhetoric solicits, it is not action in the service of a proposition. Those whom the hyperrhetoricist recognizes as brothers rather than philistines are united not by conforming behavior but by faith. And if they have come to understand something by just believing it, at least they now understand it — the net effect of the transaction is that they have received a communication.

So far I have schematically described two extremist positions that might be taken toward the roles of communication and rhetoric in philosophy, and from these descriptions I have extracted preliminary definitions of communication and rhetoric themselves. We must now turn to positions that have actually been held, and we must make needed corrections in our notions of communication and of rhetoric. Wittgenstein, in *Tractatus Logico-Philosophicus,* and Heidegger, in *Sein und Zeit,* not only take more or less explicit positions regarding the roles of communication and rhetoric in philosophy but also to some extent practice what they preach. These two books are important, however, not only because of their orientations toward communication and rhetoric but also because these orientations are representative of the broad philosophical camps to which the books belong. In spite of some major differences between Wittgenstein's *Tractatus* and the outlook of many contemporary linguistic analysts, what Wittgenstein says about philosophy in the *Tractatus* sets the tone for much of the Anglo-American linguistic analysis that has ensued upon it. Similarly, the attitude Heidegger takes toward philosophy in *Sein und Zeit* sets the tone of much contemporary continental European philosophy with respect to the issue of communication and rhetoric in philosophy. Hence reference to these books will enable us to compare two segments of the philosophical world which have often been thought impossible to compare; and possibly we will be able to suggest an area of *rapprochement* between them.

Wittgenstein declares himself early on the importance of communication. In the second paragraph of the Preface to the *Tractatus,* he writes, "What can be said at all can be said clearly, and what we cannot talk about we must pass over in silence."[1] Surely it is communication that Wittgenstein is here

[1]L. Wittgenstein, *Tractatus Logico-Philosophicus,* D.F. Pears and B.F. McGuiness (New York: Humanities Press, 1961). All my Wittgenstein quotations are from this edition.

emphasizing. The mark of something said clearly is that it is understood; i.e., communicated. His point is that everything sayable must be communicable. One for whom rhetoric had a necessary role could deny this. He would point to the philistine, to whom one can talk until doomsday without communicating anything. The mere fact that one cannot get him to understand one's doctrine by means of any amount of clear talk does not show that one must pass over these doctrines in silence.

The passage I have just quoted, however, is really about communication in every field *except* philosophy. It expresses a systematic limitation on philosophical communication. For philosophy, according to Wittgenstein, has nothing to say. It is "not a body of doctrine but an activity. . . . Philosophy does not result in 'philosophical propositions,' but rather in the clarification of propositions."[2] Wittgenstein seems to be in the position of recommending that we pass over in silence anything that we think we might have to say in the name of philosophy, for it is nothing we can really say at all.

This, however, is far from Wittgenstein's final verdict. In its very concern with the incommunicable, philosophy communicates something: "It will signify what cannot be said, by presenting clearly what can be said."[3] This clear presentation of what can be said is what Wittgenstein has in mind in speaking of philosophy as the activity of clarifying propositions rather than producing propositions itself.

The idea that philosophy is to present clearly what can be said suggests that it can present clearly what has hitherto been presented obscurely. Wittgenstein attributes much obscurity of this kind to difficulties that philosophers have had with language: "Most of the propositions and questions of philosophers arise from our failure to understand the logic of our language. . . . All philosophy is a 'critique of language.' "[4]

Philosophical activity as Wittgenstein conceives it can be illustrated profusely from his own work as well as from that of many others. Philosophical sentences are exhibited as in fact unsayable by showing that they fail to conform to the logic of our language. Even the language of the *Tractatus* itself must ultimately be left behind, because there is no position beyond our language from which we can *describe* its logic; all that we can hope to do is simply to *show* its logic, by saying as clearly as possible what can be said. Thus at the end of the *Tractatus* Wittgenstein says, "My propositions serve as elucidations in the following way: anyone who understands me eventually recognizes them as nonsensical, when he has used them — as steps — to climb up beyond them."[5]

One difference between Wittgenstein's conception of the function of philosophy and that of the ultrapositivists is that the discovery that what the philosopher is inclined to say is sayable does not undercut the former in the way that the discovery that the Verifiability Criterion is neither empirical nor tautologous undercuts the latter. Having made this shocking discovery, which amounts to the acknowledgement that the Verifiability Criterion cannot be

²Ibid., 4.112.
³Ibid., 4.115.
⁴Ibid., 4.003, 4.0031.
⁵Ibid., 6.54

communicated, the ultrapositivist can only make a rhetorical plea for its adoption; but this plea is inconsistent with his basic conviction that the function of philosophy is to communicate and not to persuade. For Wittgenstein, on the other hand, philosophy can elucidate even though it says nothing; and elucidation is clearly a kind of communication. Hence Wittgenstein's view does not have the fundamental incoherence of ultrapositivism.

Anglo-American philosophy has largely adopted Wittgenstein's conception of philosophy as an activity that eliminates problems caused by inattention to the logic of our language. According to this conception, philosophy is clearly communicative, at least when it is done properly. What philosophy has to communicate is not propositions but elucidations. It follows that we must to some extent abandon our preliminary understanding of communication as concerned with propositions. Of course, one could point to the logic that is violated by the problem we seek to elucidate by expressing this logic as a set of propositions in the metalanguage; this approach has often been taken. The fact remains, however, that this is not Wittgenstein's own approach, and his philosophy communicates as much about the sources of our philosophical ills as anyone else's. It communicates because it disseminates an understanding which is not contingent on prior belief. To put the matter in another way, no one stands in relation to Wittgenstein as an intrinsically unreachable philistine; there is always hope that the philosopher can reach his hearers by reformulating his point one more time. If he gives up it is because he is tired, not because they are philistines. Yet notice how the gap between communication and rhetoric has been narrowed. The clarity that the philosopher aims to pass on is as much a reorientation of attitudes as an intellectual reassessment. It is an understanding, but not the kind of understanding that one could put completely in words. It is a release from perplexity, and thus an enhancement of the hearer's well-being. In the last analysis one accepts Wittgenstein's elucidations not because they are true — whatever that could mean — but because one feels better about accepting them. The rhetorical dimension of the transaction resulting in this acceptance is obvious.

An early section of Heidegger's *Sein und Zeit* is entitled "The Lesson of a Destruction of the History of Ontology."[6] It is strange to see a philosopher writing of the *destruction* of anything philosophical; philosophers do not usually suppose that they *destroy* doctrines or the histories of doctrines; they do not imagine that such destruction could even be relevant to the enterprise in which they are engaged. The business in which most philosophers think they are engaged is that of *refuting* rather than destroying. To refute a doctrine is to exhibit it as incoherent and therefore unacceptable. A refuted doctrine can still be *exhibited*; indeed, if it could not, it could not be refuted, for there would be nothing to which we could then ascribe the incoherence that we want to ascribe to the doctrine. To put the matter in another way, the philosopher who regards the refutation of a doctrine as his concern must first make his hearers understand what it is he is attacking. Since the dissemination of understanding falls within the province of communication, refutation is a communicative transaction.

[6]M. Heidegger, *Sein und Zeit,* 7th ed. (Tübingen: M. Niemeyer, 1953), pp. 19-27.

How would the destruction of a doctrine differ from its refutation? If a doctrine were destroyed, it would cease to exist, and therefore could no longer be exhibited, even exhibited as incoherent. If we are too literal-minded, we may find ourselves asking how it is that Heidegger thinks he can write about the history of ontology at all if he has indeed destroyed this history. (We can of course write the history of *things* that have been destroyed, but according to Heidegger's title, it is the very *history* of ontology that is to be destroyed.) Yet we can interpret the destruction of the history of ontology in a more sympathetic way. To destroy this history is to expose it as a bad dream; it is to awaken us from this dream, which has held us in its thrall for two thousand years. Thus what is destroyed is the power of the history over us. Heidegger can write about this history as one can write about any illusion from which we have been released.

Destruction, then, in Heidegger's terms, is an awakening. To use other words that occur frequently, not only in *Sein und Zeit* but throughout Heidegger's works, it is a recall from forgetfulness. Heidegger makes it clear that he regards such an evocation as one of the primary tasks of philosophy, if not its only task. Clearly, then, he conceives of philosophy as fundamentally a rhetorical enterprise. Its function is not only to awaken, but specifically *not* to disseminate understanding. Traditional ontology, for example, is, according to Heidegger, not something that a person could simply understand, prior to deciding whether it is true or false. The person is defined by his ontology, and is held in its grip. He can dissociate himself from it only by being awakened from it; but he can be awakened from it only by becoming a new person. Heidegger's appeal is not merely rhetorical but downright homiletical.

Yet for all his emphasis on the rhetorical nature of the philosophical enterprise, Heidegger is no hyperrhetoricist. For the content and point of his doctrine is not defined simply by contrasting the doctrine with the beliefs of the philistines. In fact, Heidegger's entire position is specifically committed to the task of awakening the philistines from their ontological slumber. Heidegger refers to the philistines as *das Man* — the "they." *Das Man* expects to be told in plain language what he can in fact come to understand only by being awakened. But because Heidegger's entire thrust is *toward* the awakening of *das Man* he cannot reject as a mere philistine the man who fails to understand him. In Heidegger's own terms, he is not successful until he has reached the philistine. Hence in a sense there are no philistines at all for him.

If I am correct in arguing that Heidegger conceives philosophy as basically rhetorical, some revision in our concepton of rhetoric is called for. We can no longer think of it as an art of persuasion, except perhaps derivatively; its purpose is not to incite its hearer to action — even the action of adopting some specific belief. Instead, rhetoric totally reorients the hearer; if he listens to it he is in a position to abandon an inauthentic life in favor of an authentic one. Once we see that rhetoric has an at best incidental concern with action, we remove one of the important differences between it and communication. Rhetoric as bound to action is successful or unsuccessful; the question of its validity does not arise. If we have persuaded person A to perform act B or adopt belief C, our rhetoric has been efficacious, and it is gratuitous to ask whether he *ought* to do B or believe C. The validity question more properly arises in connection with communication, especially in the strongest sense, in which only the truth can be communicated. Here the test is not only that we have gotten A to believe C but also that C is true. But this test applies to Heidegger's rhetoric too. For it is certainly one of Heidegger's most emphatically expressed doctrines that it is the truth to which a person must be awakened. This doctrine is in fact a corollary of the Heideggerian account of truth as unconcealment.

Just as Wittgenstein's view of philosophy as primarily communicative is echoed by a large segment of Anglo-American philosophy, so Heidegger's rhetorical conception expresses an attitude toward the philosophical enterprise that is widespread on the European continent. It is doubtful that it originated with Heidegger; for the Husserlian phenomenology from which Heidegger took his departure is already fundamentally committed to a rhetorical view of philosophy. While Husserl's talk about essences may suggest that he thought the function of philosophy was to communicate about them, the epoché, or bracketing of ordinary experience that Husserl took to be the starting point of philosophical inquiry, is actually an awakening to essence — a laying aside of prosaic concerns and attitudes that permits the person to come to a more authentic form of life. We find the same basic orientation in much post-Heideggerian philosophy on the Continent, as well as in the phenomenological soil from which Heidegger's thought sprang; it is clearly an existentialistic orientation as well as a phenomenological one.

For Wittgenstein, philosophy elucidates, and in so doing engages in non-propositional communication. For Heidegger, philosophy awakens, and in so doing engages in a nonpersuasive rhetoric. The gap between communication and rhetoric has been narrowed from both sides. Is it possible, indeed, to suppose that there is any longer a gap? Wittgenstein and his followers have often spoken of the power of philosophy to remind us of what we already know, as if it were identical with its elucidatory power. To elucidate problems is simply to remind one's hearers of the logic of our language. It is to awaken them from an ontological slumber. To be sure, the slumber with which Wittgenstein is concerned is far different from that with which Heidegger is concerned. It would be a gross distortion to say that Wittgenstein is trying to call his audience to authentic existence, or that Heidegger is trying to call his to an awareness of the logic of our language. The only identity for which I am arguing is the identity of their views of the function of philosophy. Both of them emphasize the call of philosophy. At the same time, both see this call as communicative, as an elucidation or unconcealment.

I want to conclude by formulating the evocative-elucidatory function of philosophy in more general terms. If philosophy has this function in both Anglo-American and continental European philosophy, it does so because philosophy always has this function, at least when it is not caricaturing itself. Using an odd and somewhat old-fashioned word, I want to say that philosophy is the articulation of morale. Good morale is not associated with a dull or confused person. It belongs only to those who have to some extent broken out from illusion and confusion. They know what they are about, and they have a sense of their own competence. Morale is thus a certain rather explicit self-confidence. It is philosophy, in my view, that renders this self-confidence explicit, and thus distinguishes it from a mere unthinking valor. Of course we cannot point to a prior self-confidence which we then proceed to make explicit; the self-confidence is itself the result of an increasing explicitude in the way we confront the world. Wittgenstein's *Tractatus* is clearly intended to improve the morale of the thinker beset by confusions about the logic of our language. It accomplishes its purpose by making this logic explicit, and thus by giving the thinker an explicit self-confidence with respect to his ability to identify and handle the problems arising from abuses of logic. This ability, however, is more than a technical skill. This point is clearly made by Heidegger, who sees technical skill as falling within the competence of *das Man*, the inauthentic one who lacks morale. The "know-how" of *das Man*, his skill, his curiosity, and his preoccupation with jargon, may simply provide him with an excuse for evading the issues to which morale would be relevant.

Not only Wittgenstein and Heidegger, but all important philosophers, have been concerned with man's morale. In different ages they have formulated in different terms the principles upon which an explicit self-confidence can be based. If asked to amplify this remark, I would not hesitate to refer to Professor McKeon's illuminating summary of the historical progress of philosophy.[7] According to Professor McKeon, the fundamental category of ancient philosophy was Being, that of modern philosophy was Thought, and that of contemporary philosophy is Action. The generalization I would base upon this summary is that the ancient philosophers sought to provide man with an explicit self-confidence by exhibiting Man's being as continuous with Being as such; modern philosophers pointed to man's competence as a thinker as a basis for morale; and contemporary philosophers have tried to establish man's morale primarily by making him aware of his role as an agent. If we test the last clause of this generalization by applying it to Wittgenstein and Heidegger, we see that the fit is not too bad. The action that Wittgenstein is concerned with is the speaking of language; his concern with this action is to render it competent. The action that Heidegger is concerned with is of no specific kind; it is action itself, viewed under the form of time, that occupies Heidegger, and the authenticity of which he seeks to establish.

It remains to be shown what communication and rhetoric have to do with morale. My view is that they are involved in the way in which the philosopher addresses those whose morale he seeks to improve. Such hearers must both find morale desirable and unwittingly lack it. Their lack of morale unbeknownst to themselves can be the result of a relative confusion or dullness. I use the term "relative" because there is a point beyond which a person's dullness or confusion cannot be increased without depriving him of his very desire for morale. To the glassy-eyed person stumbling about in ontological oblivion, there is nothing one can say; any awakening would be a miracle. To the person thoroughly imbued with the courage of his confusions there is likewise nothing one can say, the efficaciousness of which can, to any degree, be counted on. Let us assume, then, that the philosopher's hearers are people under the erroneous impression that their pursuit of morale has been successful. Accordingly the first thing the speaker must do is to point out that

[7]See Richard McKeon, "Philosophy of Communication and the Arts," *Contemporary Philosophic Thought*, Vol. III (Albany: State University of New York Press, 1970).

those whom he addresses are living in a fool's paradise. Their attempts to formulate an explicit self-confidence have amounted precisely to a denial of the competence they are claiming. This is, for example, the message of the philosophers of Being to those who attempt to articulate man's morale by proclaiming that man is the measure of all things. It is the message of the philosophers of Thought to those who attempt to express morale in terms of man's belonging to the nature of things. It is the message of the philosophers of Action to those who think they have found morale in deductive thought. All such messages are communicative. Their aim is to point out to the hearer something he did not know.

Of course, *any* message is communicative; that is what it means to call it a message. But what philosophers have to say to their hearers are more than messages. They are arguments. Plato did not merely *tell* Protagoras that the morale he had settled for was specious. He also urged him to adopt the higher morale of identification with Being. He could go on to do this only because morale was what Protagoras wanted. Similarly, we will listen to Heidegger's evocation only if his destruction of the history of ontology has created in us the need for a newer morale.

I am obviously now speaking of the rhetorical component of philosophical argumentation. But in suggesting that it can be separated out from the communicative component I am oversimplifying. The philosopher does not first attack existing formulations of morale and then propose new formulations of it. His very attack introduces his proposal. In Wittgenstein's *Tractatus,* for example, it would be very difficult to distinguish the communicative from the rhetorical. This difficulty has characterized the writings of the more important philosophers. Even when a philosophical treatise begins with a polemical section and goes on to propose a positive doctrine, the polemic is likely to be informed with the doctrine that is to be proposed.

Even the very act of proposing a doctrine is far from being a purely rhetorical transaction. Doctrines are proposed in the name of truth; morale has often been thought to reside in the unconcealment of the concealed. It is difficult, on the other hand, to think of any philosophical statement that is purely communicative in intent. It is not the message of the philosopher that catches the attention of his hearers; it is his appeal to them to listen.

In this essay I have made some remarks concerning the nature of philosophy. I hope that these remarks will themselves be construed as philosophical. If they are, of course, they ought to exemplify the very analysis of philosophical expressions which they propound. I am confident that they do. I have not only tried to communicate something about the nature of philosophy, but have also recommended a reformulation of at least one prevailing view toward it. According to this view, Anglo-American philosophy communicates, continental philosophy exhorts, and ne'er the twain shall meet. This view constitutes a potential morale problem, or perhaps an actual one. How *can* we continue to maintain a formulation of our own competence according to which we have competence but others whom we meet at philosophical congresses are systematically barred from attaining it? Such a view, instead of articulating our morale, ends up by destroying it, because the existence of large numbers of intelligent people with whom we cannot communicate shows that we are incompetent at the very skill by which we attempted to define our competence; namely, communication. We will never really be competent at communication until we are ready to admit that in communicating we are also engaging in rhetoric.

X.
Truth, Communication, and Rhetoric in Philosophy

In an interesting paper that appeared in 1955,[1] Henri Gouhier distinguishes two phases of Descartes' philosophical activity. First Descartes had to discover the truth; then he had to communicate it to others. Gouhier points out many passages in which this second concern is distinctly enough visible that it cannot be confused with the first. "Sûr de sa raison, [Descartes] doute de sa parole,"[2] and much of his effort went toward improving his manner of presentation so as to overcome in others a natural tendency to resist the truths he had discovered. Descartes recognized these tendencies in himself as well; they stemmed from prejudices we acquire in our infancy. Gouhier argues that the large variety of literary styles adopted by Descartes, ranging from dialogues to axiomatic formulations, is an indication of the experimenting Descartes did in order to come to grips with this problem of communication.

Descartes, as Gouhier points out, rejects out of hand the rhetoric of his own time. Yet it would not be amiss to identify his concern to communicate the truth as a rhetorical one. Rhetoric and communication are very difficult to distinguish in an enterprise of this kind; they tend to fuse together. It might be thought that we could distinguish the communicative act of telling someone the truth from the rhetorical act of persuading him of the truth. But in order to succeed in telling someone the truth we have to tell him well. Mumbling the truth when the other person isn't listening, or formulating it in terms that are over his head, is not a rhetorically oriented act, but neither is it a communicatively oriented act. In order to communicate the truth at all we have to use rhetorical techniques.

My own view is that in philosophical enquiry a further fusion takes place. Not only do communication and rhetoric collapse together, but the result of this collapse collapses together with the act of discovering the truth. I believe that, Descartes to the contrary notwithstanding, one simply cannot discover a truth in philosophy without expressing this truth in a form adapted to communication. Anyone who writes philosophy knows this; I am sure Descartes knew it. One cannot find truths in philosophy except as the conclusions of arguments. To know whether you have a truth or not, you have to set up the arguments that led you to it. If the argument will not withstand criticism, you did not have a truth, only a will-o'-the-wisp. But setting up arguments and subjecting them to criticism is precisely being concerned with instruments of communication. It does not matter whether anyone else is actually listening or not; the issue is whether the claimed truth is in principle communicable.

Gouhier himself makes precisely this point when he says "La démonstration proprement cartésienne est celle qui reproduit l'itinéraire du philosophe."[3] My purpose, however, is neither to defend nor attack Gouhier's interpretation of Descartes or of philosophical truth. As a scholar, Gouhier is not concerned to refute Descartes' distinction between the discovery of truth

---

[1] "La résistance au vrai et le problème cartésien d'une philosophie sans rhétorique," *Atti Congresso Internazionale di Studi Umanistici* (Rome: Fratelli Bocca Editori, 1955), pp. 85-97.

[2] Ibid., p. 92.

[3] Ibid., p. 93.

and the communication of truth; he assumes, as Descartes does, that the distinction can be made. It is this assumption, however, that I deny. For me, the truth in philosophy is equivalent with the itinerary leading to it, and this itinerary is in principle an exercise in communication.

I have already argued in some detail that the distinction between finding the truth in philosophy and communicating it cannot be maintained.[4] There is little I could now add to those arguments. What I want to do now is to elucidate an immediate consequence of this thesis, once we admit the fusion of communication and rhetoric. This is the consequence that the distinction between finding the truth in philosophy and finding the proper rhetorical devices for propagating it cannot be maintained. In saying this, I contradict views I have long held and publicly expressed.[5]

In order to elaborate the contrast between my present view of the role of rhetoric in philosophy and my past view of it, it is helpful to explain why the latter attracted me for so many years. I supposed that the essentially communicative act by which one arrived at philosophical truth was an argument addressed, in a certain sense, to the reason of the reader, and I regarded such an appeal to reason as entirely different from any attempt to persuade the reader. In order to spell out the *sense* in which I supposed the argument in question to be addressed to the reason of the reader, let me say that I regarded it as an *argumentum ad hominem,* and the latter as the ideal argument in philosophy. Such an argument exposes an inconsistency between what one's interlocutor has explicitly said or done and what his statement or act presupposes. It is an appeal to reason in the sense that it appeals to everyone's abhorrence of inconsistencies. It pivots on the expectation that any interlocutor to whom one has pointed out an inconsistency of the kind I have in mind would revise or abandon either his explicit words or acts, or their presuppositions, in order to resolve the inconsistency and thus to remove the threat to reason.

At the same time that I regarded the communicative act in philosophy as addressed to reason, I supposed that rhetoric is not so addressed. I thought of the rhetorical act as fundamentally unilateral — as an attempt by one person to manipulate the beliefs of another without at the same time exposing his own beliefs to manipulation. Only in a nonrhetorical discussion, I thought, could the argumentative techniques be genuinely bilateral. Here each interlocutor, precisely in his use of an argument of a certain sort, would be making that argument available to the others. If an argument is valid, I thought, it must be valid for all who use it.

My view was rationalistic. It had much in common with the Cartesianism it attacked. Like that Cartesianism, it assumed that there are valid arguments in philosophy — arguments whose conclusions must be accepted. It differed from Cartesianism only in denying that there is a difference in principle between discovering the truth and communicating it. Both acts, I would still say, must make use of essentially the same argument.

[4]"Argument and Truth in Philosophy," *Philosophy and Phenomenological Research,* 18 (1957), 228-36.
[5]"Persuasion and Validity in Philosophy," *Philosophy and Argument* (University Park: The Pennsylvania State University Press, 1959), ch. IV.

But such a view suffers from a defect common to many rationalisms: It makes the unwarranted assumption that all humans reason in the same way. In particular, it assumes that what I call your inconsistency you will necessarily admit to be an inconsistency. In fact, however, one of the hardest things to do in philosophical argumentation is to get another person to admit that he has been inconsistent. Pinning him down is like pinning down a droplet of mercury. For it is usually child's play for him to find a distinction that will resolve the contradiction. If I charge you with having said "A and not-A," you can always retort that you meant the first "A" in one sense and the second in another. More fundamentally, however, your very view of the nature of contradictions may differ from mine. You may refuse to consider it important that your expression is syntactically a contradiction; or you may refuse to take seriously any alleged contradiction that can *not* be expressed in the syntactical form "P and not-P." As a kind of Hegelian or Marxist, you may refuse to take contradictions seriously at all, so that my polemic leaves you altogether untouched.

I have made several attempts to patch up this difficulty, one of them on the pages of this journal.[6] I am ready now, however, to say that it cannot be patched up. At the same time, I am not ready to abandon my belief in the fundamental efficacy of *argumentum ad hominem* in philosophical argument. What sort of view emerges, then, and how are truth, communication, and rhetoric related in it?

The view that I would now want to defend still makes a basic distinction between *argumentum ad hominem* and *argumentum ad rem*. When the truth can be discovered through an act wholly distinct from that of communicating it, then the act of discovery can be formulated as an *argumentum ad rem*, an appeal to the truth in the form of a fact. But if a philosophical truth does not exist in the form of a fact, it cannot be appealed to in this way. And there are many ways of arguing for the nonfactual status of philosophical truth. One might point out, for example, the curious status of an alleged fact that one cannot, in principle, get another person to acknowledge as a fact, because it has no place in his systematic point of view. Or one might develop the point that I made at the beginning of this paper — that one never *has* a philosophical truth unless one knows how to express it. This is hardly the case with the facts to which an *argumentum ad rem* would be relevant. They are *there,* waiting to be appealed to whenever we are ready.

If *argumentum ad rem* is unavailable, then only *argumentum ad hominem* is available. Let us see what kind of an argument this must be if it cannot be, or cannot be merely, an appeal to consistency.

My present view is that a successful argument in philosophy is one that is intended to evoke, and does evoke, a response of a certain kind in the man to whom it is addressed. Throughout the history of philosophy this act of evocation and its consequences have been characterized in various ways. Plato spoke of reminiscence, and Spinoza of blessedness. Wittgenstein seeks to *remind* his reader of something he already knew, and Heidegger speaks of calling people to authentic existence. Some mode of life or thought more

[6]"Argumentation and Inconsistency," *Revue Internationale de Philosophie*, XV (1961), 353-65.

authentic than that of common sense is the aim in each case. *Argumentum ad hominem* as I previously conceived it was a special case of this evocation; here the call is to a life of reason, a life in which consistency matters and one can't duck one's responsibilities by making trivial distinctions.

How does this sort of argument figure in the discovery of philosophical truth? Let me begin by saying that I feel that our search for truth in philosophy is always a search for morale. We are demoralized by shabby thinking, by sophistry, by revolutions that destroy an old world but bring no new one into being, by the sort of talk that obliterates distinctions, by relativism, scepticism, and by many other tendencies. We are interested in philosophy only as a way of regaining morale — of tightening our thought and sharpening our perceptions. Philosophy is always the attempt to regain the world, or at least to see it afresh, and the truths we seek are truths appropriate to such a purpose. Hence we could hardly seek them without considering how to communicate them to others. The only way to tell whether what I have is a truth or a falsehood is to contemplate its evocative power.

Communication and rhetoric, on my view, are even more closely bound up than I suggested at first. The function of rhetoric is not merely to get the other person to listen to what I want to communicate to him. Rather, the communicative act is itself rhetorical. At one and the same time I tell a truth and evoke a basis for morale. Hence discovery, communication, and rhetoric all collapse into a unitary philosophical act.

This collapse implies that my view of the nature of rhetoric has undergone changes over the years, just as has my view of the nature of philosophical argumentation. I used to see rhetoric as fundamentally the art of persuasion. I see it now as the art of evocation. While persuasion is basically a unilateral act, there is no reason why evocation should necessarily be unilateral. Indeed, if I try to call another to authentic existence without myself being open to such a call, I am a hypocrite. I am entitled to address you only to the extent that I give you the right to address me. The ideal participants in a philosophical discussion are friends of the sort characterized by Aristotle as engaged in a common pursuit of the good,[7] and friends must necessarily address each other *ad hominem*. Aristotle puts the point quaintly by quoting the proverb that men cannot know one another "til they have eaten the requisite amount of salt together."[8]

---

[7] *Nicomachean Ethics,* bk. VIII, ch. 3.
[8] Ibid., 1156b 26-27.

XI.
Rationality and Rhetoric in Philosophy

In a discussion of philosophical reasoning, Passmore refers to the fact that "Bradley is a philosopher in a sense which, say, a theosophist is not; even if their final conclusions look almost indistinguishable."[1] What distinguishes Bradley from the theosophist, according to Passmore, is his refusal to assert any conclusion that he has not reached through the use of reasoning. In taking this position, Passmore is in effect endorsing the characterization of philosophy as a rational enterprise — a characterization that has been very common, if not universal. Certainly the most influential thinkers in the Western tradition since the time of Plato — thinkers like Aristotle, Kant, and Hegel — have regarded philosophy as rational. Even philosophers who have primarily depended on some mode of thought other than rational thought have used reason to articulate and defend the ultimacy of this other mode, and to attack the thesis that reason is ultimate. One thinks here of Pascal, Kierkegaard, Nietzsche, Bergson, and Heidegger. And in some of these cases it is clear that the alternative non-rational mode of thought was not itself regarded as philosophical in the first place.

We must distinguish between two senses of the rational. In the strong sense, to speak of philosophy as a rational enterprise is to imply that its conclusions are non-trivial, and result from formally valid arguments with true premises. Descartes and Hume alike regarded rationality in this sense as the standard of philosophy. The geometrical method of Descartes presupposes this interpretation of rationality, and it was Hume's failure to find arguments of the requisite sort in contemporary metaphysical treatises that led him to urge that they all be consigned to the flames. Hume's reaction has, in fact, occurred throughout the history of philosophy. Although few philosophers have attempted to construct deductive systems in the mode of Descartes, many of them have criticized their colleagues as if they had expected *them* to have constructed deductive systems. For their criticism has taken the form of challenging the premises of the argument under attack, or else of raising doubts about the formal validity of the argument, or else of holding that the conclusion of the argument is trivial.

In the weak sense of "rational," to say that philosophy is rational is only to imply that it reaches its conclusions as the result of using arguments. Thus if we find flaws in an interlocutor's argument, we can still regard him as a philosopher; what bestows this status upon him is just the fact that he has argued. The use made by Plato and Aristotle of the idea of dialectic points to this conception of the rationality of the philosophical enterprise; Aristotle specifically distinguished dialectical from formal reasoning.

There are at least *prima facie* difficulties, however, in maintaining that philosophy is rational in either of these senses. For whenever anyone proposes a philosophical argument, someone else is almost certain to contend that it does not measure up to the standards of rationality in the first sense. The argument under attack is exposed either as a *non sequitur* or as a set of

[1]John Passmore, *Philosophical Reasoning* (New York: Scribners', 1961), pp. 14-15.

premises either not all true or such that the most that can be validly deduced from them is an extremely trivial conclusion. Few if any are the philosophical arguments whose formal validity and soundness have been attested to by any except their authors. If we adopt this interpretation of rationality, then for all practical purposes there has never been any philosophy.

On the other hand, if to be rational is simply to argue, then anyone who uses the word "therefore" becomes an instant philosopher, however out-rageous the argument containing the "therefore." On the assumption that it is possible to identify certain issues as specifically philosophical, we might restrict the arguments bestowing this instant status to those concerned with philosophical issues. But this restriction does not go nearly far enough. We do not engage in philosophy merely by using the word "therefore" in front of philosophical conclusions. Hence just as the first sense of "rational" was far too narrow, this sense is far too broad.

Can we escape between the horns of this dilemma? Are there arguments which, although not formally valid, can still be distinguished from pieces of discourse in which "therefore" is inserted in any place we choose, just as long as what follows it is philosophical? In science there can be valid arguments that are not *formally* valid. (I have in mind, of course, valid inductive arguments.) If not all valid philosophical arguments must be *formally* valid, perhaps we could characterize the rationality of the philosophical enterprise as its use of valid arguments the validity of which cannot be established through the use of for-mal criteria. I have on several occasions[2] suggested such a conception of validity, a conception according to which a philosophical argument is valid if it forces the thinker to whom it is addressed to revise or abandon his position. The term "forces" here is not, of course, being used in a psychological sense; a valid philosophical argument is one exploiting the principles of a position un-der attack in such a way that whoever holds this position is exposed as logically inconsistent whether he admits it or not.

To illustrate, let us consider one form of the Verifiability Criterion of meaningfulness: a proposition is meaningful only if it is a tautology or has con-sequences that could be verified or disconfirmed through observation. This principle can be exploited by asking whether it is itself a meaningful proposition. Clearly it is not a tautology. Nor does it have consequences that could be confirmed or disconfirmed through observation. Hence the Verifiability Criterion is, in its own terms, meaningless. Since the propounder of the Criterion clearly believes that all philosophical propositions ought to be meaningful, he has contradicted himself. Thus he must revise or abandon his position. The revision evoked has sometimes taken the form of asserting that the Verifiability Criterion is not a proposition, but a convention. This assertion can in its turn be attacked, but not by the argument I have sketched. If it is to be successfully attacked, a new valid argument must be found.

The question remains, however, whether it is not otiose to talk about validity of this kind. For it is at least very often the case that a thinker attacked by an argument intended to exploit his principles can reply that these were not

---

[2]"Self-Refutation and Validity," *The Monist*, 48 (1964), 467-85, and "Can Philosophical Arguments Be Valid?" *Bucknell Review*, 11 (1963), 89-98.

really his principles at all, that the arguer missed the point and thus argued invalidly. Indeed, the reaction of revising one's position to meet a valid argument cannot in the end be distinguished from the maneuver I have just described; to meet a valid argument is to turn it into an invalid one. What difference does it make whether a supporter of the Verifiability Criterion is prepared to call that Criterion a convention *before* he is attacked or *as a result of* the attack? And yet if he was already calling it a convention before he was attacked the attack is invalid; it begs the question.

It is possible that some arguments forcing the revision or abandonment of a position even though not formally valid have occurred in the history of philosophy. Perhaps such an argument on the part of Hume awoke Kant from his "dogmatic slumbers." Yet if the rationality of the philosophical enterprise were reduced to the use of arguments valid in this sense, we should have to say that genuine philosophy is at best an uncommon phenomenon. It is clear in any event that many texts and discussions generally regarded as philosophical contain few arguments, if any, valid in this sense. Philosophy is full of arguments and counterarguments, but it is also full of charges that one's opponent has missed the point. Where in a dialogue of Plato, for example, do we find a single instance in which an interlocutor is, strictly speaking, compelled to revise or abandon his position? And is there nothing Hylas can say to answer Philonous? Revisions and abandonments do of course occur, but are largely to be explained in psychological or dramatic rather than logical terms. It is likely that even Kant could have found a way to slumber on. It is a safe bet that he took on Hume's problem because he chose to, not because he was compelled to in some non-psychological way.

We can develop the same point in another way without relying on a specialized conception of validity such as the conception I made use of in the preceding two paragraphs. For assume that there are valid philosophical arguments, understanding "valid" in any way you choose. Suppose a position P is supported by such arguments. Then, as the most cursory reading of the history of philosophy shows, there must also be arguments against P answering to the same criteria of validity, whatever they are. No position in the history of philosophy is so strong that we should want to say that only the arguments favoring it are valid; and none so weak that we should want to say that only the arguments opposing it are valid. For every argument there has been an equally strong counterargument. It follows at once that neither the argument nor the counterargument could really have been valid. Our assumption has led to a *reductio.*

There is one further way of approaching the question of the existence of valid arguments in philosophy. So far I have tried to answer this question by making a sort of inductive appeal to philosophical texts and discussions. But there is also a metaphilosophical answer. Not many thinkers who have rigorously analyzed typical philosophical arguments have been able to offer much hope that such arguments could legitimately lead to non-trivial conclusions. Thus, for example, J. L. Mackie, in his examination of Passmore's account of the "Self-refutation argument,"[3] concludes that this argument is in-

[3]"Self-Refutation — a Formal Analysis," *Philosophical Quarterly,* 14 (1964), 193-203.

capable of supporting any interesting conclusion. Passmore himself admits that "every valid argument 'forces,' in the sense that it restricts freedom of movement, but . . . no argument forces absolutely."[4]

Metaphilosophy is itself, of course, philosophy; a metaphilosophical argument can claim no special immunity from the disease fatal to philosophical árguments in general. So perhaps Mackie, Passmore, and others who have labored with them should not be taken too seriously after all. But to say this is simply to illustrate again the thesis that valid arguments occur very rarely if at all in philosophy.

And yet it is clear that when we speak of the philosophical enterprise as rational, we have in mind *some* aspect or consequence of the ways in which philosophers argue. If philosophers did not argue at all, what would be the grounds on which we could call their activity rational? I am not suggesting that every rational activity must depend on argument. Chess is an exercise of reason in which no explicit arguments, at any rate, are needed. And it is likely that they are not needed in all forms of scientific inquiry. But philosophy without explicit arguments would not be philosophy. It might, as Passmore suggests, be no more than theosophy.

The position for which I want to argue is that in the very process through which philosophical arguments are demolished, the rationality of the philosophical enterprise is established. The process takes place only because philosophers have a deep and pervasive concern with the validity and cogency of the arguments which they find themselves and their colleagues using. No activity besides philosophy has ever shown such a concern. Scientists, to be sure, discuss on the pages of learned journals the validity of the arguments propounded by their colleagues. But it is not such discussions that establish the *rationality* of the scientific enterprise. Such discussions are rather an outgrowth of the factors that do render science rational — the experimental method, the repeatablity of its experiments, its explanatory power. But the entire rationality of the philosophical enterprise reduces to its concern — almost an obsession, a monomania — to examine arguments. To be taken in by an invalid argument, even when its conclusion seems acceptable, is for the philosopher an unconscionable surrender to unreason. No one, of course, wants to be taken in, but only the philosopher claims that he is being rational only insofar as he is avoiding being taken in. For others, rationality can reside in activities other than the examination of arguments; it can reside, for example, in the discernment of patterns or in the pursuit of established standards. But the philosopher demands to know *what arguments* have sensitized us to the patterns we happen to discern, and *what arguments* are thought to establish the standards we pursue. Once he has elicited the arguments, he asks whether they are valid. For it is conceivable to him that we have allowed ourselves to be sensitized for the wrong reasons (even though the patterns we discern are in fact there), and that we have failed to establish our standards (even though our pursuit of them is in fact justifiable). If the philosopher did not proceed in this way, he could not, in his own terms, be rational.

It is not only the analysts and the systematists who have been dedicated to

---

[4]*Philosophical Reasoning,* p. 36.

the examination of arguments. Unsystematic philosophers like Kierkegaard and Nietzsche find their way into the histories and anthologies of philosophy because they, too, in their ironic and oblique way, have expressed a concern not to be taken in. Indeed, they have shown that they can be formidable examiners of argument.

It is perhaps misleading to speak of the philosopher's concern with the validity of arguments as an obsession. This suggests that those who pursue philosophy face a strange occupational hazard. But it is no accident that philosophers should be so preoccupied. The preoccupation is essential to philosophy itself. A *philosophical* interest in a topic, as opposed to an interest of some other sort (say a scientific or an economic interest) is just an interest in examining the arguments that cluster around this topic. Conclusions on the topic matter to the philosopher only if they are supported by arguments, and his interest as a philosopher is to see what support, if any the arguments provide. This examination is a continuing task. Whoever dismisses philosophical arguments wholesale, on the ground that he suspects that they are all invalid, is a phobosopher, not a philosopher. We can pursue wisdom only by giving it the benefit of the doubt and assuming at least the bare possibility of its turning up in some hitherto unexamined argument. Or better: It is in the pursuit of wisdom, not in wisdom as such, that the rationality of the philosophical enterprise resides.

The rationality of philosophy, then, consists in its examination of arguments. Such examination of course presupposes the *use* of arguments by philosophers. So this use contributes to the rationality of the enterprise. It might indeed be thought that it would make more sense to ascribe the rationality of the enterprise to its *use* as such of arguments than to ascribe it to its examination of the arguments used. But as we have already seen, the use of arguments by the philosopher does not in itself guarantee the rationality of what he does. Such use might consist of nothing more than the insertion of "therefores" in a disconnected text. Furthermore, if the philosopher's use of arguments were to be exempted from scrutiny, the arguments themselves would function as no more than elaborate assertions. The unexamined pronouncement "The Heavens declare the glory of God" is no more rational than the unsupported statement "God is glorious," even though the former is a version of the teleological argument.

I have been arguing that the philosophical enterprise can be rational even though none of the arguments used by philosophers are formally valid and few if any are valid in any other sense. If my argument has been convincing, I have driven a wedge between rationality and validity in philosophy. Does this mean that there is nothing further that we can say about the rationality of philosophy? Is rationality an indefinable property that simply inheres in the activity of philosophers, as green inheres in my blotter? That would be strange. No attribution seems more in need of rational discussion and defense than the attribution to any activity of the very property of rationality. So it is incumbent upon me to say *in what way* the very process through which philosophical arguments are demolished establishes the rationality of the philosophical enterprise.

If the rationality of philosophy has escaped the gravitational field of logic, into what gravitational field is it falling? I know of no conclusive way to answer this question. But let us try "rhetoric." This experiment is plausible if we reflect that if it makes sense to talk of studying the success of successful arguments in general, without regard to the fields in which these arguments occur (chemistry, political science, art criticism, etc.), there are really only two disciplines that carry out this study; namely, logic (including the logic of science) and rhetoric. In other words, if we think that an argument has succeeded, there are only two explanations of its success that do not focus on the field-dependent features of the argument; these are the logical explanation and the rhetorical explanation. It goes without saying, of course, that the success that can be explained logically is not the same as the success that can be explained rhetorically. All that I am arguing is that since in the case of philosophical argumentation and the critique of philosophical argumentation the sort of success that might have had a logical explanation (in terms of valid structures, for example) never occurs, or at least very seldom occurs, it follows that if we think philosophical arguments and criticisms of them are successful at all, their success must be accounted for in rhetorical terms.

I am, of course, making several assumptions. The first is that to say that the rationality of the philosophical enterprise is established in the critique of philosophical arguments is to imply that this critique is in one way or another successful. This seems to me to be true in two senses. The critique succeeds in that it persuades those to whom it is addressed that the arguments it examines are defective. It also succeeds in that it is constitutive of the rationality of the philosophical enterprise. The latter point can be amplified by pointing out that it would be odd if rationality were somehow regarded as a failure or as a symptom of failure. There are, of course, those who claim that reason is incompetent as an instrument for achieving knowledge of certain sorts. What this means is that it would be irrational to use reason in quest of such knowledge, and rational not to use it. Reason can fail where rationality succeeds. This is, in fact, the case in philosophy, the rationality of which is established by the failure of reason.

Another assumption I am making is that it is not field-dependent features of the critique of philosophical arguments by virtue of which this critique succeeds. If that were the case, we would have to say that the explanation of the success of the critique belongs to particular fields rather than to rhetoric as such. This assumption can, I think, be buttressed only inductively. When we examine attacks upon philosophical arguments, we find that these attacks seldom if ever involve the trundling out of evidence from chemistry, political science, art criticism, or any other field. They are concerned only with the structures of the arguments themselves. They consist in such comments as "That argument is a *non sequitur*," "This argument begs the question," and "Your premises are open to doubt on general philosophical grounds," rather than in comments drawn from specific fields.

Supposing that the rationality of the philosophical enterprise requires a rhetorical explanation, what is the explanation? This I find an extremely difficult question. The rhetorical explanation that one gives depends on one's rhetorical theory, but I have no particular rhetorical theory in mind. The most I can do is to make some comments on the philosophical enterprise which I think might be compatible with several rhetorical theories.

A rhetorical explanation appeals to such parameters of discourse as the attitude of the speaker, the way in which he presents his message, and the audience to which he presents it. In its concern with these parameters, it is totally unlike an explanation of the success of a successful argument from the point of view of formal logic. For none of these has any bearing on the analysis of the formal validity of an argument. The valid moods of the syllogism are formulated without reference to speaker, audience, or style of presentation. With regard to this last point, in particular, we can be most confident in our logical explanation of the success of an argument when we have eliminated style altogether in favor of an aseptic symbolism.

I am contending that it is precisely because the success of the philosopher's examination of philosophical arguments has a *rhetorical* explanation that it is *rational*. This contention will no doubt shock those inclined to limit rationality to successful discourse the success of which has a *logical* explanation. But in philosophy there is either an insignificant amount of such discourse or none at all. If we believe that philosophy is rational, therefore, we undercut this belief when we attempt to explain such rationality in terms of logic.

So far, my argument has been negative. It has been only by default that rhetoric has emerged as the locus of the rationality of the philosophical enterprise. What can I say positively about the function of rhetoric? Recall my remark that it is rational to want not to be taken in. A critic who examines a philosophical argument is urging his hearers (perhaps including the propounder of the argument) not to be taken in by it. He can succeed only if he formulates his criticisms clearly; his style matters. And he can succeed only if his audience consists of people for whom not being taken in is a value. As Peirce showed in "The Fixation of Belief," many people simply settle for the most comfortable conclusion; to them it is a matter of no consequence whether they are being taken in or not. Finally, although the critic perhaps need not have the charisma of an evangelistic preacher, he must at least have the right attitude. I will develop this point later; suffice it to say here that the critic will fail if he is merely trying to punch logical holes in the argument he is examining.

The critic's invitation to his audience to consider how it may have been taken in is, of course, an argument and, in view of my preceding remarks, one not very likely to be valid in any sense. There are almost certainly escape-routes for the propounder of the argument it criticizes. Is the rhetoric I have been describing, then, based on a fraud? In representing itself as valid criticism, does it con its audience? This is the case only if as a result of it the audience is convinced willy-nilly that it has been taken in, regardless of the merits of the argument criticized. But I have not been arguing that the rationality of the philosophical enterprise depends on the exercise of such control over the audience of the critique of an argument. It is rational to *consider* whether one has been taken in; it is irrational to conclude automatically in all cases that one *has* been. It is rational to give any philosophical argument the benefit of the doubt unless and until its invalidity has been shown; it is irrational to assume in advance that all such arguments *must* be invalid.

The remarks I have just made reflect a view of rationality that is by no means universally held. My view is that there is at least a kind of rationality that cannot manifest itself apart from its embodiment in people. Human beings are rational in a way in which God could not be because God is not concerned to examine arguments. As sovereigns in the kingdom of ends, humans bring rationality of this kind into the world. This is why a certain rhetoric, which is, like all rhetorics, addressed to people, can serve as the locus of the rationality of the philosophical enterprise. It serves this role simply by calling on its listeners to consider whether they may not have been taken in.

The view that rhetoric is the locus of the rational in philosophy, however, if not further qualified, opens the door to activities that we would hesitate to call rational. For the argument of a philosopher can be challenged sophistically as well as responsibly; and we would not want to be forced to consider the sophistical challenge as an activity of the kind that establishes the rationality of the philosophical enterprise. Yet if rhetorical theory is to be the sole rubric under which challenges to philosophical arguments fall, how shall we distinguish the sophistical from the responsible challenge?

It might be supposed that we could reply that the responsible challenge does demolish the argument, while the sophistical one does not. Let us remember, however, that few challenges, if any, however responsible, really demolish any argument. For as I have just pointed out, the challenge must itself take the form of an argument, subject to all the afflictions of arguments in philosophy. And if perchance the challenge is valid and thus incapable of being waived, we ought to be prepared to find sophistical criticisms with exactly the same merit. For it is not on the basis of logical power that we make the distinction between sophistical and responsible criticisms of philosophical arguments, even though we feel that many sophistical criticisms are patently invalid.

The basis on which we do make the distinction, I think, is the interest of the critic in maintaining the philosophical enterprise. In criticizing, he is implicitly appealing to his interlocutor to do better, to produce a better argument. He criticizes *con amore*. He is like the inspector of products coming off the assembly line, who discards items only in order to raise the standards of the manufacturing process. (And if he discards them all, he can still be said to be raising the standards.) The sophist, on the other hand, would like to see the assembly line shut down. His purpose is not to encourage his interlocutor, but to silence him.

The remarks I have just made show why the attitude of the critic of philosophical arguments must be taken into account. Whether a critic is criticizing *con amore* or not cannot be determined from his criticisms as such. His intention either to shut down the assembly line or to keep it running is not revealed in descriptions of the defects of the articles he rejects. It is revealed only in the way he goes about his work — lovingly or viciously. There is nothing arcane about our knowledge of this intention, provided we look for the knowledge in the right place.

My argument in this paper (which is of course subject to the limitations of all philosophical arguments) has been that the rationality of the philosophical enterprise consists in the use of a rhetoric. I can now specify this rhetoric to some extent by calling it a self-perpetuating rhetoric. The arguments and criticisms of the philosopher must always establish the conditions for their own continuation. Otherwise it is not a philosopher we are dealing with; it is rather a sophist.

The self-perpetuating rhetoric of which I have spoken is easy to ex-emplify. It has been at work throughout the history of philosophy, for it has *been* that history. If we think of later positions as emerging from the critique of the arguments of earlier ones we shall see them as arising from an interest in maintaining the philosophical enterprise. The rhetoric that demolishes the arguments of the past does so in such a way as to show respect for these arguments; it demolishes them *con amore.*

It is the self-perpetuating feature of the rhetoric that is the rationality of philosophy which distinguishes it from rhetoric occurring in other domains. A point is never reached at which the rhetoric of the critique of arguments can-not be reinjected into the argumentative situation, thus generating further movement. The rhetor, on the other hand, moves his audience to the threshold of action, and then expects it to act. To reason with it after it has reached the moment of decision is to take the risk of undoing the work he has struggled so hard to accomplish.

I have been attempting to analyze the rationality of the philosophical enterprise in terms of the use of a certain sort of rhetoric in the pursuit of this enterprise — a self-perpetuating rhetoric. But I do not intend to offer this analysis of the *rationality* of an enterprise as in any way an analysis of the enterprise itself. It would clearly be insufficient to attempt to define philosophy by saying merely that it is a rational enterprise. What else ought to be included in the definition is open to discussion lying beyond the scope of this paper, but might make use of such terms as the articulation of insights, the perception of general patterns, the establishment of norms, or the com-munication of *Weltanschauungen.* Some of the activities I have just mentioned have no obvious connection with examination of arguments. All of them, furthermore, can be carried out in a way not specifically claimed to be rational. If we bear in mind, however, that when they are carried out in that way they are likely to be regarded as religious or artistic activities rather than as con-tributions to philosophy, we shall know where to look for its credentials when we want to show that an activity *is* philosophical. What has no obvious con-nection with the examination of arguments may still have *some* connection.

XII.
A New Theory of Philosophical Argumentation

In a heterodox age such as our own, for every philosophical outlook there is another which raises doubts about it, and the ingenuous thinker may well come to feel that only the reality of controversy itself is ultimately undeniable. This insight has often been tantamount to a cynical repudiation of all philosophies. A more hopeful and, indeed, more thoughtful alternative, however, would consist in developing the philosophical consequences of supposing that controversy is ultimately real. What is needed is a general theory of philosophical argumentation, a study of the conditions under which disputes among philosophers arise, are conducted, and may be assessed. For many reasons, the principles of philosophical argumentation seem *suorum generum*; they do not appear to be strictly identifiable with the canons of formal logic, scientific method, or any other hitherto established discipline. The most important of these reasons is that it is precisely the canons of logic and science which are among the controversial issues of contemporary philosophy. Other reasons will be discussed shortly.

In this situation, it is surprising that in recent years so little work has been done on the theory of philosophical argumentation. Indeed, the only sustained inquiry into it has been that undertaken by the logical positivists. But this inquiry is circumscribed by that very assumption whose doubtfulness has just been indicated; the assumption, namely, that the principles which govern philosophical disputes can be strictly identified with those of hitherto established methodologies.

The recent book *Rhétorique et philosophie*[1] offers an alternative to the positivistic approach. It accuses the positivist of adopting too narrow a conception of proof. "We are prepared to accept other arguments than those with which traditional logic, deductive or inductive, concerns itself. We shall consider as proof ... any argument that diminishes our doubt, that quells our hesitations" (p. 123).

The basic task to which the authors of this book devote themselves is to explore the principles and important ramifications of the art of allaying philosophical doubts and hesitations — an art which they identify as rhetoric. This version of rhetoric is said to contrast with formal logic in several ways. In the first place, "while in logic, one always reasons at the interior of a postulated system, considered as taken for granted, in a rhetorical argument anything can at any time be called into question; one can always withdraw his adherence" (p. 26). Another difference is that in logic, one proof is sufficient to establish a given assertion, while in rhetoric many may be necessary. But the fundamental distinction is that although a logical proof is constraining, a rhetorical proof is not, but results only in a degree of assent to the thesis which the rhetorician proposes. And since degrees of assent are distinct from degrees of probability, rhetoric is independent of the theory of probability. Nor is it, furthermore, to be equated with the psychology of suggestion.

---

[1] Ch. Perelman and L. Olbrechts-Tyteca, *Rhétorique et philosophie: pour une théorie de l'argumentation en philosophie.* Throughout the present discussion, parenthesized numbers will be used to refer to the pages of this work.

The class of phenomena which we shall wish to study could undoubtedly serve as the object of a psychological research, seeing that the result at which [rhetorical] arguments aim is a particular state of consciousness, a certain intensity of adherence. But our concern is to grasp the logical aspect, in a very broad sense of the word, of the methods used, under the title of "proof," in order to obtain this state of consciousness (p. 3).

The use of the term "rhetoric" to connote the discipline which they do have in mind the authors attempt to justify in terms of its employment by ancient writers, especially Aristotle, whose third or panegyric kind of rhetoric[2] is said by them to correspond closely with the subject of their own investigation.

All eight chapters of *Rhétorique et philosophie* had appeared previously in various journals. Six of these articles were written by Professor Perelman alone; these are entitled, respectively, "Freedom and Ratiocination," "Absolute Philosophies and Relative Philosophy," "The Quest of the Rational," "On Proof in Philosophy," "Sociology of Knowledge and Philosophy of Knowledge," and "The Problem of Good Choice." These are largely preparatory or peripheral studies. In the two articles which seem most directly to develop the thesis of the book, "Logic and Rhetoric" and "Act and Person in Argument," M. Perelman is joined by Mme Olbrechts-Tyteca. In these chapters two important matters are discussed: the nature of the audience[3] in philosophical rhetoric and the techniques effective in dealing with this audience.

It is necessary to consider the audience of rhetorical argumentation because "rhetoric, in our sense of the word, differs from logic in that it is concerned not with abstract truth, categorical or hypothetical, but with adherence" (p. 18). And "since rhetorical argumentation aims at adherence, it essentially depends upon the audience to which it addresses itself, for what will be conceded by one audience will not be by another" (p. 19). And to produce or increase such adherence to his doctrine, the speaker can do no more than to exploit the assumptions or prejudices of his particular audience. The difference between philosophical and nonphilosophical rhetoric is only that in the former, "one may make use only of premises admitted by everyone, or at least by that hypercritical assembly, independent of the contingencies of time and place, which one supposes oneself to be addressing" (p. 21) The universal audience to which the philosopher makes his appeal contrasts with the opposite extreme of the single respondent dramatized in the Socratic dialogue. In this case the rhetorician can readily ascertain what premises are actually conceded by his audience and, in making capital of these, can create the illusion that the argument concerns objective fact rather than opinion. But the universal audience affords no such assurance; it is in the last analysis only an image in the mind of the philosopher. "We invent a model of man — the incarnation of reason . . . which we seek to convince, and which varies with our knowledge of other men, or other civilizations, of other systems of thought, with what we take to be incontrovertible facts or objective truths" (p.

---

[2] Aristotle, *Rhetorica, 1358b 21-29.*
[3] Throughout the present discussion, the words "audience" and "speaker" should be understood to cover situations involving the written as well as the spoken word.

22). If certain individuals remain unmoved by his solicitations, the philosopher's only ultimate recourse is to regard them as irrational and thus excluded from the ideal audience which he supposes himself to be addressing. In so doing, "we shall pass, in reality, from the universal audience to the elite audience" (p. 22).

An obvious epistemological question arises here: how shall we distinguish the *bona fide* philosopher from one whose "elite audience" consists merely of figmentary interlocutors, who by definition will capitulate to his arguments? The reply is that "to address itself to this [elite] audience constitutes, in the case of an honest mind, the maximum effort of argumentation to which it can lay claim" (p. 39). To the extent that this statement appeals to the unexamined notion of the upright man, it seems unsatisfactory. But the suggestion that the genuine philosopher, as opposed to the charlatan, will use all the effective resources of rhetorical argumentation is helpful, since many of these devices are discussed at some length.

For Perelman and Olbrechts-Tyteca, most of the important techniques of rhetoric depend upon the fact that there is, in the mind of the audience, an interaction between the personality of the speaker and the propositions he asserts. If the speaker is trusted, his thesis will be received with less hesitation than otherwise, and if the thesis seems obviously true, the trustworthiness of its propounder will appear to be enhanced. La Bruyère is quoted as evidence that the complement of this latter relation likewise holds: "An error of fact throws a wise man into ridicule. A fact is more respectable than a lord-mayor." Objective fact is indeed one of the limiting points of the interaction; it is impersonal in the sense that its credibility is unaffected by the personality of the speaker. The other limit is the speaker regarded as perfect, since his sway over an audience cannot be diminished by any of his utterances, however absurd they may be. Thus science and theology represent extreme cases of the rhetorical situation. Most argumentation falls somewhere between these.

The rhetorical techniques which make use of this principle do so in striving either to inhibit or to reinforce the interaction. In the first case, the speaker will attempt to steer the argument toward either of the limits just mentioned; he will address his audience with an air of high authority, or he will efface himself in an attitude of objectivity. Both limits would seem to be involved when the acknowledged expert disqualifies himself; for "The incompetence of the competent man can be used as a criterion to disqualify all those whom one has no reason to believe more competent than him who has declared himself to be incompetent" (p. 69). This type of argument is often used by philosophers to establish the incompetence of man in general.

The relationship between a speaker and his utterances may, on the other hand, be reinforced by a constant reference from one to the other. This presupposes, of course, that both tend in the first place to be trusted by the audience. The authors discuss the ways of dealing with the interaction between a *proposition* and its *proponent* primarily in the wider context of the relation between the moral criticism of a *person* and that of his *acts* ("Act and Person in Argument"), but the former pair is a special case of the latter. "The connection between act and person seems to us the prototype of a series of relationships which give rise to the same interactions and the same arguments" (p. 84).

Various other modes of rhetoric are referred to, but not in any systematic fashion. The more closely an argument approaches the limit of pure mental suggestion, and the further it is from formal validity, the more important it will be to conceal rhetorically the use of rhetoric. "A fundamental procedure — well known and much used, but very effective — is to insinuate from the very beginning that one is not a persuasive speaker" (p. 37). Another procedure, which seems largely independent of the personality of the speaker, is to argue that a given proposal involves a difference of kind rather than one of degree, or vice versa. "When General Marshall was . . . fighting the 25% reduction of credits to Europe which the American Congress wished to impose, he asserted that from that time on it was no longer a question of 'reconstruction' but of 'assistance' " (p. 35). Again, one may attempt to disqualify a value by exhibiting it as merely a means to an end.

An interesting *obiter dictum* concerns the rhetorical tactic of accusing one's opponent of *petitio:* "Begging the question is not a logical fallacy . . . for [logic] has never forbidden the use of the principle of identity. . . . The fact is that to commit a *petitio principii* is to regard as conceded a premise which one's interlocutor contests. The truth of the premise is not at issue, but only the adherence of the interlocutor" (pp. 127-28). And the matter of adherence is, of course, the essence of rhetoric.

Among the ramifications of this central theory of rhetoric are its bearings upon the contrast between absolute philosophies and relative philosophy, upon the sociology of knowledge, and upon the problem of freedom. Absolute ("premières") philosophies are those resting on unquestioned assumptions regarding reality, veridical cognition, or the nature of value, and would be exemplified by most traditional metaphysics. Such philosophies seem incapable of accounting for subjectivity, error, appearance, and other modes of disorder, and appear to be locked in endless contention with each other. Philosophical disagreements can be resolved only within relative ("régressive") philosophy; i.e., that whose postulates are open to revision when newly encountered facts reveal incoherences in a previous formulation. But the revision "is neither automatic nor arbitrary; it is arrived at by a mind conscious of its own effort and of its responsibility, by a mind conscious of its engagement with the real and of its ultimate freedom of judgment" (p. 98). (This is a quotation from an article by Gonseth.) Genuine choice is involved, and choice is influenced by argumentation. So relative philosophy is ultimately a product of rhetoric.

While absolute philosophies have been typical of times of social stability, ages of upheaval are characterized by a predominately relativistic temper of thought. This observation is intended to show the relevance of the sociology of knowledge to the study of philosophical argumentation. In general, the idea which the philosopher has of his universal audience "has varied in the course of history, [and this idea] has been influenced by the milieu in which one has lived, by the education he has received, and by all the other elements which determine the conceptions of the individual" (p. 140).

Intellectual freedom is neither submission to an externally imposed order nor absolute indeterminism; it is rather a feature of the rhetorical situation. In the case of two interlocutors, "we may consider as manifestations of freedom, in the first place, the attitude of the one who devises the arguments . . . and, in the second place, the behavior of the one who is content to grant or withhold his adherence to the theses which are presented to him" (p. 44). The first attitude corresponds to spontaneity of invention; the second to that freedom of commitment which is "the foundation of a community of minds" (p. 44).

The idea of rhetoric, then, sheds, some light on traditional types and problems of philosophy — this much may be granted. And that *Rhétorique et philosophie* makes a solid contribution to the general theory of rhetoric is indisputable. In particular, the use the authors make of the concept of interaction is original and enlightening. But whether they have really succeeded in illuminating, to any considerable extent, the nature of philosophical argumentation itself, is open to question. A general impression of the book is that most of the statements it makes about rhetoric, and most of the rhetorical techniques it discusses, do not apply peculiarly to the arguments of philosophers. The methods for inhibiting or reinforcing the interaction between a speaker's personality and his thesis are a case in point. These seem rather remote from any significant device of philosophical polemic. Whatever we may know of a philosopher's character has little to do with whether we accept or reject his position; the credibility of the Leibnizian theory of monads, for example, is not diminished by the statement that its author was somewhat of an opportunist in his personal conduct. Perhaps the rejoinder would be that such a theory approaches the impersonal limit of objective fact. But this is not satisfactory, for there is an obvious difference between a theory of monads, however "objectively" it may be presented, and objective fact as such — a difference which it would not be possible to conceal from any audience sufficiently enlightened to understand the theory of monads in the first place. This may be expressed by saying that the latter could not be confirmed or disconfirmed through any observation or series of observations; in Whitehead's phrase, it "could not fail of exemplification."

The ultimate reply might well be that the techniques based on interaction are not generally applicable to philosophical argumentation. This would bring into sharp relief the need for a clear-cut distinction between philosophical and nonphilosophical rhetoric. The authors themselves regard this as a crucial problem and attempt to solve it by stipulating that the philosopher must address a "universal audience." The epistemological difficulties with this conception have already been pointed out. In addition, it may be asked whether, even supposing these difficulties overcome, the stipulation makes any real sense; this question is especially justified in view of the fact that not a single concrete example of a genuine "universal audience" of philosophical rhetoric is given in the course of the entire book. (The audience which Pascal attempted to interest in the problem of the immortality of the soul is mentioned, but it seems clear that the intent here was didactic rather than purely philosophical.) If one tries to think of examples, he will be likely to think of moral appeals to the human race, like the Sermon on the Mount and the *Communist Manifesto*. But the "universality" of the audience in such cases is not at all what the authors seem to intend it to be. It is primarily a rhetorical impression of universality insinuated by the speaker into the minds of his audience for the sake of united action, rather than an idea of "reason incarnate" grasped by the speaker himself. Nor is it clear that this type of appeal is really philosophical, since neither analysis nor speculation is likely to be involved. In any event, no theory of philosophical argumentation which omits these traditional activities of philosophers can be regarded as adequate.

The point may be pressed further by asking what audience *is* addressed by the arguments of analytic or speculative philosophers. For the present writer, an irresistible reply is that it consists of those whom the philosopher wishes to disabuse of error. For Plato, it included the Sophists; for Hume, the Rationalists; for Hegel, the Intuitionists. But in no case would it include the whole world. It would exclude at least those whom the philosopher regarded as his allies. But oddly enough, the authors insist that "The author ought . . . himself to be included in this [universal] audience"! (p. 21).

M. Perelman and Mme Olbrechts-Tyteca might well reply here that philosophical argumentation may be not only polemical or negative but also constructive, and that only the latter variety of it is addressed to a universal audience. If this is what they meant, it is a serious defect in their exposition not to have said so, for the distinction between "argument" in the sense of "attack" and the same word in the sense of "proof" is fundamental. And, aside from the interesting question whether there has ever been an effective philosophical "proof" which was not actually an attack, the objection may be raised that it is not very helpful to suppose that seemingly constructive philosophical arguments are addressed to a universal audience. For of all proofs, those which have the clearest claim to a universal audience are scientific demonstrations; here all of the authors' observations, including those on the passage to an elite audience as the result of the speaker's identification of recalcitrance with irrationality, are borne out with complete success. Mere universality gives no clue as to how one might distinguish constructive philosophy from scientific exposition.

In discussing the relations between philosophy and science, M. Perelman does distinguish the "responsibility" of the former from the "technicity" ("technicité") of the latter (pp. 98, 115, 117). He does this in such a way as to suggest the traditional view that philosophy is concerned with Reason and science with the Understanding. If Reason and Understanding could be regarded as distinctive modes of the universal audience — and the authors do refer to this audience in its philosophical version as "the incarnation of reason" — then perhaps the difference between philosophy and science could be maintained. But is it not a distortion of the philosopher's purpose to say that he addresses his arguments to Reason? A much more natural description of philosophical argumentation is that it is addressed to an unspecified or, if specified, particular audience, and that Reason is the means, mode, vehicle, or language of the argument.

If all the foregoing objections are valid, one wonders whether there is really any promise after all in the attempt to define philosophical argumentation in terms of rhetoric. This doubt is fortified by the reflection that the philosopher's aim in arguing has usually been more than merely to secure adherence to his thesis. More specifically, no conscientious philosopher would be satisfied by assent brought about by methods concealed from his audience. Philosophical controversy is essentially a bilateral affair; it is genuine only when each party to it makes available to the other all the argumentative devices that he uses. The authors, in fact, are careful to point this out (p. 18). But they also realize, indeed emphasize, the fact that "rhetoric" has commonly been used in a sense at least neutral to the distinction between unilateral and bilateral persuasion. And at no point in the book is it made clear that the rhetorical techniques employed in philosophical argumentation would be essentially bilateral.

It should be stressed, however, that the problem here does not arise from any mere oversight on the part of the authors. It is rather a consequence of a systematic refusal to suppose that there is any difference, except one of degree, between Rhetoric and the discipline which has traditionally been called "Dialectic." Aristotle, whom it is germane to quote here, in view of the importance which the authors attach to his *Rhetorica*, defined "Dialectic" as "a line of inquiry whereby we shall be able to reason from opinions that are generally accepted about every problem propounded to us,"[4] and went on to define "Rhetoric," "the counterpart of Dialectic,"[5] as "the faculty of observing in any given case the available means of persuasion."[6] But an age of "Relative Philosophy" distrusts the notion that there is any *bona fide* "reasoning" from "generally accepted" (i.e., philosophical) opinion. To it, such reasoning smacks of the inflexibility and intellectual despotism of "Absolute Philosophies." Because they regard all philosophical positions as the product of a free and tentative choice, the authors are satisfied to suppose that no objective dialectic of ideas is operative in this area. Yet the fact that there must be such a dialectic is shown not only by the results but also by the method of the present criticism; for the statement that certain difficulties arise from·a systematic repudiation of the distinction between rhetoric and dialectic is not intended necessarily to persuade anyone; it is only a kind of reasoning from generally accepted opinion. The final account of philosophical argumentation will have to be given by a philosophy which endorses dialectic while avoiding the absolutism which this book justly opposes.

The preface to *Rhétorique et philosophie* had been undertaken by the late Professor Emile Bréhier, who unfortunately died before he had finished writing it. The paragraphs which are printed, however, suggest a line of criticism similar to that adopted here. The very last passage seems especially relevant; it reads: "Rhetoric seeks to justify a thesis by relying upon a general knowledge of men, of their characters, of their passions; it is an art of obtaining assent. The dialectician seeks to try ("éprouver") the intellectual force of . . ."

Never, to the present writer's knowledge, has death interrupted a more interesting sentence.

---

[4] *Topica,* 100a 18-20, Pickard-Cambridge translation.
[5] *Rhetorica,* 1354a 1, Roberts translation.
[6] *Ibid.,* 1335b 25-26.

XIII.
New Outlooks on Controversy

Two books about argumentation have recently appeared.[1] Each includes a resolute and systematic examination of the nature, scope, limits, and techniques of controversy in all areas of discourse. The documentation of each book is so extensive and so exactly to the point that the reader feels that the footnotes are merely a fragment of a universe of references all of which would constitute evidence for the thesis of the book. Yet the bibliographical universe environing one book has almost nothing in common with that in which the other is immersed. In fact, the author of one of the books never refers to either of the co-authors of the other; and there are only two or three passing references in the opposite direction. There is nothing mysterious about this disjunction, however; the two books appeal to evidence of radically different kinds because their theses are radically different.

Crawshay-Williams defines the scope of his book as the study of statements "put forward with a sort of claim to general acceptance by the company [to which they are addressed]" (MCR, pp. 8-9). Perelman and Olbrechts-Tyteca would certainly agree that only such statements are capable of giving rise to controversy. But this point, and one other that I shall mention shortly, are nearly the only ones on which the two books agree. And there is profound disagreement about how even this point is to be interpreted. Crawshay-Williams is interested only in the extent to which the claim to acceptance can be *satisfied*. The phrase I have just quoted is his definition of statements that are *testable*. His book is largely a discussion of the tests that can be used to determine the correctness of such statements. The implication is, of course, that any genuine controversy can, in principle, be adjudicated by applying such tests to the statements over which it arises. Perelman and Olbrechts-Tyteca, on the other hand, are primarily interested in ways of *expressing* the claim to general acceptance. Their book is mainly a study of the means by which a statement, or a series of them, can be *put forward* so as to claim general acceptance by the company to which it is addressed. For them, controversy consists in claims and counter-claims. It can thus be decisively settled only when a claim is sufficiently overpowering to silence all counter-claims. But such a result can be accomplished only by force or hypnosis, and these settle controversy not by adjudicating it but by abolishing it. Controversy cannot therefore be adjudicated at all, except in relatively trivial cases.

Such trivial cases, in the view of Perelman and Olbrechts-Tyteca, are those in which the correct answer to a problem can be deduced by applying the laws of logic to the axioms of a formal system. In this situation it is altogether irrelevant how the claim to acceptance is expressed, or even whether it is expressed. The validity of a formal deduction is independent of its acceptance by any mind or community of minds. But once we move from formal to non-

[1]Rupert Crawshay-Williams, *Methods and Criteria of Reasoning: An Inquiry into the Structure of Controversy* (New York: The Humanities Press, Inc., 1957); and Ch. Perelman and L. Olbrechts-Tyteca, *La nouvelle rhétorique: Traité de l'argumentation,* 2 vols. (Paris: Presses Universitaires de France, 1958). I shall abbreviate the former as "MCR" and the latter as "TA."

formal reasoning, the success of any argument will depend upon the manner in which the particular audience[2] to which it is addressed responds to the claim it makes on behalf of its conclusion.

For Crawshay-Williams, too, the trivial cases are those in which logical deduction is directly applicable. "There is no room for dispute about the logical truth of the answer to a question. Either it is logically true, in which case its truth can be demonstrated indubitably in a matter of minutes — or it is false" (p. 177). The correctness of most statements involved in controversies, however, cannot be tested so immediately; for the required tests depend upon the correct identification of the contexts of the statements or upon knowledge of objective facts, or both, rather than simply upon deductive logic. If logic be thought of as the lower limit of controversy, there is also, in Crawshay-Williams's view, an upper limit, reached in *untestable* discourse. Here "Statements are put forward for consideration, but the claim to consideration need not necessarily be a claim to general acceptance" (p. 9). It might instead simply call attention to the fact that the speaker thought the statement important. Many of the controversies analyzed by Perelman and Olbrechts-Tyteca revolve about statements that Crawshay-Williams would regard as at least very nearly untestable. On the other hand, many of the controversies analyzed by Crawshay-Williams concern questions that Perelman and Olbrechts-Tyteca would regard as trivial — not in the sense that these controversies could be decisively adjudicated through the use of formal logic, but rather because the questions themselves have no practical significance.

Only a hyper-rationalist would deny that a speaker who attempts to persuade an audience to choose a given course of action, but avoids the use of force or pure suggestion in making this attempt, is *reasoning* with his audience. The most important philosophical thesis explicitly stated in *Traité de l'argumentation* is that the traditional view of reason must be rejected in favor of one capable of accounting for the rationality of argumentation aiming at action. The traditional view of reason is the one inherited from Descartes, according to which reason is essentially characterized by self-evidence. To search for self-evident data is, in fact, to withdraw altogether from argumentation. Nor is reason simply a faculty of calculation. If it were, there would be an impassable gulf between theoretical knowledge, viewed as rational, and action, viewed as irrational.

Crawshay-Williams, too, takes issue with tradition. What he rejects is not so much the traditional view of reason as it is the traditional view that there are precisely two criteria for the correctness of a statement, viz., conformity to the laws of logic and correspondence with the facts. The criteria that Crawshay-Williams proposes to substitute for these in dealing with testable statements (the only statements to which it is relevant to apply any criteria of correctness) fall into three basic categories. There are, in the first place, conventional tests, i.e., those that depend upon "a general agreement among the members of a given company" (MCR, p. 10) as to the acceptability of certain statements. In the second place, there are logical tests that use conventional rules to deduce

---

[2]The authors use "auditoire" — and I use "audience" — to refer to any individual or group to which spoken or written discourse is addressed. Similar remarks apply to "speaker."

conclusions from premises that may themselves fall under one or another of the categories under consideration. There are, finally, empirical tests, which may be either *factual* or *methodological*. The former consist in "observation of what are normally called 'the facts'" (p. 12), and the latter in "trying out methods of treating things and observing whether they produce desired results" (p. 12).

The bulk of *Methods and Criteria of Reasoning* discusses particular types of statements and controversies in terms of criteria of these three sorts. Much of this discussion revolves about a central paradigm. A typical dispute arises when one person states that A is a B and another that A is not a B. If the statements are empirical, however, they may often be expanded so as to show that they are not really contradictories. Thus "A is a B" can be regarded as shorthand for "the neutral facts are such that for such and such a purpose A should be treated as a B" (p. 73). The author usually speaks of "context" instead of "purpose." The problem of resolving controversies is to a considerable extent that of making explicit the contexts of seemingly inconsistent statements. Implicit contexts may be *environmentally determined* or *self-determined*. In the first case, "The physical or intellectual environment of the discussion . . . in which a statement occurs . . . indicate[s] the context of the statement so obviously to the company that there is no chance of misunderstanding" (p. 42). The statement "This is the same book as that" may be false if uttered in an environment in which differences of editions, printings, bindings, etc., are naturally discussed but true if uttered in a more literary environment. When "the words contained in the statement itself [are] normally used only in a certain context, and thus serve to specify that context unambiguously" (p. 42), the context of the statement is self-determined. "This piece of dress material is three yards long" belongs to a self-determined context, because "the words 'dress material' show that the purpose for which the measurement is being given is that of dress-making" (p. 54). This statement could not therefore be relevantly challenged by stating that the material is in fact 109.4 inches long. To be sure, the latter statement is more *precise*. But it is not more *correct*. Indeed, it is misleading, since it suggests that the context is not, after all, that of dress-making. The difference between correctness and preciseness is related to "the strictly speaking argument." Strictly speaking, "every empirical statement of the form 'A is different from B' is . . . true" (p. 143). But the omission indicated by the ellipsis here is that of the adverb "trivially." For given any A and any B, there is always some context in which they are different. But often such a context is irrelevant to the subject under discussion. In any event, almost every statement of the form "A is B" is vulnerable to the strictly speaking argument, which is therefore two-edged, since it can ordinarily be used to refute whatever statement a person may claim to defend through its use. Yet "philosophical speaking is almost by definition strict" (p. 153). Eddington's argument that the plank on the floor is not solid and Russell's to the effect that solipsism is tenable only in its most drastic form are cited as examples. Even when, in the hope of saving appearances, a philosopher endorses Butler's dictum that "Everything is what it is, and not another thing" — as Moore does, for example, in discussing the Naturalistic Fallacy — he may make use of the argument-schema, "Strictly speaking, the process or activity A cannot be reduced to B" (see p. 153, n. 1).

Another common technique of philosophical discussion is to speak in terms of "really," "merely," and "simply." Such talk assumes that there is a Universal Context — thus "the correctness of an empirical statement is in no way related to the purpose for which its subject is being paid attention to" (p. 63). The statement "A is really B," for example, suggests that A is B regardless of context. "And unless [the context of] the statement is already more than adequately determined . . . an indeterminate statement will be made more so" (p. 156). Since the context of "Empirical statements are hypotheses" is far from obvious, for example, we are readily taken in by "Empirical statements are really hypotheses" (p. 156).

It is clear that the author rejects the Universal Context assumption. But the rejection is never justified except methodologically. Now a methodological recommendation could not be incompatible with a factual assertion. Hence the author must be thinking of the Universal Context assumption as itself a methodological recommendation rather than as a factual assertion. Indeed, he suggests that it is simply an inferior way of treating empirical statements for the purpose of testing them. But what if the Universal Context assumption is not, in fact, a methodological recommendation made for this purpose? What if it is not a recommendation at all, but an assertion claiming to be true? In such a situation, can the assumption be properly treated as a methodological recommendation for the purpose the author has in mind? Doesn't this beg the question?

I am not arguing in favor of the Universal Context assumption. My point is only that I do not believe that a contextual analysis such as is advocated in Methods and Criteria of Reasoning is adequate for the purpose of understanding the motives for making philosophical statements (including those that presuppose a Universal Context), even though it may be adequate for the purpose of testing such statements. Crawshay-Williams concedes that philosophy has a value (p. 259) even when the statements in which it is expressed turn out, on analysis, to be either untestable or dully factual. But he seems to feel that it would be in principle possible for a sufficiently cautious person to avoid making philosophical statements altogether. Yet it is not, in fact, possible for Crawshay-Williams himself to avoid making them. The statement "There is always some purpose for which A can be shown to be different from B" (p. 143), for example, not only expresses a philosophical thesis but also is crucial to the argument of the book. So is the "postulate" that "at any position in space and time there is a certain 'structure of events' which is peculiar to that position — as, for instance, the structure of events in my pen is peculiar to the pen and differentiable from the structure of events in my hand" (p. 25), without which it would be impossible for the author to discuss "the objective criterion" required for testing empirical statements (pp. 35ff). It is difficult to see how the correctness of either of these philosophical statements could be tested — or even what it would mean to say that they were "correct." But it is easy to understand why Crawshay-Williams makes them. If he did not, there would be no point to most of his other statements.

In discussing Methods and Criteria of Reasoning, I have been able to do no more than to trace out one line of thought that is at least typical of the expository structure of this compact and deftly written book. There are many other lines of thought that deserve close attention; for instance, the role in controversy of convention and of logic, the theory of distinctions, and the author's treatment of philosophical paradoxes, puzzles, and disputes. What he has to say about contemporary philosophical analysis, in particular about the part played by "informally analytic" statements in controversies over the scope of analytic truth (pp. 205-13), I find particularly illuminating.

Uneasy as I am about the results of my attempt to summarize this book within the space I have been able to give it, I find the task of composing a judicious précis of *Traité de l'argumentation* even more appalling. The latter is more that twice as long as the former, and is about twice as compact. Its singular richness and variety of content is partly explained by the fact that the book is actually the digest of a manuscript of over 3000 pages, the product of ten years of work on the part of its authors. It would be foolish to try to digest this digest. I shall content myself with a rough outline, in the hope that what I have already said about the book will suggest the inner logic giving rise to this sequence of topics.

An introductory section discusses the scope and limitations of argumentation, along lines that I have already suggested. The second main division of the book is concerned with the agreements between a speaker and his audience from which all argumentation must be launched. Among other things, these may concern *facts* (once questioned, though, a fact loses its privileged status), *values* and *hierarchies of values,* and *commonplaces,* the treatment of which here follows Aristotle's *Topics.* Some initial agreements are peculiar to restricted audiences. The use of technical language is symptomatic of this situation. *Argumentum ad hominem,* furthermore, is the exploitation of what a single individual has agreed to. In this connection, the valuable remark is made that *petitio principii* is not a logical fallacy, but rather "consists in a use of argument *ad hominem* when such use is not permissible because it presupposes that the interlocutor has already assented to a thesis that one is just now attempting to make him admit" (TA, p. 153).[3]

A third chapter considers ways in which a speaker may select from the material at his disposal and adapt it to the purposes of argumentation. While "Rhetoric" in its ancient sense was specifically concerned with such purposes, the term has more recently referred to the study of literary style, whether argumentative or not. But "we refuse to separate form from substance within discourse, to study the structures and figures of style independently of the purpose they must serve in argumentation" (p. 192). Among the techniques examined by the authors in the light of this purpose are repetition, synonymy, negation, and the uses of families of words, questions, tenses, pronouns, and conjunctions, and of each entry in the standard catalogue of figures of speech. Students of style should find this section especially interesting.

The next chapter deals with argumentative techniques over and above those involved in presentation and interpretation. The main techniques are those of *liaison* and *dissociation.* The former comprises "schemata that bring together distinct elements and permit the establishment between them of a

---

[3]Inspired by a previous statement of Professor Perelman's about the nature of *petitio,* I had already reached the same conclusion regarding its relation to *argumentum ad hominem* in "Hume's Arguments Concerning Causal Necessity," *Philosophy and Phenomenological Research,* XVI (1956), 332.

solidarity that aims either to structure them or bestow value positively or negatively on each element by means of the other" (p. 255). Liaison is exemplified by "quasi-logical arguments," by arguments based on the (alleged) structure of the real, and by those that aim to *establish* the structure of the real. Quasi-logical arguments aim at liaison with formal logic. "Yet whoever submits them to analysis immediately sees the difference between these arguments and formal demonstration" (p. 259); this is why they are only *quasi*-logical. Examples include the attempts to exhibit contradictions, to identify concepts with one another, and to prove that an opponent's statement is merely tautologous.

The difficulty I find with the notion of quasi-logical arguments is that I do not see how they could have any effect upon anyone unacquainted with formal logic and thus unable to transfer its prestige to the arguments in question. A person could surely grasp the idea of validity without being aware of the existence of formal demonstrations. It is such persons, indeed, who are likely to be most receptive to what are here called "quasi-logical arguments."

Among "arguments based upon the structure of the real" are causal inferences and arguments depending upon the relation between a person and his acts.[4] In order to "establish the structure of the real," one can argue from a particular case. This may serve as (1) an *example,* giving rise to a generalization, (2) an *illustration,* lending support to a regularity already discovered, or (3) a *model,* inspiring imitation. Or one can argue by *analogy* — a type of reasoning that is here analyzed in terms of its persuasive force, rather than in terms of the customary textbook criteria for deciding whether an analogy is "good." But I should like to pass on to what Perelman and Olbrechts-Tyteca have to say about arguments that use the technique of *dissociation.* This is to be distinguished from the attempt to break up a liaison:

> The technique of breaking up a liaison consists . . . in asserting that elements that should remain separated and independent are improperly associated. On the other hand, dissociation presupposes the primitive unity of elements confused within the same conception, designated by the same notion. Dissociation . . . brings about a more or less profound modification of the conceptual assumptions that serve as a foundation of argumentation; it is no longer a question here of breaking the threads that connect isolated elements, but of modifying the very structure of the latter (pp. 550-51).

Dissociation always arises from an incompatibility. When appearance was first dissociated from reality, for example, "doubtless the necessity [of making the distinction] arose from certain difficulties, from certain incompatibilities, among appearances; it could no longer be supposed that all of the latter expressed reality if one assumed that all aspects of the real are mutually compatible" (p. 556).

All dissociations, according to *Traité de l'argumentation,* result in contrasting notions whose relation to one another corresponds to the relation between appearance and reality. The "Term I" of any dissociation has the same

---

[4]The account of this relation given in TA does not differ substantially from what appears in the authors' earlier book, *Rhétorique et philosophie* (Paris, 1952), and I have already summarized this earlier account in "A New Theory of Philosophical Argumentation," *Philosophy and Phenomenological Research,* XV (1954), 244-52.

function as "appearance," and "Term II" corresponds to "reality." But the authors face a serious problem in attempting to say anything more about "Term I" and "Term II." In connection with the former, they use phrases like "what is presented in the first place," "the present," and "the immediate" (p. 557). "Term II" is characterized as "criterion," "norm," and "never given but a *construction*" (p. 557). But they are quick to note that the roles may be reversed. *Because* it is a construction, what has been regarded as reality may be dismissed as appearance. And reality may be identified with immediacy. Indeed, it has been asserted that appearance is the sole reality.

Among the examples of philosophical notions related as Term I/Term II are means/end, accident/essence, individual/universal, language/thought, and theory/practice. Even "rhetoric/truth" belongs in the list, as the authors themselves urge; this accounts for the fact that the cardinal principle of rhetoric is to conceal the use of rhetoric. It is difficult to understand, however, how two authors who have devoted a long book to the attempt to establish the status of rhetoric as a Term II could be prepared to see it reduced to a Term I *en un clin d'oeil.* If dissociations are inevitable, as they seem to think they are, there is no defense against this one. Nor could the difficulty be eliminated by revising this one section. It is symptomatic of the fundamental ambiguity of the entire book. One is never sure whether the authors are thinking of rhetoric primarily as a technique or primarily as a mode of truth. One wonders, too, what status the authors are claiming for the book itself.

The failure of the authors to give any ultimately tenable general characterizations of Term I and Term II is also significant. To my way of thinking, it means that neither Term could possibly be characterized at all prior to the distinction between them. I doubt, for example, that the assumption that "all aspects of the real are mutually compatible" is antecedent to the original distinction between appearance and reality. What is antecedent to this distinction, in my view, is just an inarticulate problem, which it is the function of the distinction to articulate. Thus I doubt that there is any general logic of dissociation; there is only the logic of each particular dissociation, generated in each case by a particular problem.

After making a detailed study of dissociation in all its applications, both within and outside of philosophy, the authors consider the ways in which arguments interact. The final section comes to general conclusions, to some of which I have already referred.

My comparison of these two books leads me to make two comments. The first has to do with the main point on which they agree; namely, that formal logic is devoid of the characteristics that give rise to genuine controversy. This point seems altogether doubtful. No formal system can be evaluated, or even understood, except in terms of an intuition of what it is supposed to formalize,[5] and intuitions are notorious sources of controversy. The second comment is this: both controversy that is always in principle adjudicable and controversy that is never in principle adjudicable are pointless. Controversy has a point only if its participants are entitled to hope both that their dispute can be

---

[5]My reasons for making this remark can be found in "Systèmes formels et systèmes ontologiques, *Logique et analyse,* I (1958), 24-27.

settled and that the conditions under which it arose can be maintained. But this hope is warranted only in a context that is altogether lacking from both books; to wit, the context of history.

XIV.
The Idea of a Universal Audience

The New Rhetoric: A Treatise on Argumentation. Ch. Perelman and L. Olbrechts-Tyteca. Translated by John Wilkinson and Purcell Weaver. Notre Dame: University of Notre Dame Press, 1969.

This is not the first time I have commented on this book.[1] My previous bouts with it, however, have mainly been tendentious: they have been largely concerned with how the view of the nature of philosophy it expresses conflicts with my own. In other words, ignoring my own precepts, I have argued against the book from a point of view external to it. This time, I want to leave my own position wholly aside, and simply address myself to the question whether the work is coherent in its own terms.

Ever since I had the privilege of reading the French manuscript in 1957, before the original edition of the book[2] was even in proof, I have been puzzled about the role that the idea of *audience* plays in the book. My own tendentious attacks centered on the authors' claim that the philosopher addresses a "universal audience." But at a deeper level, I did not know what was even *meant* by a "universal audience," how it was supposed to be related to particular audiences, or what the authors were trying to assert concerning the function of audiences of *any* sort in the exercise of rhetoric.

It is clear that this book is intended to be the systematic presentation of an audience-centered rhetoric. "*It is in terms of an audience that an argumentation develops*" (p. 5; italics in text). In fact, it is claimed to be the *first* systematic presentation of an audience-centered rhetoric. Although the authors acknowledge an immeasureable debt to Aristotle throughout the book, it is their supposedly revolutionary shift away from the message-centered character of Aristotle's approach to argumentation which justifies, in their minds, the title *The New Rhetoric*.

I can begin to express my puzzlement by sketching, with broad strokes, my impression of the book as a whole — an impression that has not changed in any important way in fourteen years. The book begins by distinguishing demonstration and argumentation, contrasting the irrelevance of audience to formal proof with its indispensability to argumentation. A distinction is made between the universal audience and particular audiences — a distinction to which I will revert later. In Part Two, "The Starting Point of Argument," some of the initial agreements from which any argument must begin are ascribed to the universal audience and others to particular audiences. When we get to Part Three, "Techniques of Argumentation," we find that audiences are referred to

---

[1] See "New Outlooks on Controversy," *Review of Metaphysics*, 12 (1958), 57-67; *Philosophy and Argument* (The Pennsylvania State University Press, 1959), esp. Ch. IV; and "Theory of Argumentation," *Contemporary Philosophy* (ed. Klibansky) (Florence: La Nuova Italia Editrice, 1968), pp. 177-78. My article, "A New Theory of Philosophical Argumentation," *Philosophy and Phenomenological Research*, XV (1954), 244-52, is a critical study of an earlier book by the same two authors that is essentially a preliminary sketch for *The New Rhetoric*.

[2] Paris: Presses Universitaires de France, 2 vols., 1958.

infrequently and usually only in passing. Yet Part Three is thoroughly systematic. It is a masterpiece of presentation and documentation; the techniques of argumentation are thoroughly laid out and their relationships to one another exhaustively explored. This, if anything, deserves to be called "The New Rhetoric." But the suspicion develops that the idea of audience is really derivative from that of techniques of argumentation. There are certain techniques, for example, for arguing as if one were simply stating facts; it is such arguments that are said by the authors to be addressed to "the universal audience." Similarly, if one claims, implicitly or explicitly, that *any* rational person ought to believe what one is saying, it is the universal audience that one is addressing. But to make this claim is again to use a technique. And through the use of other techniques one can argue for preferences, thus addressing "particular audiences," which may differ from one another in their preferences. In each case, it is the technique we use that determines whether it is the universal or particular audience we are addressing. The organizing principle of the book, it seems to me, is not *audience* at all, but *technique*.

Yet if Perelman and Olbrechts-Tyteca have failed to produce what they thought they were producing, their failure is by no means unique. It is hard to think of a rhetoric that is *not*, in the end, a systematic presentation of techniques of argumentation. Many of the classics begin with brave assertions regarding the organizing principles of rhetoric, which may be message, speaker, psychology, symbolism, or what have you, but by the time the end of the treatise is reached, the organizing principle has dropped out and the reader is being led through one more systematic presentation of techniques. I know of no presentation more complete than that of Perelman and Olbrechts-Tyteca — here is their real claim to fame — but they have had the advantage, of course, of being able to sift through the rich literature on techniques that has appeared over the past 2400 years. Their scholarship is impressive; there is no book I know of more abundantly supplied with examples that are exactly to the point. Nor is their work by any means limited to sifting; there are myriads of rhetorical techniques that they seem to have noticed for the first time. This book may not be surpassed for another hundred years. But when it is, it will be surpassed by another book on techniques, not by a book on audiences — for such a book would not be to the point.

I want now to make a few somewhat less impressionistic comments on the concepts of *audience, universal audience,* and *particular audience,* in an effort to show that these concepts do not in fact play the role in the book that the authors think they do. We are put on our guard, to begin with, by the statement that "Every speech is addressed to an audience, and it is frequently forgotten that this applies to everything written as well" (pp. 6-7). But must not an audience-oriented rhetoric maintain at all costs the distinction between hearers and readers? Clearly the audience of a live speech is more than merely the set of people to whom the speech is addressed; it is a social organism within which complex interactions can take place, and which can interact in complex ways with the speaker. But the audience of written material need not be a social organism at all; it can be merely a scattered collection of people sitting in their armchairs reading a certain document at various times and in various moods. One would think, however, that an audience-centered rhetoric would deal with the audience as an organism, treating it sociologically and phenomenologically, making clear the nature of the interactions to which it is susceptible. Many of these interactions, of course, come about through causes other than discursive language; they arise simply from the nonrational sociological and psychological nature of the beast that the audience is. But when they say "Our treatise will consider only the *discursive means* of obtaining the adherence of minds" (p. 8; italics in text), Perelman and Olbrechts-Tyteca are declaring their refusal to consider the parameters that an audience-centered rhetoric ought to concern itself with. (They do make passing comments on some of these parameters — for example, on the *sizes* of audiences — but these comments are never systematic.) What they mean by "audience" comprises simply those to whom any speech or piece of writing is addressed. Of course, in some cases it is impossible to say to just what people a piece of writing *is* addressed; an example that the authors use is that of a philosophical treatise. In that case, they assert that it is addressed to the universal audience. The universal audience, then, is simply brought in to make "Every speech is addressed to an audience, and it is frequently forgotten that this applies to everything written as well" come out true. But in this process, the idea of *audience* is altogether deprived of content; it is vacuous. And "Every speech . . . " turns out to be a tautology.

A rhetoric that considered written as well as oral messages might still take the sort of interest in audiences that would entitle it to be called "audience-centered." In a recent article,[3] Carroll Arnold has brought out some remarkable differences between actual speeches and their transcripts. In many cases, the transcript does not have at all the appeal that the actual speech had. One might ask how the transcript would have to be rewritten in order to have the same effect upon an audience of readers that the speech itself had upon its audience of hearers. This question presupposes the possibility of studying as a coherent class the readers of certain kinds of written material (but certainly not all kinds), in distinction from the hearers of this material. But Perelman and Olbrechts-Tyteca are not fundamentally interested in the differences between oral and written messages ("We shall not dwell on whether or not the presentation is spoken or written" — p. 7); so once again they fail to qualify as sponsors of a genuinely audience-centered rhetoric.

The concept of *universal audience* has a variety of uses in *The New Rhetoric.* I have already suggested two of them: (1) as the audience of what a speaker presents either as facts or as what any rational person ought to believe, and (2) as the audience of writing to which we cannot otherwise assign an audience. The universal audience is also an audience that we *convince,* rather than merely *persuade.* Now when we have persuaded some particular audience, there are some fairly palpable signs of our success; its members vote the ticket we are presenting, or rush out into the streets and put up barricades. But how can we test the assertion that we have convinced the universal audience? What sort of evidence is possible? The authors do not make it easy to answer this question; for the universal audience exists only as a "construction" of the speaker; its agreement is "not . . . an experimentally proven fact,

[3]"Oral Rhetoric, Rhetoric, and Literature," *Philosophy and Rhetoric,* 1 (1968), 191-210.

but . . . a universality and unanimity imagined by the speaker" (p. 31). It would seem, then, that he could hardly fail to convince it. Yet it is precisely in his failure that the *elite* audience arises — the audience consisting not of everyone but just of those in a position to know. "If argumentation addressed to the universal audience and calculated to convince does not convince everybody, one can always resort to *disqualifying the recalcitrant* by classifying him as stupid or abnormal" (p. 33; italics in text). But it is hard to see either how such a failure could occur or how this move would help if it could. Such a move could help only if the elite audience is actually some particular audience that we could watch being persuaded.

Perelman and Olbrechts-Tyteca sometimes speak as if *all* audiences, not just the universal audience, were "constructions" of the speaker. In fact, the universal audience is not brought up until after a section on "The Audience as a Construction of the Speaker." "The audience," they say here, "as visualized by one undertaking to argue, is always a more or less systematized construction" (p. 19). In the case of a particular audience I can understand, as in the case of a universal audience I cannot, how the speaker's construction of his audience could be tested. I wonder, however, how the test of whether I had properly *constructed* my audience would differ from the test of whether I had actually *persuaded* it. In some cases, of course, the difference is clear; but these are cases in which a speaker is attempting not to persuade an audience at all, but just to find out what kind of an audience it is. If the speaker who has argued in a certain way is greeted by jeers and brickbats, he can say "That is not the audience I thought it was," but if his intention was actually to persuade the audience, his statement becomes a rueful remark equivalent in meaning with "I have failed to persuade my audience." In other words, the speaker's construction of his audience does not in most cases seem to be different from the process of addressing it; and one wonders whether it is not otiose to speak of "constructing" at all. In a section late in the book, called "The Order of the Speech and the Conditioning of the Audience" (pp. 495-502), the authors seem to suggest that instead of *constructing* his audience at all, the speaker simply encounters it as it actually is. If this is what they mean, I think they are on the right track.

Perhaps one could say that before facing his audience, a speaker "constructs" it, but that the process of constructing comes to an end when he actually stands on the podium and addresses it. If this is the distinction the authors intend, it does not seem a very important one to me. Surely the constructive process is part and parcel of the persuasive process. The speaker must continue constructing as he engages in persuading.

In the case of universal audiences, moreover, it is not always clear that the authors mean to assert that the speaker *does* "construct" his audience. "The agreement of a universal audience is . . . a matter, not of fact, but of right" (p. 31). I can only interpret this statement to mean that the universal audience is not the product of the speaker's *imagination* at all. Instead of *imagining* the world at large, and supposing that this audience agrees with him, he simply thinks that the world at large *ought* to agree with him. Surely such an evaluative judgment cannot be assimilated to the imaginative "construction" of an audience. But nowhere in the book is this ambiguity resolved.

Another use of the concept of *universal audience* is in the role of audience of scientific discourse. And the more formal the discourse, the more appropriate the role. "The maximally efficacious rhetoric, in the case of a universal audience, is rhetoric employing nothing but logical proof" (p. 32). But this statement collides with the contrast between demonstration and argumentation with which the book opens. The contrast is exclusive: "*All argumentation aims at gaining the adherence of minds*" (p. 14; italics in text), but this is not the aim of demonstration. (Of course, the authors might protest that it was "the maximally efficacious rhetoric" that they were talking about, not "the maximally efficacious argumentation." Yet can we conceive of a rhetoric that does not "aim at gaining the adherence of minds"?) It would seem, then, that there are occasions on which argument addressed to the universal audience is not argument at all. Clearly, it is *sometimes* bona fide argument, as when it aims to establish facts. But this aim is itself inconsistent with that of the logician engaged in demonstration, for whom it is irrelevant to ask whether the propositions with which he deals are facts. (See pp. 13, 14.)

All these ambiguities and perplexities in the concept of *universal audience* make me wonder whether the concept is after all really necessary to the project that the authors of *The New Rhetoric* have undertaken. What would the book be like without it? It seems to me that the concept of *particular audience* would then drop out, too. For then it would no longer be possible to distinguish between *convincing* (i.e., obtaining the agreement of a universal audience) and *persuading*. But if all we do in arguing is to persuade, then all we do is to address a particular audience, and there is no longer anything distinctive about the concept of that audience. It is a fact of grammar that in order to persuade, we must persuade *somebody,* and a fact of life that there is nothing of which we can persuade *everybody;* the particular audience thus serves trivially as the object of the verb "to persuade," and the important task becomes that of eliciting the techniques of persuasion.

In fact, all the examples that Perelman and Olbrechts-Tyteca attempt to give of arguments intended to convince a universal audience can be reinterpreted as examples either of discourse not intended to convince anyone at all or else of arguments intended to persuade a particular audience. Consider, for instance, the technique of arguing as if one were simply stating facts. It is misleading to assert that the user of such a technique is addressing the universal audience. He is rather addressing whatever *particular* audience is listening to him, trying to persuade it that he has the facts. Similarly, although the argument that *any* rational person ought to believe what one is saying may *invoke* the idea of a universal audience, it is *addressed* to a particular audience. The authors' failure throughout the book to distinguish between audience invoked and audience addressed is, I believe, at the heart of the confusion surrounding the concept of *universal audience.*

Anyhow, one should not have to use a technique *at all* to convince a universal audience, which is supposed to be purely rational. Yet on page 491 we find this baffling passage: "The order adopted [in a speech] is crucial. . . . This is as true of the different incarnations of the universal audience as it is of particular audiences. . . . The universal audience is no less than other audiences a concrete audience, which changes with time, along with the speaker's conception of it." Perhaps the kindest interpretation of this passage is that what the authors mean by "different incarnations of the universal audience" *are* particular audiences.

My conclusions, then, are that if the universal audience had never been mentioned, there would have been no need to mention particular audiences either; and that, as a matter of fact, there never was any need to mention the universal audience. The idea of this audience is not only unnecessary, it is inconsistent and ambiguous in ways I have attempted to point out. Why, then, have the authors insisted on alluding to it? Very likely because they thought their compendium of rhetorical techniques needed a philosophical underpinning which the concept of *universal audience* could supply. This hypothesis, however, is not intended as an elucidation of the actual order of their work. Perhaps the idea of the universal audience actually dawned on them before much of their work on techniques had been done, seeming to offer a key to the understanding of the techniques. But this account, if true, is merely of psychological significance. In fact, the idea offers no key whatever to the understanding of rhetorical techniques.

It is likely that many or all of my points have been made before, and that the authors have already reacted to them. But a reviewer must retain, as much as possible, a scrupulous ignorance of what other reviewers have said. And if the authors have revised their position in response to previous criticisms, one would suppose that they would have taken the opportunity to record that revision in a translation appearing more than a decade after the original work. A one-sentence warning in the Preface to the English edition would do. But none appears.

XV.
Some Reflections on Argumentation[1]

When we wish to control the action or belief of another person, but either lack an effective means of control or have an effective means that we nevertheless do not wish to use, we argue with the person. Argument is therefore not effective control. To argue with another is to regard him as beyond the scope of effective control, and hence is precisely to *place* him beyond the scope of effective control, provided he is capable of listening to argument and knows how it is that we are regarding him. We give him the option of resisting us, and as soon as we withdraw that option we are no longer arguing. To argue is inherently to risk failure, just as to play a game is inherently to risk defeat. An argument that we are guaranteed to win is no more a real argument than a game that we are guaranteed to win is a real game. An adept arguer can feel certain that he is going to win an argument against someone, but if the certainty is an objective consequence of the very procedure he is using, then this procedure is not an argument.

I do not mean to suggest that the non-argumentative control of action or belief is necessarily infallible. We can command the obedient child but not the disobedient one. But our failure to command the disobedient child is not the result of our regarding him as beyond the scope of effective control. His resistance does not arise from our having given him the option of resisting. It arises from a technical shortcoming on our part. Perhaps with further research we can find the procedure that will guarantee the child's compliance. If we cannot, we may even have to turn to argument.

Argument is a pervasive feature of human life. This is not to deny that there are occasions on which man can appropriately respond to hypnotism, subliminal stimulation, drugs, brainwashing, and physical force, and occasions on which he can appropriately control the action and belief of his fellow-man by means other than argument. But only the sort of person whom we would characterize as inhuman would take pleasure in a life spent controlling the behavior of others through non-argumentative means, and only an idiot would willingly obey him. We do not even exercise power over people when we merely manipulate them — except in the extended sense in which we can be said to exercise power over robots. We normally say that we have power over people only when we are treating them as people.

One typical way of exercising power is by means of threats. A threat is a form of argument because whoever uses a threat in the attempt to obtain action of a specific sort runs the risk that the other will choose to accept the threatened reprisal rather than to act as desired. It is only a person who can respond to a threat, and when we threaten a person we at least treat him as a

---

[1] The view of argumentation to be presented in this paper is in many respects indebted to that of Professor Perelman; but there are important differences in emphasis which make it difficult to compare the two views. For example, it will be seen that I emphasize the element of risk in argumentation. Perelman does not. But I do not know whether this difference amounts to a disagreement between us. In this paper I have thought it best just to present my own view with its peculiar emphases, and to let the reader decide to what extent Perelman and I disagree.

person. We treat him as capable of envisaging the consequences of non-compliance. Perhaps some animals are capable of responding to threats. This would imply the capacity to comprehend a conditional proposition. To the extent that we actually can deal with animals in this way, we are certainly treating them as persons.

A threat is, however, a degenerate form of argument. It is degenerate because its appeal to the person is only momentary. Once the threat has been uttered, there remains only to carry it out, or, if it has succeeded in bringing about the desired action, to break off contact. The one who is threatened has no opportunity to treat the propounder of the threat as a person at all unless he can utter a counter-threat.

Commands are sometimes of a mixed status. They are usually efforts to control behavior and sometimes belief by non-argumentative means. Sometimes a command carries an additional implicit threat, however, and so is partly an argument. This is much more likely to be the case when the command is addressed to a human than when it is addressed to an animal. The automatic, unquestioning compliance that we expect of an animal is the response to a more purely non-argumentative technique than any we would ordinarily use when dealing with a human being.

I have said that the arguer takes a risk. But he is not the only one who does. The person to whom the argument is addressed may or may not elect to run the risk of having his behavior or beliefs altered by the argument. By closing his mind to the argument, he can avoid the risk altogether. Then anyone wishing to control his behavior or beliefs must resort to non-argumentative modes of control if he is to have control at all. There are issues to which all of us must to some extent close our minds. We cannot argue everything out, or always be available to arguments addressed to us. But we cannot always have closed minds, either, for the person with the totally closed mind cuts himself off from the human race. Such a person is inhuman, although he is not beastly, for we do not accuse animals of having closed minds, any more than we say that their minds are open.

On the other hand, the person willing to run the risks involved in listening to the arguments of others is open-minded and, to that extent, human. The differences between man and the animals are typified in man's open-mindedness. Open-mindedness is not merely an added means of accomplishing what the animal can to some extent already accomplish by other means. It is an entirely new possiblility. In making himself available to arguments, man transcends the horizons of his own perceptions, emotions, and instincts. Within these horizons the risks of argument do not occur; there is no arguing over what I immediately see, feel, or do. No arguer can take away from me what I immediately experience or feel, because this bears no relation to the conclusions for which he is arguing. These conclusions consist of argued beliefs, evaluations, and lines of conduct, and they can come into conflict with my views only to the extent that these are themselves argued rather than immediate. I do not mean to suggest that the solitary individual, out of the range of other arguers, could not rise above immediacy. As I shall shortly point out, in deliberating about the meaning of his experience, and thus transcending it, he is arguing with himself.

It is only to the open-minded person who has transcended the horizons of immediate experience by taking the risks implicit in argument that knowledge and morality are possible. The animal perceives and expects, but has no knowledge, because it cannot expose to argument its interpretation of what it perceives or its reasons for expecting. The animal cannot behave morally because it cannot argue for its conduct. The animal, in short, has no world. The world is revealed only to an open-minded person.

I have spoken of open-mindedness as involving a risk. The risk that the open-minded person takes is that of having his belief or conduct altered. This risk, of course, is strictly correlative to the risk the arguer takes that his arguments might fail. The question arises whether it is necessary to characterize the possibility that the arguer might fail or that his interlocutor might fail or that his interlocutor might be persuaded, as a *risk*. Is it not sufficient to characterize it as a *possibility,* and say simply that the open-minded person faces the *possibility* that argument might alter his belief or conduct?

The difference between a risk that a person takes and a possibility that he faces is that he has an interest or stake in the outcome of activity in which he is taking a risk, whereas he is unconcerned with the outcome of activity that he merely supposes to present various possibilities. To say that it is merely a *possibility* that argument might alter his belief or conduct is to suggest that the person plays a wholly passive role in the transaction — that "he couldn't care less." It is to suggest that he has resigned from the control of his own action and belief — that he has transferred this control to the hands of the arguer, saying, in effect, "You must decide for me." But what such a person has done is simply to withdraw from the argument. And having withdrawn from it, he brings the argument itself into question. For it now appears that the arguer possesses direct control over the belief and conduct of the person with whom he is arguing. The former takes no more of a risk than the latter. Thus the argument itself collapses into a non-argumentative type of control.

Thus genuine argument can occur only where the respondent is neither impassive to the utterances of the arguer nor passive to them. It can occur only when the respondent is himself interested in the outcome of the argument; that is, where the respondent takes a risk, and thus forces a risk upon the arguer. What, then, is the interest that the respondent has in the argument? We might be tempted to say that it is an interest in maintaining his own belief and conduct. To some extent such an interest does account for the risk a person takes in allowing himself to become involved in an argument. He takes the palpable chance that his belief or conduct may be exposed as questionable and overthrown. But this cannot be the whole story. For one thing, it is not clear why anyone should feel any resistance to the abandonment of his position once its defects have been revealed. Why does he not cheerfully say "good riddance" and adopt the recommendations of the arguer? For another thing, there can be risk in arguments over issues concerning which a person has no prior opinion. In this situation there is no present belief or conduct to be maintained. What, then, is the risk? It is that the respondent, in his belief or conduct, may have to take account of something that he has not had to take account of before. What he would like to maintain is the relative simplicity of his own position. And in general the risk a person takes by listening to an argument is that he may have to change himself. It is the self, not any specific belief or mode of conduct, that the arguer's respondent wishes to maintain.

But his interest in maintaining it cannot be absolute, for if it were he would be presenting a closed mind to the argument.

The open-minded person, then, is one in whom there is tension. On the one hand, he wishes to maintain himself. On the other hand, he must expose himself to the risk of change implicit in argument. Such tension is necessary to any human being who wishes to transcend the horizons of his immediate experience and inhabit a world.

The person who listens to argument is not the only one to take a risk. I have already suggested what risk is taken by the arguer. The arguer risks failure to control the belief or conduct of another. This risk, too, implies a tension. The arguer wants control over another but is willing to see that control limited by the negative responses of the other. That this is a genuine and precarious tension becomes obvious when we consider each of its terms to the exclusion of the other. An arguer who wants control pure and simple does not argue; he controls by non-argumentative means and avoids risk. An arguer purely and simply willing to be limited by the responses of the other does not argue, either; in his subservient passivity he abdicates from argument. To argue, a person must maintain the tension between control and what limits control. This tension may be characterized as tolerance, intellectual generosity, or respect. It is isomorphic with the tension I have already characterized as open-mindedness, the terms of which are self-maintenance and change. The tolerant person must find the limits to control in the act of controlling, and he must control in terms of these limits. The open-minded person must maintain himself through change, and change by maintaining himself.

The give-and-take of argument sheds light on the function of logic and the meaning of validity. When sophistries and fallacies are used by one disputant or all, the discussion soon degenerates into a form in which open-mindedness and tolerance are no longer possible. The fallacious argument is disrespectful; it does not treat its listeners as people but either deliberately or unwittingly aims to extort their assent. Logic is the discipline that prevents the discussion from degenerating. The valid argument is the one that maintains the possibility of arguing.

I have written so far as if one could make a final distinction between the arguer and his respondent. Of course one cannot. For the respondent can also be an arguer. When this is the case, the negative responses that limit the control of the arguer will themselves be arguments, and he will submit to this limit in the role of a respondent. In other words, open-mindedness will have become a condition for tolerance. In the dialogue between two or more arguers tolerance and open-mindedness simply become different ways of characterizing the same basic willingness to maintain the argument and follow it wherever it leads.

The arguer and the respondent may also be the same person, as in deliberation. In this situation it is the same person who seeks control and submits to control, who imposes limits and accepts limits. The tension that must be maintained here is extremely precarious, and readily collapses into habit, impulse, or panic. Deliberation eventuating in a change or reaffirmation of belief is probably capable of existing in a purer form than is deliberation eventuating in conduct because our habits and impulses constitute unargued lures to possible action in a way in which they do not necessarily constitute lures to possible belief. What I am constitutionally capable of doing will cast a stronger spell over my arguments to action than it will over my arguments to belief.

A common view of argument is that it is a transaction that has no essential bearing on the characters of those who engage in it. The arguer attempts to persuade the listener. If he succeeds, well and good; if he fails, he may either resort to non-argumentative techniques or else give up the effort. But the argument is in no way definitive of either the arguer or the listener. It is simply a kind of communication among minds that already exist and already inhabit the world — a device that they may or may not choose to employ. And one can always choose argument without simultaneously choosing himself.

My own position is that argument is in fact essential to those who engage in it — a person who chooses argument does in fact choose himself. For the tension between conservation and change which is felt by the interlocutors is precisely what enables them to inhabit the world. Immediate experience makes no claims and raises no questions; it is transparent. It is only when action and belief become subject to argument that an opacity is introduced into experience — the opacity which is the self. There is no self for immediate experience. There is a self only when there is risk. I do not want to claim that argument provides the *only* sort of relevant risk. But when people argue, they take risks that raise them above the level of immediate experience and put them on the map. And unless they take risks of one kind or another they are not people. So argument does seem to me to be constitutive of those who participate in it.

Non-argumentative forms of control do not establish the self. Instead, they by-pass it. They proceed on the assumption that the self is not present to interfere with their effective administration. The command, the subliminal suggestion, the hypnotic pass, avoid the risk of dealing with the self. The cajoler, the advertiser, and the hypnotist not only operate on the basis that "nobody is at home" in the body of the interlocutor, but are not even "at home" themselves. One who wheedles instead of arguing does not himself quite deserve to be treated as a person, and neither does one who secures the assent of another when the latter has his guard down or is looking the other way. When a man is given to using non-argumentative means of control we have no compunctions about using non-argumentative means against *him,* on the ground that he has not shown himself to be a person.

Shall we say, then, that argumentation is a device for avoiding the need to resort to violence? That when we assume that another is "at home," and argue with him, our conduct is a *substitute* for non-argumentative forms of control including the use of force? This is a common account of argument. According to it, men argue only by virtue of a prior agreement, either explicit or implicit, to substitute the conference table for the battlefield. But this fragile agreement may collapse at any time, and, when it does, the first man to return to the battlefield will have the advantage. This is a cynical view of human nature, since it regards man's capacity for argument as no more than the product of a transient enlightenment — an unstable victory over the irrational forces that define him — and it regards argument itself as no more than an expedient. If argument is in fact a mere expedient to avoid violence, then we ought to consider as most successful that argument which has the greatest soporific effect. More fundamentally, this view is in direct contradiction to the history of

human hostility. Throughout recorded time, men have always based their conflicts upon arguments. Every war has been preceded by the search for an excuse for fighting. To find examples of violence not based upon argument we
must look to the annals of psychopathology. This shows that normal human
violence already presupposes argument. Indeed, if the capacity to argue is not
present from the outset, how is it possible to reach any agreement, whether
explicit or implicit, to suspend hostilities in favor of argument?

A similar common account of argument hardly does justice to the human
need for rhetoric, advertising, and propaganda. It presents rhetorical technique as mere poses or postures that can be taken by the arguer. For every
rhetorical posture, there is another that can be used to counteract it, so that
human controversy appears as sequences of meaningless gestures. They are
meaningless because the arguer himself can stand altogether outside them. As
devices at his command, they express no feature of his ego. The arguer's ego
can remain inscrutable throughout his argumentation, according to this
traditional view of the role of argument in human life. It is only necessary for
the arguer to *appear* to be committed to his own argument. Indeed, only a fool
would really be committed to his own arguments, because for every argument
there is in fact an equally effective counter-argument. This, too, is a cynical interpretation of human nature.

My own interpretation does not require me to deny that for every
argument there is an equally effective counter-argument. It merely derives a
new conclusion from this premise. Instead of concluding that no one should
be so foolish as to become committed to his own argument, I conclude that
argument is a defining feature of the human situation. A being not capable of
arguing or of listening to argument would simply not be human. Such a being
would, as we have seen, lack a self. Any reflective arguer knows, of course, that
all of his arguments can be met by counter-arguments. But to condemn all
argument on the basis of this reflection is completely to miss the point of
argument. The point of argument is not to provide effective control over
others, as might be the case if there were some arguments that could not be
met by counter-arguments. It is rather to introduce the arguer into a situation
of risk in which open-mindedness and tolerance are possible. This is the
human milieu which the arguer supports through his fervent commitment to
his own arguments. If he were not committed, his arguments could have no
more than a strategic function, and the milieu would collapse into a game in
which open-mindedness and tolerance would no longer be possibilities.

An arguer can both be fervently committed to his arguments and know
that all of them can be met by counter-arguments. This is possible because the
reflection with regard to the counter-arguments represents a momentary dis-
engagement from the milieu in which the arguer lives. Similarily, a thinker can
disengage himself from manners and mores and pronounce that manners and
mores are all equally arbitrary. This pronouncement would have a point if it
had ever been claimed that they were *not* equally arbitrary. But in the absence
of this claim, it misses the point that a human milieu is sustained by manners
and mores in much the same way as it is sustained by argument.

I have just been considering how according to a common view the existence of a counter-argument for every argument is evidence of the futility of
argument. Sometimes it is the alleged datum of futility that makes those who

share this view feel that for every argument there must be a counter-argument. The history of philosophy is an alleged datum of this kind: because no philosopher has ever been known to have secured general agreement to his position by means of arguments, it follows that for every philosophical argument there is a counter-argument. Now if general agreement were in fact a desideratum or alleged achievement of the philosophical enterprise, there would be some point in being concerned with the possibility of a philosophical argument admitting no counter-argument. The layman attributes this goal to philosophy, and there are some philosophers who join him in doing so. But most philosophers are not interested in securing general agreement to their views. To them the observation that general assent has never been attained would simply seem to miss the point of the philosophical enterprise. The point of it is not to get everyone to agree but to argue for conclusions to which general agreement would be irrelevant. What could such conclusions be? Evidently they cannot be concerned with facts. In a broad sense they are indeed concerned with values. A philosophical argument may deal with such values as knowledge and morality. These are values because they enable man to transcend the horizons of immediate experience and hence to inhabit a world. Other philosophical arguments deal with other ways of moving beyond the immediate. If it is argument *sans phrase* in the first place that opens the world to us, philosophical argument deals with the fruits of argument *sans phrase*. Argument *sans phrase* may well aim to secure general agreement. It can do this because general agreement is one of the possibilities of the world it opens up. We can escape from immediate experience into general agreement just as we can escape from it into knowledge or morality. But philosophical argument is not an escape from immediate experience. It is only an attempt to expand and consolidate the world into which the escape has been made. Thus it may examine the concept of general agreement as well as those of knowledge, morality, and so on. But general agreement with regard to the results of the expansion and consolidation achieved by philosophy would be beside the point.

What I am trying to say can be put more positively. I have said that argument reveals the self by confronting it with risk. Philosophy makes clear the structure of the risks faced by a person who argues or listens to argument. It articulates a world of people and of things. It tells the self who it is and where it stands. Thus philosophy may be said to serve the emerging self by contributing to its morale. Philosophical arguments, then, have a morale function rather than an information function. If we expect general agreement regarding their conclusions, we simply do not understand them correctly. Philosophical argumentation will continue with unabated force as long as there are selves confronted with a world in which they must take a stance.

My conclusion is that neither the existence of a counter-argument for every argument nor the alleged futility of philosophical arguments is, if rightly interpreted, a reason for adopting a cynical view of man's argumentative nature. Indeed, without that nature he could not be man.

XVI.
Controversy and the Self

Like Rogge,[1] McKeon,[2] and Hall,[3] I believe that between two rival philosophical systems there is at least sometimes a gulf which neither position can cross if it insists on pursuing the discussion in its own terms. "Each . . . can claim the virtues of the other. . . while denying that [the] other. . . in fact possess[es] those virtues," as McKeon says.[4] I have myself expressed this view by asserting that the partisan of each system is, in principle, incapable of conceiving the system espoused by the other. "For each, in stating his own systematic position, is in effect claiming that this position includes all the relevant evidence and therefore no statement adducing evidence against it is possible."[5] To some readers, this assertion has sounded strange. Surely, they have objected, one can conceive of a rival system, even though one violently disagrees with it. Indeed, how could one disagree with it at all unless one could conceive of it? This is a problem to which I wish to address myself in this paper. But I see no reason to withdraw my assertion that a philosopher who espouses one system is incapable of conceiving of a rival system. If it were merely the case that he had reviewed the evidence for the rival system, and found it unconvincing, I would certainly admit that he could conceive of the rival system. But when a philosopher — say, Smith — is in principle committed to the thesis that nothing that his antagonist submits as evidence can possibly be evidence for anything except Smith's own view, then to say that Smith literally cannot conceive of his antagonist's system seems to me an accurate way of describing the situation. Another way of putting the matter is to point out that philosophical positions are not hypotheses. If one frames a hypothesis, one can regard a rival hypothesis as a possibility. But one does not take a philosophical position as the result of choosing among positions regarded as possible. The position one takes is really the only one that one sees as possible; and one sees one's rivals' positions, accordingly, as impossible. But one cannot conceive the impossible. One can no doubt talk, and perhaps in a sense even think, about round squares, even if one cannot conceive of them, but no one is in fact able to form the idea of a round square. Similarly, no philosopher taking a systematic position is in principle able to form the idea of a position contradicting his. A statement expressing a philosophical system is like a tautology in logic. Any tautology includes all the possible evidence; it is true regardless of the evidence. Hence no evidence against a tautology is possible. And if we contradict a tautology, the result is a contradiction, i.e., a statement the meaning of which we literally cannot conceive. The difference between tautologies and philosophical systems, however, is that while all rational beings admit the

[1] Eberhard Rogge, *Axiomatik alles möglichen Philosophierens* (Meisenheim/Glan, 1950).
[2] Richard McKeon, "Philosophy and Method," *The Journal of Philosophy*, 48 (1951), 653-82.
[3] Everett Hall, *Philosophical Systems, A Categorial Analysis* (University of Chicago Press, 1960).
[4] McKeon, p. 673.
[5] *Philosophy and Argument* (The Pennsylvania State University Press, 1959), p. 1.

same set of tautologies, not all rational beings endorse the same philosophical system.

In a recent article,[6] Duane Whittier has reviewed a number of situations in which a philosophical system cannot envisage the possibility of evidence contradicting it. One of these is the dispute over the "incommunicability of content":

> It has been asserted that there is no way of knowing for certain that when two persons name color-sensations alike they are actually experiencing the same sensation-quality. It is said that it is *conceivable* that color-sensations between persons might differ systematically in such a way as to elude any test for the difference. Critics of this view argue that this state-of-affairs is not conceivable because what we *mean* by the expressions "the same" and "different experience" is determined, and can only be determined, by public criteria. To speak of a color-blindness that no test can detect is to speak idly. What we *mean* by "color-blindness" or "sensation-discrepancy" is precisely those things which certain tests reveal. For one party to this dispute such color-experience discrepancy is *conceivable*. To those committed to a verificationist theory of meaning it is not conceivable.[7]

From the point of view of the philosopher who interprets color-blindness as a phenomenon exhaustively defined in terms of public criteria — the verificationist — it is logically impossible that there should be any cases of color-blindness not satisfying these criteria. His interpretation of color-blindness renders him incapable of conceiving such cases, just as the standard definition of a circle renders us incapable of conceiving a square circle. It might be objected that this analogy is defective, since although we *cannot* interpret circles in such a way as to be able to conceive a square circle, we *can* interpret color-blindness in such a way as to be able to conceive cases of color-blindness not satisfying the public criteria. But the verificationist, unlike other people, *cannot* in fact conceive any cases of color-blindness not satisfying the public criteria. It is his very commitment to his position that cuts him off from this possibility.

To say that the verificationist cannot conceive of any cases of color-blindness not satisfying the public criteria is precisely to say that he cannot conceive of any evidence against the view that all cases of color-blindness satisfy the public criteria. Whatever he will accept as evidence must already satisfy the public criteria. Hence all the evidence that is possible is evidence for his own view. He is in much the same position as that of a person who, on being told that circles can be square, asks for evidence of this possibility. All that he, or anyone else, is willing to regard as evidence at all must take the form of circles that are not square.

But there is an important difference between asserting that no circles are square and asserting that no cases of color-blindness fail to satisfy the public criteria. The latter assertion is polemical. It is made in order to challenge the contention that there might be cases of color-blindness not satisfying the public criteria. The former assertion, on the other hand, is not made in order to challenge the contention that circles can be square. For this is not a serious

---

[6]"Basic Assumption and Argument in Philosophy," *The Monist,* 48 (1964), 486-500.
[7] Ibid., p. 488.

contention at all. The reason why we assert "no circles are square" is that we deduce it from a definition of "circle" the function of which is regulative rather than polemical. Such a definition is not the formulation of a view about circles. It expresses the nature of a circle, but this expression is not a view. There are alternatives to any view, just because it is a view and not a grasp of a fact; but all correct expressions of the nature of a circle (at least in Euclidean space) are equivalent, because they all express the same fact. Since the definition of "circle" is not a view, it cannot be used to *attack* a view about circles.

In fact, if anyone contends that circles can be square, he is neither expressing nor attacking a view about circles. He is not saying "I interpret circles in this new way." All that he is doing, in effect, is proposing that the term "circle" be broadened to include squares. We can argue with him over the usefulness of this proposal, but our argument will not be an attempt of any sort to get our hearers to interpret circles in one way rather than another. There is only one way to interpret circles — and hence we do not interpret them at all.

The assertion "No cases of color-blindness fail to satisfy the public criteria," however, arises in the effort to combat a certain interpretation of color-blindness, and thus is itself an interpretation. It interprets color-blindness as nothing more than a certain sequence of responses to certain tests capable of being conducted in public. This is not only an interpretation of color-blindness, it is a very narrow and tendentious interpretation; many people would call it altogether perverse. It certainly does not answer to what most people mean by "color-blindness." The only excuse for making such an assertion as this is that in making it one intends to attack another interpretation that seems to have consequences at least equally perverse. In this case the unwelcome consequence is the possibility of undetectible cases of color-blindness.

I have said that for the verificationist there can be no evidence contradicting his view. He literally cannot conceive of any case of color-blindness not satisfying the public criteria. If anyone contends that such cases are possible the verificationist may, of course, imagine that his interlocutor is proposing that the term "color-blindness" be broadened. But as in the case of the proposal that the term "circle" be broadened, such a proposal is not seen as an interpretation of color-blindness, and hence is not regarded by the verificationist as an interpretation at variance with his own. As a purely verbal proposal, it does not, so far as he can see, express a genuine alternative to his view.

But if a philosopher literally cannot conceive of any genuine alternative to his view, then he cannot understand his own position as a view that has arisen as a response to an alternative view. Asked why he takes the position he does, he is not entitled to say "There is a perverse view that I wish to attack." All that he can say is "I am simply stating the nature of color-blindness." But to an onlooker this explanation is obviously wrong. No one who was simply stating the nature of color-blindness would define it in terms of the satisfaction of public criteria. Anyone who defined it in such a perverse way could have done so only in order to attack an alien view. A definition as strange as this does not arise in a vacuum.

In fact, the verificationist is aware of the context of his own definition.

Even though his position does not *entitle* him to conceive of any genuine alternative, yet he will cheerfully admit that it arises from a concern with an alternative, and will sincerely impugn this alternative as perverse. The notion of developing his definition in total isolation from the alleged error that it aims to correct will seem just as queer to him as it does to others.

The verificationist has contradicted himself. He has said, in effect, both "my position is not a view" and "my position is a view, which attacks a rival view."[8] He both can conceive of an alternative to his position and cannot conceive of an alternative to it.

Let us analyze the contradiction in greater detail. It arises from two considerations. In the first place, as I have already said, a philosopher does not take his position as the result of choosing among positions he regards as possible. The position he takes is actually the only one that he sees as possible. It follows that he must regard all rival positions as impossible. "Impossible" here means "logically impossible"; it is not merely a psychological block or a defect in imagination that prevents the philosopher from conceiving a rival position. His inability to conceive it is instead like anyone's inability to conceive a logical contradiction.

The second consideration is that the philosopher's position is polemically oriented; it does not arise in a vacuum. It is a view that arises in the attempt to combat an alien view. But no one would think of attempting to combat a view that he did not regard as logically possible. If someone tells me that some squares are not squares, I simply do not know what he means. If I do not know what he means, I am not in a position to regard his statement as the expression of a perverse or dangerous doctrine that I want to attack. I can want to attack a doctrine only if I see it as logically possible.

Another way to put this second consideration is in terms suggested earlier. If I cannot conceive any alternative to my view, then my view, like a logical tautology, conveys no information; it is true for all possible worlds. But again, like a tautology, it is trivially true. If my view is to be true in a nontrivial way, then at least one alternative to it must be conceivable.

Hence the verificationist must see the view he is attacking as both logically impossible and logically possible. This is a contradiction. One's normal reaction to a contradiction is to look for a distinction in terms of which it can be resolved. But it is clear that in the present case no saving distinction can be found. It is in precisely the same sense of "logically possible" that the alternative to the philosopher's position must be both logically possible and logically *impossible*. In fact, it is because the alternative is logically possible that it is logically impossible, and it is because it is logically impossible that it is logically possible. A view can be negated (i.e., called logically impossible) only if it exists (i.e., is logically possible); and it can exist only if it is negated (for any philosophical view exists only as a radical denial).

If there were a way of resolving the contradiction, the dialectical tension between the position that all cases of color-blindness must satisfy public

---

[8] Notice that I use the term "position" to include both definitions that are not interpretations — e.g., the definition of "circle" — and views, such as the verificationist's view.

criteria and the alternative to this position would be broken, and both the position and the alternative would collapse into inanity. Either the philosopher would find himself entertaining the alternative to his position as one possibility among many, or he would find that the point of taking his position had vanished.

It would be preposterous to argue that verificationists, or philosophers who take any other view, are explicitly aware of embracing a contradiction. Most philosophers would be angered if not horrified by the very suggestion. Throughout the history of philosophy only a handful of thinkers have made the accusation that I am making. In a somewhat different version, however, the accusation is slightly more palatable. This version is a consequence of some reflections on argumentative strategies open to the philosopher. I have pointed out that if a philosopher defines color-blindness in terms of the satisfaction of public criteria, he will be unable to accept as evidence any alleged evidence of the existence of color-blindness failing to satisfy the public criteria. He can thus argue by pointing to all the evidence amassed in favor of his view, and by disqualifying any alleged evidence against it. But an astute opponent will soon see that in carrying out each of these strategies the philosopher is doing no more than begging the question. If the proposition to be proved is that all the evidence is in his favor, the proof cannot consist in any application of that proposition itself. Hence the philosopher may turn to a new strategy. This consists in exposing an incoherence internal to the view that some cases of color-blindness do not satisfy public criteria. One might argue as follows. If there can be cases of color-blindness not satisfying public criteria, then there is no reason in principle why there should not be cases of insensateness of other sorts not satisfying public criteria; e.g., tone-deafness or a corresponding olfactory defect. There is no reason, for that matter, why it should simply be *defects* in sensation that might be undetectible. For the same principle that leads us to suspect that undetectible defects are possible should also lead us to suspect that undetectible differences in *qualia* are possible. Perhaps what you call red is what I call green. The fact that there are public criteria to determine whether a person sees red is irrelevant; even when you behave in such a way that according to these criteria you are seeing red, you may still be seeing what I call green. This brings us to the final and fatal extension of the position, which has been well expressed by Max Black:

> . . . The very same considerations which inculcate scepticism concerning the individual *qualia* of another person's experiences ought to raise insuperable doubts concerning the character of the classes to which they belong. If we cannot be sure that another person means by "red" or "middle C" the same as ourselves, we have no better grounds for believing that such relatively general terms as "sensations," "sense-quality," or "feeling" mean the same to hearer and speaker. We cannot even be sure that the names of colors and tastes apply at all to sensory experience rather than to some features of, say, logical deduction.[9]

But exactly the same considerations apply to the entire vocabulary of the man who has said that there may be undetectible cases of color-blindness. Given any word that he uses, there is no way of being sure that he means by

[9] *Language and Philosophy* (Ithaca, New York, 1949), p. 6.

the word what we do. On his own view, then, "we ought to be in no position to understand *any* of his own statements. . . . Only [he] can ever know what he means by his sceptical assertions; and he can never tell us."[10]

Black summarizes by saying of the view under attack that it "involves a very peculiar type of *reductio ad absurdum*. For if [the] thesis were true, it would be *meaningless* to us; therefore we cannot be expected to understand it; therefore we cannot be expected to believe it."[11] The argument that exposes this *reductio* might also be said to be of a peculiar type. It is peculiar in that it is an *argumentum ad hominem*, an argument of a type that is not usually regarded as rigorous. But the reason why *argumentum ad hominem* is not usually regarded as rigorous is that stronger arguments are available which appeal to evidence; they are *ad rem* rather than *ad hominem*. Where every appeal to evidence is question-begging, however, as all would be in the case of the verificationist, there can be no stronger argument than *argumentum ad hominem*.[12]

Yet there is an *argumentum ad hominem* against this very use of *argumentum ad hominem*. For I have just said that the validity of this use arises from the invalidity of any appeal to evidence. The appeal to evidence is invalid because by hypothesis no evidence in favor of the view that there may be undetectible cases of color-blindness is possible. But this is tantamount to saying that this view is inconceivable. The *argumentum ad hominem*, however, is precisely an exercise in conceiving the view under attack. It is essentially a sympathetic argument — one that slays by delivering "the kiss of death." To destroy a view, its opponent simply assumes its leading principle and elicits the fatal consequences of that principle. But one cannot assume a principle if one cannot conceive it. Thus a dilemma arises. Either the verificationist can conceive the view he attacks or not. If he can conceive it, *argumentum ad hominem* is no longer an effective argument; a far more relevant attack will be one that appeals to evidence. But if he cannot conceive the view he wishes to attack, he cannot formulate an *argumentum ad hominem*. That this dilemma is itself addressed *ad hominem* is shown by the way in which it exploits the assumption that any *argumentum ad hominem* must exploit an assumption. The dilemma exploits this assumption by pointing out that one cannot exploit any assumption without first conceiving it.

Hence the verificationist is caught once again in a contradiction. He must be both unable to conceive the view he attacks and able to conceive it. There is no way in which he can avoid this contradiction.

Exactly the same considerations that apply to the particular philosophical views on which I have chosen to dwell thus far in this article would apply to any philosophical view whatever. Whoever adopts a philosophy adopts a contradiction, whether he knows it or not. This fact is seen most clearly when we consider the argumentative strategies open to a philosopher, as we have just done.

---

[10] Ibid., p. 7.
[11] Ibid.
[12] I have defended this contention in "Philosophy and *Argumentum ad Hominem*," *The Journal of Philosophy*, 49 (1952), 489-98.

Either of two different responses to this situation would be entirely natural. One is to give up philosophy. But the difficulties inherent in this response are well known. Anyone who deliberately sets out to give up philosophy takes a view that only can be regarded as itself philosophical. The other response is to abandon the attempt to avoid contradiction. But this irrationalism undercuts itself too. For it is only as a consequence of attempting to avoid contradiction that we fall into it. If the rational expression of our views were never a desideratum, the very concept of contradiction could not arise. There are no contradictions in nature; whatever natural thing we choose, it cannot both have a certain property and not have it; in nature, the Law of Noncontradiction reigns supreme. There are no contradictions in the utterances of animals or idiots. Contradictions exist only in the language of men attempting to be consistent. To waive the goal of consistency is thus to abolish the very possibility of contradiction.

The response that I want to recommend — the only response, I think, that does not undermine itself — is to accept the fact that in espousing a philosophical view one has contradicted oneself, while at the same time maintaining consistency as the standard and goal of discourse. The philosopher who regretfully accepts the fact that in taking a view and opposing other views he has contradicted himself differs markedly from the one who does not accept this fact. The latter is a kind of schizophrene. Sometimes he regards a view that he opposes as logically possible. Sometimes he regards the same view as logically impossible. He thinks of it as logically possible when he wants to attack it. His attack, however, consists in exhibiting it as logically impossible. He vacillates between these two assessments of the view he opposes. He adopts one after the other, failing to see that in fact both assessments apply to the same view at the same time and in the same respect. By introducing a specious temporal interval between the assessments, he has managed momentarily to evade the contradiction by keeping its poles apart. But the evasion is not a genuine escape; it is only a dissimulation. To stop dissimulating, one must accept the contradiction; one must acknowledge that both assessments coincide. One must be willing to unify the poles. Indeed, the contradiction itself presupposes this unification. Unless there is a single perspective from which an opposing view can be seen as both logically possible and logically impossible, there is no contradiction — there is only a vacillation. It might be objected that the contradiction exists regardless of perspective. Unsuspected contradictions, after all, have been known to lurk in mathematical systems. But I have already pointed out that contradictions exist only for people attempting to avoid them. Men concerned with mathematical systems are obviously attempting to avoid contradictions. It is this very attempt, however, that results in the single perspective from which it is possible to assert that p and not-p are both true at the same time and in the same respect. It is because the vacillator is not interested in avoiding contradictions, on the other hand, that there are no contradictions for him to avoid.

Let us examine more closely the perspective from which the poles of a contradiction are unified. This perspective is a locus of responsibility. For it is clear that only the thinker who refuses to vacillate between the poles is a responsible thinker. He has assumed responsibility for his own philosophical view. Indeed, the mode of existence of a responsibility closely resembles the mode of existence of a contradiction. Just as contradictions exist only for those attempting to avoid them, so responsibilities exist only for those willing to assume them. Neither contradictions nor responsibilities exist in nature.

The perspective from which the poles of a contradiction are unified is also a locus of transcendence. For the philosopher who sees an opposing view as both logically impossible and logically possible stands both inside his own view and outside it. The assessment of the opposing view as logically impossible is one that the philosopher must make from within his own view, since it is the way in which his view defines its terms that renders any alternative view inconceivable to him. The assessment of the opposing view as logically possible, on the other hand, presupposes that the philosopher stands outside his own view, observing how the latter is saved from triviality by the existence of meaningful assertions inconsistent with it. The kind of transcendence that is involved in the philosopher's acceptance of the two contradictory assessments of a rival view has in recent years been referred to as "ecstasis."[13] It is a characteristic of a being which in its being is what it is not, and is not what it is. The responsible philosophical thinker is both totally immersed in his point of view and not totally immersed in it — and thus his being as a responsible thinker consists in his being what he is not and not being what he is.

In addition, the perspective is a locus of subjectivity. As I have said several times, contradictions do not occur in nature. They do not occur in any objective domain. Indeed, a domain has objectivity to the extent that the law of noncontradiction is valid within it; even a fantasy world is objective to the extent that within that world nothing both has a certain property and fails to have it at the same time in the same respect. It follows that the sole source of contradictions must be subjectivity. When we accept a contradiction we accordingly acknowledge the subjectivity of our perspective.

Finally, the perspective from which the poles of a contradiction are seen as unified is a locus of identity. To be aware of myself, I must distinguish myself from others. This means that I must have a point of view which I know to be distinct from the points of view of other persons. I must take a position, but at the same time be aware that other positions are possible. Yet any such awareness naturally threatens my absolute commitment to my own position. If other positions are possible, how can I hope to justify my own? Identity thus presupposes an ecstasis, which is precisely the ecstasis that I discussed above.

The conclusion that I wish to draw is obvious. It is the *self* to which responsibility, transcendence, subjectivity, and identity have traditionally been ascribed. The *self,* then, is the perspective from which the poles of a contradiction are unified. The contradiction presupposes the self. At the same time, it takes a contradiction to evoke the self. When there is a contradiction, a burden is felt; and the self arises to take up this burden. There is no other occasion on which the self is called for.

The self is the pivot of philosophical controversy. One can address arguments only to the thinker willing to acknowledge a contradiction when one occurs and yet committed to the principle that discourse should be consistent. It would be impossible, for example, to argue with the schizophrene,

---

[13] Cf. Martin Heidegger, *Sein und Zeit* (Tübingen, 1957[8]), p. 329.

who sometimes sees his opponent's view as logically possible and sometimes sees it as logically impossible, but sees no contradiction. I do not mean to be suggesting, however, that it is only the philosopher under attack in whom the self must have arisen. It must also have arisen in the attacker. Otherwise, the attack will be no more than an exercise in logic-chopping. An attacker who insists that those whom he attacks take seriously the contradictions into which they have fallen, but who refuses to apply the same standard to himself, can be safely ignored, for he is in fact a schizophrene. Unless a man is willing to reveal the stake he has in criticizing another position, we need not listen to his criticism. I have already suggested the nature of that stake. All effective philosophical arguments are *ad hominem,* but there is an *argumentum ad hominem* against the use of any *argumentum ad hominem* — a meta-*argumentum ad hominem* — that consists in pointing out that in order to use *argumentum ad hominem* one must stand both inside one's own view and outside it. The price the philosophical critic must pay for his use of *argumentum ad hominem* is to be subject to this meta-*argumentum ad hominem.* If he refuses to pay this price his talk becomes mere schizophrenic babble. It takes a self to evoke a self.

The act in which the self is evoked is essentially an act of philosophical criticism because it is only in responding to such criticism that we are forced to stand outside ourselves. The proper response to non-philosophical criticism is not ecstasis but the correction of our errors. Hence not only is the self the pivot of philosophical controversy, but also philosophical controversy is the life-sustaining atmosphere of the self. A community of selves is one whose members are open to criticism that is distinctively bilateral, in the sense that every member is responsive to criticisms of exactly the kind that he addresses to others.

I have said that the self arises only in a person both willing to admit that he has contradicted himself and committed to the standard of consistent discourse. This statement may seem to suggest that one can come to rest in a permanent contradiction permanently evoking the self. But no contradiction can be permanent; for it is part of the meaning of any contradiction that it is to be overcome. Whatever we are willing to settle for in perpetuity cannot be a contradiction — or else, in settling for it, we are in fact evading it. If a contradiction exists to be overcome, then we must take steps to overcome it. To illustrate such a movement, let me return to my example. The philosopher who holds that undetectible cases of color-blindness are possible has contradicted himself, as is revealed by the *argumentum ad hominem* addressed against him. Therefore there are no undetectible cases of color-blindness. But this view, too, is vulnerable to an *argumentum ad hominem.* If color-blindness is to be exhaustively defined by the public criteria in terms of which we can detect it, then neither color-blindness nor color-sensitivity has any subjective counterpart. Each is wholly a matter of a person's behavior, not of anything that might be said to be present to his mind or absent from it. But on the same principle, the meaning of any term referring to a mental state must be exhausted by publicly observable behavior. Hence if the philosopher says that he believes that there are no undetectible cases of color-blindness, he is only reporting his own behavior. But while a belief can be true or false, behavior cannot. Yet surely he supposes his belief to be true (Lovejoy called this contradiction "The

Paradox of the Thinking Behaviorist").[14] The possibility of making a philosophical claim evaporates in the pan-objectivism implicit in the verificationist's view, just as it does in the pan-subjectivism implicit in the view of his rival that undetectible cases of color-blindness are possible.

So far we have not yet taken any forward step of the kind I said is necessary to overcome the contradiction. There is no one uniquely required step. But a step that would be possible at this point is to declare that the objectivity and subjectivity of color-blindness are conditions for each other. Unless color-blindness had a public meaning, it might be contended, it could not have a private meaning. Nothing can be undetectible unless we can know what it would mean to detect it. Conversely, unless color-blindness had a private meaning it could not have a public meaning. We cannot set up a criterion for something without knowing what that thing is of which it is the criterion.

We have arrived at a dialectical view of color-blindness. As a philosophical view, it is certain to have its own defects. But these are not the defects of either of the views from which it has emerged. It represents novelty. Progress has been made. Although we face a new contradiction, it is one that results from the overcoming of an old one.

[14] A.O. Lovejoy, "The Paradox of the Thinking Behaviorist," *Philosophical Review*, 31 (1922), 135-47.

XVII.
The Philosophical Basis of Rhetoric

I want to begin by distinguishing between what has a philosophical basis at all and what has none. Science, history, morals, and art have a philosophical basis. Fishing, tennis, needlecraft, and carpentry do not. The criterion that determines membership in each list is simple: an activity has a philosophical basis if, and only if, the practice of it distinguishes man from the animals. It must be necessary to man but not necessary to any other creature. Fishing is of course disqualified on the ground that some animals, as well as men, fish. It might be argued, however, that there is an art of fishing requiring tools utilizable by man alone, and that the ability to fish in this way distinguishes man from the animals. To be sure, in some cultures fishing with appropriate tools is necessary. In others, carpentry is. But if we came across a culture in which fishing did not occur, we would not say, "This creature does not fish; hence he is not a man"; and the same for carpentry. It may seem that the same question arises for science and history. Not all cultures are scientific. If science is indeed, as I maintain, necessary for men, what then prevents us from visiting some primitive tribe and saying "These creatures have no science; hence they are not men"? The answer is that the culture we have encountered is prescientific. Even though its participants have at the moment no science, science is somehow "in the cards" for them. We would not characterize the nomads of Afghanistan as being in a pre-fishing era. We would not say that fishing was in the cards for them. Of course if the desert should become a sea, they will become fishermen, and there will have been a pre-fishing era. But it is not *necessary* to the character or status of the nomad that he represent either a pre-fishing or a fishing, or, for that matter, a post-fishing era. It is necessary for man, however, that he be either prescientific man or scientific man or postscientific man. I add the last rubric to accommodate not only the tragic possibility of a cataclysm that could wipe out all humans capable of maintaining the tradition of science but also the ironic possibility that man might some day simply turn away from science. In either eventuality, man would be essentially characterized as a being living in a postscientific era; that is, not merely as a being bereft of science, but as a being living a life either oriented to the cataclysm that had shattered the tradition of science or else oriented to the conviction that science is a thing of the past. The non-fishing nomad, on the other hand, need not take any position at all with regard to the nature or value of fishing. The possibility of fishing need receive no mention in any characterization of him.

The principle I have roughly stated and exemplified implies that if rhetoric has a philosophical basis, it is necessary to man, in the sense that all men live in either a pre-rhetorical culture, or a rhetorical culture, or a post-rhetorical culture. Each of these cultures is characterized by a disposition toward rhetoric. In the pre-rhetorical era, even though man does not engage in any form of rhetoric that we can recognize, we can see rhetorical activity as in the cards for him. Perhaps someone will object that there never has been such an era; as long as man has existed, he has engaged in rhetoric. So much the better for my argument; for then it is all the more clearly the case that rhetoric is necessary to man. But if man has gone through a pre-rhetorical phase, he is distinguished from all nonhuman creatures in this respect. No one would say of rats, cats, or cows that they are not yet engaged in rhetoric, but that once the idea occurs to them they will be. But man is either rhetorical from the outset or fated to become so once a certain idea dawns upon him — this, at any rate, is what anyone would be claiming who asserted that rhetoric has a philosophical basis. The assertion also implies that if man ever ceases to be rhetorical, his cessation will not be a mere turning of attention from rhetoric to some other activity — as a primitive tribe might turn from fishing to hunting — but will take the form of a positive attitude; the belief, for example, that rhetorical activity is out of date or is immoral.

Although there is some *prima facie* plausibility in the thesis that rhetoric is necessary to man, the thesis is not easy to prove. The two main attempts to prove it have been those made by naturalists and pragmatists. According to the naturalists, man is by nature a bellicose being, and rhetoric arises as a substitute for his warlike propensities — a temporary transfer of hostility from the battlefield to the halls of disputation.[1] This theory seems doubtful at best; I am sure that a careful reading of history would show that most wars are caused by rhetoric rather than the other way around. Even if the theory were true, furthermore, it would not establish that rhetoric is necessary to man — it would simply show that rhetoric is an expedient sometimes tried out in the attempt to gain a surcease from fighting, but in principle doomed to failure.

The pragmatic view defines rhetoric in terms of the fundamental category of action.[2] Action, on this view, is intrinsically fraught with risk. We cannot know what the ultimate consequences of our acts will be. Our estimates are at best probable, and rhetoric is argumentation over the probabilities. Personally, I prefer this view to the naturalistic one, because it seems to me to reflect a sounder judgment concerning what it is to be a man; but in the last analysis I cannot accept it. The pragmatic view is unable to show the necessity of rhetoric to man, and this is for a very simple reason: it cannot show the necessity of anything other than statements that are trivially true. Where all nontrivial statements are at best probable, it can hardly be *necessary* for man to use rhetoric.

My own argument for the necessity of rhetoric to man is that rhetoric is implied in the very activity which is supposed to supersede it; to wit, the communication of objective fact. In attempting to spell out this argument, I may seem at times to be moving rather far afield; much of what I want to say I find I can most conveniently say by discussing computers. But having disposed of computers, I will eventually turn to rhetoric as such, and I hope my readers will then agree that what appeared to be a digression was not a digression at all.

What, then, can we say of a situation in which rhetoric has been totally suppressed in favor of communication? In such a situation there would be no need for persuasion. Information would replace argument. Instead of

---

[1] For a recent expression of this view, see Th. Kotarbinski, "L'Éristique — cas particulier de la Théorie de la Lutte," *Logique et Analyse*, 6 (1963), 19-29.

[2] An articulate and forceful expression of this view is to be found in the writings of Ch. Perelman. See, for example, his definitive work *La nouvelle Rhétorique: Traité de l'argumentation* (with L. Olbrechts-Tyteca), 2 vols., Paris, 1958.

attempting to convince me of the truth of a certain proposition or the correctness of a certain course of action, my interlocutor would simply tell me.
My readers may feel that this situation is already familiar to them, in the
writings of Orwell if not in accounts of past and existing monolithic states. But
these are not situations without rhetoric; they are rather situations which
ironically must be sustained by rhetoric. Only through the official rhetoric can
private and deviant uses of rhetoric be rigorously suppressed. A situation totally devoid of rhetoric would be more appropriately exemplified by a system of
devices designed to receive, store, manipulate, and transmit information. Certainly rhetoric could have no effect on such a system. One can't argue with a
machine — one can only control it. The question I want to ask is whether a
machine of this kind or a system of them does in fact represent a situation in
which we have succeeded in suppressing rhetoric in favor of communication.

It might be supposed that no more perfect vehicle of communication
could be imagined than a deck of punched cards constituting a computer
program. There is no ambiguity whatever about the information conveyed to
the machine. Nor would it make sense to suppose the machine in any way
reluctant to receive the information. A rhetoric of belief would be absolutely
gratuitous even if it were possible. Nor is there any need for a rhetoric of action. Some of the cards in this deck formulate commands to the machine. For
example, if a certain statement is true, the machine is told to go to another
statement designated as "200" and execute the command therein expressed;
otherwise, it is to go to "300." The machine does not need to be convinced of
the correctness of this course of action. Indeed, the very notion that a course
of action would be correct for it is tenuous, to say the least.

Using a deck of punched cards, or some other input device like a
magnetic tape or a light-pen, I establish absolute communication with the
computer. Is it not obvious, though, that this absolute communication is identical with absolute noncommunication? I "tell" the computer that the initial
value of the variable N is 15. But have I really communicated anything to it? It
has no choice but to accept 15 as the value of N. Perfect communication, and
hence noncommunication, characterizes the transmission of messages from
man to machine and from the machine to other machines. In order to show
why it amounts to noncommunication, let us contrast it with the transmission
of a message from machine to man. Suppose that "N = 15" is not the initial
datum of a problem, but rather the solution to a problem that a user has
programmed a computer to solve. Accordingly, the user in question will
receive from the machine a sheet of paper on which is printed the expression
"N = 15." One might suppose that this, too, is perfect communication. Certainly there is no ambiguity about it. But the fact remains that the user need
not accept it. He may say, "Hey! Wait a minute! That can't be right!" Anyone
who has had experience with computers will recognize this situation. Computers do not always tell the truth; they do so only when they are correctly
programmed and given data that are correct. Even if "N = 15" is actually the
correct answer, the user need not accept it; his past dealings with the machine
may have made a doubting Thomas of him. And even if the user does not reject "N = 15" as the solution to the problem, he need not accept it, either. His

mind may simply be on something else. Perfect communication presupposes a perfect listener. But, as I will try to show, a perfect listener would hear nothing.

The question before us is whether we can replace rhetoric by communication. A likely instrument for carrying out the replacement is the computer. It turns out, however, that in the process of getting rid of rhetoric, we have gotten rid of communication as well. For we can actually communicate nothing to the machine; we can at best get it to accept the data we feed into it. Nothing can be communicated to a recipient who is not, in principle, free to reject or to ignore the datum he is invited to accept. The issue here is not whether the datum is true or false; it is only whether the recipient can judge it false, or ignore it altogether. Hence, in our dealings with a computer, we have not suppressed rhetoric in favor of communication; we have simply been discussing a situation to which rhetoric and communication are alike irrelevant.

The machine in the version we were just considering failed to serve as an appropriate model of a kind of communication with no rhetorical component because it did not engage in communication at all. It might be thought, however, that by modifying the machine we could create the needed model. If the fault lies in the perfection of perfect communication, let us undo that perfection. Receiving communications imperfectly, the modified machine will, we hope, at least receive them. Rhetoric, however, will still play no part in the message we address to the machine. We can address it rhetorically no more than we can preach to the waves — at least, success in the one enterprise is as unlikely as it is in the other.

Accordingly, let us try to construct a machine to which we cannot communicate perfectly. In fact, we may feel that we do not need to devote much effort to this task. We have merely to shift our perspective on existing machines. When we avowed that we could communicate perfectly to them, what we really had in mind were ideal machines. For it is only in theory that a computer would always and of necessity accept, say, the information that N is 15. Now, shifting our perspective slightly, we acknowledge that existing machines are fallible; mechanical parts wear out, short circuits occur, unexpected "bugs" develop. One cannot at all be sure that an existing machine will accept the information that N is 15.

It does not follow, however, that we are able to communicate with it. For the explanation of its failure is nothing at all like the explanation of human failure. The man fails to accept the datum that N = 15 either because he refuses to believe it or because his mind is not on the printed sheet before him. We could communicate with him if his mind were on what we told him and he believed it. The machine, however, can neither have its mind on what is being transmitted to it nor receive this datum absent-mindedly; and it can neither believe nor disbelieve what it is told.

Conversely, we may ask whether we would regard ability on the part of the human to accept or reject information as the machine accepts or rejects it as evidence that we could communicate with him. The machine accepts information by passing into a certain state — a certain piece of iron in the machine, for example, is magnetized. Perhaps the closest parallel in the case of a person is post-hypnotic suggestion. If the hypnotist succeeds in putting me in a state in which my nose itches whenever I hear the word "freight," he has stimulated me in exactly the way in which a punched card bearing the message "N = 15" stimulates a computer. But no one would say that he had communicated anything to me — indeed, the very point of post-hypnotic suggestion is that I be unaware of the suggestion.

We have failed to communicate with the machine because our communication is still perfect. The computer had to accept whatever it *did* accept. Suppose that instead of accepting the datum that N is 15, the computer stores the value 14 in the location identified with the variable N. This malfunction can undoubtedly be explained. And to explain it is to show why the machine *had* to accept 14 as the value. This value is thus perfectly communicated to it by errant features of the situation (for example, by a card reader with a short circuit), even though it is not the value the user intended to communicate to it. The machine's failure, furthermore, is not like the failure of a human to accept a datum. It is not *either* because the machine believes that 15 is not the correct value *or* because its mind is not on what it is doing that it stores 14 as the value. But it is only when communication can fail in ways like these that it can occur at all.

It might be supposed that a computer could simulate these human failings. Computers do in fact comment on the programs that are given to them, pointing out syntactical errors and inconsistencies. Why could not a machine be designed to criticize the data fed into it, rejecting those which, on one criterion or another, were unacceptable? For example, if N has already been assigned the value 14, it may be inconsistent to assign it the value 15. The machine I am envisaging would say, in effect (and could say quite explicitly, if we wanted it to), "Hey! Wait a minute! That can't be right!"

When we tell the machine we have just constructed that N is 15, we run a risk. Perhaps it will accept the datum. But it need not, and if it does not it will print out the error message that I have just phrased in a colloquial form. In view of this risk, have we not at last managed to avoid perfect communication with the machine and thus managed to engage in genuine communication with it? If so, we have communication without rhetoric, for, short of magic, we cannot persuade the machine.

There is a difference, however, between the machine's refusal to accept 15 as a datum and a similar refusal on the part of a person. The machine's refusal consists in *telling the user* that 15 is not an acceptable value for N, and in not storing 15 in the appropriate location. The person's refusal, on the other hand, involves *telling himself* that 15 can't be right. (He may also tell others, but he need not.) The machine does not tell *itself* anything. In other words, it is not *conscious* of anything. An individual incapable of telling himself, in images if not in words, whatever he is claimed to be conscious of, is not conscious of it. The mere ability to blurt it out is no criterion of consciousness. Now if the computer cannot be said to be conscious that 15 is not an acceptable value of N, even though it tells *us* that it is not acceptable, then it cannot be conscious that a datum *is* acceptable when it *is*. But we do not succeed in communicating anything to anyone unless he is conscious of what we are communicating. To say that he must be conscious of what we are communicating is just another way of saying something I said before — that he must be free to accept or reject the datum. The nature of consciousness is the root of the paradox of perfect communication. The communication of a datum could be perfect only if it were in principle impossible for the recipient to tell himself otherwise. But in this case, he would be unconscious, and no communication at all would have taken place.[3]

My argument so far has been that we cannot use machines, or systems of them, to illustrate the thesis that there are cases of communication requiring no rhetoric, because machines do not exemplify communication in the first place. As soon as we approach genuine communication, we depart from the world of the machine, and we set foot in a domain requiring rhetoric as an inextricable adjunct or aspect of communication. But this point I have so far made only in a negative way. It cries out for positive argumentation and illustration. Why is rhetoric necessary? What is the indispensible role it plays?

I have just claimed that communication entails consciousness. Without further ado, let me state my main thesis: *Rhetoric is the evocation and maintenance of the consciousness required for communication.* The reason rhetoric does not work when applied to the machine is that the latter cannot be conscious of anything. But it is required whenever there is genuine communication. Let us recall the computer user who received the printed statement "N = 15" from the computer. We might be tempted to wonder what role rhetoric could possibly have in this act of straightforward communication. But it was just the fact that the man could have failed to accept the statement that certified his acceptance as the consummation of a genuine act of communication. And rhetoric, whatever else it is, is certainly concerned with the acceptance or refusal to accept statements. There is a rhetoric of factual communication as well as a rhetoric of exhortation. The facts never speak for themselves; they are always spoken for or against by the rhetorical ambiance of the situation in which they are asserted — an ambiance that is the suppressed premise of the rhetorical enthymeme. Even computer output has rhetorical force, the source of which is in the user himself. If I trust the machine, and feel competent to handle it, and am familiar in addition with the general range of values within which the solution of my problem must fall, I endow the machine's output with authority. I can raise questions about the correctness of the output only if I am not completely under the spell of the machine. Most programmers are not; they know that the computer is no more than a device for confronting them with the consequences of their own thinking, exposing its shoddiness to the full light of day when it has been shoddy.

Supposing that all genuine communication does require rhetoric, what does all this have to do with the evocation and maintenance of consciousness?

---

[3] Some readers may wonder why I have gone to such lengths to show that it is impossible to communicate with machines. To such readers it seems obvious that since machines cannot think we cannot communicate with them. There are those, however, who are not convinced that it is impossible for a machine to think. See, for example, Feigenbaum and Feldman, eds., *Computers and Thought*, New York, 1963. Furthermore, the mathematical theory of communication treats a machine's acceptance of data as a perfectly legitimate example of communication. Not only does such acceptance meet the specifications for communication stipulated by this theory, but it meets them in a certain ideal way — the communication is "noiseless." See Colin Cherry, *On Human Communication* (Cambridge, Mass., 1957), especially ch. 5.

The machine is once again a handy model to serve as the basis of the discussion. Let me begin by mentioning the concept of an *interface*. An interface is the point at which a message passes from one form into another. For example, the card-reader, which converts holes in punched cards into electrical impulses, is an interface. So is the output printer, and so is a cathode-ray tube into which output might be fed. Now if the phenomenon of *being conscious of* is something that is to occur, or is to have an analogue, in the machine, it seems plausible to look for it in the relation between what lies on one side of an interface and what lies on the other. If there is to be consciousness anywhere in the machine, for example, one might expect to find it in the machine's acceptance, in terms of an electrical response, of the datum on a punched card. For it might seem that the response is the acceptance of a datum quite similar, at least formally, to a person's acceptance of a datum of which he is conscious. But in fact, the analogy does not hold; for, as we have seen there is in fact a radical difference between a person's acceptance of a datum and a machine's acceptance of it. I want to argue that the analogy collapses because, in the sense of "interface" in which interfaces are actually involved in communication, there are really no interfaces at all in the machine; or, alternatively, if we insist on maintaining a sense of "interface" in which there are interfaces in the machine, these latter separate activities that are not separated from each other by any distance of a relevant kind. The relevant kind of distance is that between a person and what is communicated to him. It is this distance that permits him to accept or reject the proferred datum. The only reason why such distance is not available to the machine is that it is impossible to maintain the distinction between the two sides of the interface. For if the card-reader is an interface between punched card and computer, why can we not say, with equal justice, that whatever connects any two elements of the computer is an interface between them? We thus immediately push the concept to triviality. Conversely, we can show that there are in principle no interfaces at all in the system in which the machine is involved. For we can regard the printer as the interface between the output and all of the earlier parts of the train taken together. But if we take these parts together, what is there to prevent us from taking the printer along with them? It seems altogether arbitrary to call the printer an "interface."

Yet even if the concept of an interface cannot be consistently applied to the machine, for the benefit of which it was invented, it can be applied to the reception of messages by people, even though not invented for this purpose. If we elect to say that consciousness is an interface between the computer's output and a person's acceptance or rejection of this output, this statement is not obviously trivial or false in the way that the statement on which it is modeled is. The interface in this case can be neither endlessly proliferated nor eliminated. There is a distance between the person and the datum, but this distance is not to be found everywhere.

We can imagine, furthermore, what it would be like if the interface between the person and the datum were eliminated. One is very often confronted with data of which one is not conscious — the weather report one is not listening to, the striking of the clock; for that matter, any background sound (which is always a datum of *something*). To say that one is not conscious of such data is just to say that there is no distance between oneself and the data — one accepts the data only in a sense in which one could not reject them. Who is to say in this case which is the interface? Is it the vibrating body, the sound waves, the vibrating eardrum, or the cochlea, which converts mechanical into electrical energy? Or is there no interface at all to interrupt the unity of this seamless fabric? Whichever way we look at the activity in question, it is one in which the person is sometimes engaged and in which the machine is always engaged.

It now becomes evident what would be required if we were to succeed in communicating with the machine. We would have to introduce a genuine interface between the machine and the datum we wished to communicate to it. Is it not clear, however, that in the entire world of physical things, of which the machine is a part, there is no genuine interface? Nothing is sufficiently *other* than the machine to be communicated to it. Only what is *other* than a person can be communicated to him.

To be conscious of something is always to interrupt the unity of the transaction between subject and object. Consciousness confronts the person with something radically other than himself. I have the power to accept or reject a datum only because I am not the datum. The question that now seems most imperative to deal with is "How can two beings that are radically different be brought into relation to each other at all?" I myself believe that no consistent answer to this question is possible. Consciousness is a contradiction which consists in bringing together the poles of a contradiction. But without consciousness there could be no distinction between the person and a datum other than the person; no interface could ultimately be maintained. For that matter, without the distinction between person and datum there could be no consciousness of anything. If consciousness is a contradiction, let us not presume that it accordingly does not exist; it is only in a world in which all problems have been swept under the rug that there are no contradictions.

To get back to rhetoric, I have so far characterized it as the evoking and maintaining of consciousness insofar as consciousness is involved in communication. This characterization distinguishes rhetoric both from suggestion and from the aesthetic experience. The former is specifically not an evocation of consciousness, but a technique of getting a person to accept data in just the way that a machine accepts them. Suggestion attempts to dissolve the interface between person and datum. Aesthetic experience, on the other hand, does invite consciousness, but it is not consciousness arising à *propos* of an attempt to communicate.

An interface is a kind of wedge as well as a kind of bridge, and rhetoric is the technique of driving this wedge between a person and the data of his immediate experience. We have seen how the rhetoric of factual communication can drive it. Just as the data of sensuous experience can constitute a background from which the person is not separated, so can data in a more technical sense. The computer operator sits idly by while the machine spews forth page after page of numbers arranged in columns. To him, this flow of printed paper is just an aspect of the metabolism of a healthy machine. He takes it in, just as the machine itself has taken in the data on the punched cards fed to it. The user to whom the printed sheets are eventually handed may also merely take in the numbers. He may simply accept them as the machine accepts data. But he need not. A distance may be interposed between him and the numbers. The force that interposes it is the rhetoric of objective communication. The source of this rhetoric, as we have already seen, is in the user himself. He has an idea what the numbers ought to be like, and if they fail to conform to his idea, he suddenly begins to view them with suspicion. If he does, his consciousness of the numbers has been evoked by his own previous state; he has moved himself. Objective data are communicated, of course, by other persons as well as by machines. In both cases, the sole source of the rhetoric required to evoke consciousness in the recipient is the recipient himself. The fact that the person who communicates the data does not engage in rhetoric in the act of communicating them — or at least does not properly do so if the communication is objective — has made it appear that no rhetoric at all is involved in objective communication. If it were not, however, communication would collapse into the mere acceptance of data à la machine.

A reflexive rhetoric of objective communication has not generally been recognized. It is perhaps more plausible, however, to characterize the irreflexive rhetoric that applies to the other domains of discourse in the same terms as those in which we have characterized the reflexive rhetoric. It, too, seeks to evoke and maintain consciousness — in this case, consciousness on the part of someone other than the user of the rhetoric. What is attacked by both the irreflexive rhetoric of belief and the irreflexive rhetoric of action is just unconsciousness in all its forms: unawareness, naive acceptance, shortsightedness, complacency, blind confidence, unquestioning conformity to habits of thought and action, or lack of appreciation of the personal qualities of a distinguished man. The senses have long been held to dull the mind, and the rhetoric of the Puritan is once again intended to evoke a heightened consciousness. Of course consciousness is a matter of relativity; he who is conscious of some things will perforce be unconscious of others. This is precisely why the use of rhetoric generates controversy. If I take the position that you are unconscious of the suffering and the waste of human lives in Viet Nam, you may find me unconscious of the moral issues that account for our country's being there.

I have neither the space nor the inclination to compare my conception of the nature of rhetoric with all the others that have been widely adopted. But it is surely incumbent upon me to compare it with the conception of rhetoric as the art of persuasion, since this has been by far most widely held. One of the shoals on which this conception continually threatens to founder is the distinction between the persuasion that is the legitimate concern of rhetoric and the persuasion that is not. Where shall we draw the line between subliminal stimulation, coercion at gunpoint, and brainwashing, on the one hand, and rhetorical persuasion on the other? I would argue that it is natural to draw the line in terms of the evocation of consciousness for purposes of communication. Subliminal stimulation deliberately avoids consciousness. The armed bandit evokes fear, not consciousness, although perhaps he incidentally communicates something in the process. Brainwashing depends upon a physiological deprivation. Although we may say that it *causes* a state of consciousness, it would be incorrect to hold that in *evokes* the state. Unless we are taking poetic liberties we do not say that A evokes B when A merely causes B. The wind does not evoke the slamming of the door.

If rhetoric is no more than the art of persuasion, we will have a difficult time convincing the rationalists and positivists that it is really necessary — we will have and indeed have had such difficulty throughout the centuries. When men see the truth, say the rationalists and positivists, they do not need to be persuaded of anything. Persuasion holds sway only in that twilight zone in which there is neither formal truth nor objective fact. But that zone will some day be abolished.

I think I have indicated how I would reply to the rationalist and the positivist. Rhetoric, in my view, permeates even formal truth and objective fact. Even in the utopian world envisaged by my interlocutors, people must still manage to remain conscious. If they do not, communication will become perfect and collapse into noncommunication, and there will no longer be a world at all — only a system comparable to a machine or system of machines.

This reply serves also to show why I regard rhetoric as an activity distinguishing man from the animals, and hence why it has a philosophical basis. Any effort to prove rhetoric unnecessary would already involve rhetoric — the rhetoric of factual communication, if not of exhortation. Another way of indicating the necessity of rhetoric is to point out that without it there can be no consciousness of fact or value, and hence no human experience at all. Rhetoric is necessary to man, and is unnecessary only if man is unnecessary.

Having shown *that* rhetoric has a philosophical basis, I turn to the question of *what* that basis is. I think that question can be disposed of quite briefly. For what could the philosophical basis of anything *be,* over and above the manner in which it is shown to have such a basis? The philosophical basis of rhetoric cannot be some objective situation external to and prior to rhetoric; for rhetoric would be required to make us conscious of this very situation. In philosophy, content is expressed by the very argument for the existence of the content. In arguing for the existence of a philosophical basis of rhetoric, I think I have revealed what that basis is, and I know no other way to reveal it.

XVIII.
Epilogue

I now want to indulge in some self-analysis. I want to try to describe the main changes that have taken place in my position from the time of "Philosophy and *Argumentum ad Hominem*" to that of "Rationality and Rhetoric in Philosophy," and to give some reasons for these changes. This is not an easy task, but there is in principle no reason why it should be harder for me than anyone else to understand the considerations that led me, from time to time, to revise my own point of view.

The causes of those changes in philosophical positions that are worth attending to are not likely to be natural events. If a person changes his mind about his philosophy merely as the result of a physical process such as growing older or becoming senile, we should not expect the change to be much of an improvement. At most it will seem an arbitrary shift from one viewpoint to another. The change is saved from arbitrariness only if it is a response to criticism rather than to some natural stimulus. Such criticism can come from the very thinker himself whose viewpoint is changing, or it can come from critics other than he. In my case, the relevant criticism stemmed from both these sources.

The criticism of a philosophical position may or may not take account of the presuppositions of that position. In my view, however, it cannot be valid unless it does. *Argumentum ad hominem,* which I have continued to regard as the only valid argument in philosophy, if any is valid, is precisely the criticism of a position in terms of its own presuppositions. Hence if I wish to exhibit the changes in my position as responses to valid criticism, it is important for me to exhibit the presuppositions of my position at various stages of its development.

The task of exhibiting some of these presuppositions has a strangely involuted character. For example, one of my presuppositions is precisely that philosophical criticism must take account of presuppositions. A criticism failing to do this would, in my terms, be at best an *argumentum ad rem;* i.e., an attempt to assess a philosophical position as true or false regardless of its presuppositions. I regard any such criticisms as invalid because I do not think there are any facts such that we can affirm that the position is true or false to these facts. Nor is it likely that we could judge it true or false on logical grounds alone. It is my belief — and a presupposition of my inquiry into philosophical argumentation — that a philosophical position can be true or false only insofar as it is true or false to its own presuppositions.

This presupposition of mine has been fairly stable during the course of the development of my views on argumentation and rhetoric. Other presuppositions have had briefer careers. One of these was the rationalism of my early writings. I supposed that the validity of certain philosophical arguments could be conclusively established. That could only have meant that I regarded validity as an objective property of these arguments, though not necessarily a property to be equated with formal validity. What I took this objective property to be is pretty clear. A valid philosophical argument, I supposed, asserted an inconsistency between a position and the presuppositions of that position.

Chief among the difficulties with my early notion of validity is the problem of securing agreement on the identification of inconsistencies. If I assert an inconsistency between a position taken by an opponent and the presuppositions of that position, how can I be sure that my opponent will acknowledge there to be an inconsistency where I see one? If the inconsistency had the status of a fact, he would of course have to acknowledge it just as one must sooner or later acknowledge any fact, but in this case my argument would be ad rem. If I am to maintain the ad hominem character of my own argument, I must be prepared to admit that what I call an inconsistency my opponent might not acknowledge to be an inconsistency at all. What are inconsistencies for him will depend upon his presuppositions.

The problem is a dilemma. Either the inconsistency I aim to exploit is a fact or it is not. If it is, my argument is ad rem, and I have violated my own principles of argumentation. If it is not, there is no assurance I can get my antagonist to agree with me that there is an inconsistency. Let us call this dilemma "The Consistency Problem."

Several papers in this volume are at least in part attempts to grapple with the Consistency Problem. These are "Argumentation and Inconsistency in Philosophy," " 'Philosophy and Argumentum ad Hominem' Revisited," and "Controversy and the Self." In "Truth, Communication, and Rhetoric in Philosophy," I declare that I do not see how the problem can be solved at all, and I switch to a different version of argumentum ad hominem, a version in which the problem does not arise because the argument is not regarded as attempting to exploit an inconsistency. But if the validity of a philosophical argument is defined in terms of inconsistency, it would seem that to get rid of the Consistency Problem is at the same time to get rid of the thesis that philosophical arguments can be valid. In fact, the role of validity in my thinking about philosophical arguments has undergone a profound change, the result of which is expressed in "Rationality and Rhetoric in Philosophy." Here I argue that the rationality of the philosophical enterprise is determined not by the validity of philosophical arguments, but by the philosopher's concern for validity. Validity, in other words, enters our understanding of the arguments of philosophers not as an objective property of those arguments, but as a regulative ideal.

If it had occurred to me at the beginning to consider why I was at all interested in the validity of philosophical arguments, I might sooner have grasped the regulative function of the idea of validity. At the periphery of my intellectual field of vision was what has been called "The Strife of Systems," the alleged fact that no philosophical system has ever reached conclusions not open to cogent challenge by other systems; hence that no progress has ever been made in philosophy. It would be easy to conclude from this situation that no argument promulgated by any system has ever been valid. The constructive arguments are invalid because rejected by the other systems; the negative arguments are invalid because ineffective against the claims they attack. The whole enterprise is a logomachy, a war of words in which the systems that have prevailed are merely those whose advocates have shouted the loudest.

One who accepts the picture I have just drawn as an accurate characterization of philosophy has no alternative except to regard the rise of philosophy as a strange aberration. Perhaps he will wish to study the Strife of Systems as a psychological or sociological phenomenon. But he will certainly eschew the acceptance of any of the warring systems themselves.

In my newfound idealism, however, I believed that the picture was not quite accurate. Even the psychological or sociological account, I supposed (and still suppose), must have philosophical presuppositions. There must be systems, even if it follows that there must be strife. And the necessity arises from no mere aberration. There must be systems because systems are authoritative expressions of the standards of thought, knowledge, and human association. Without them there are no standards at all. Philosophy is inescapable. So the problem is to see how systems can be understood as authoritative even though they are at war with one another.

I thought that an account of the validity of the arguments by which systems build themselves and attack one another would be a contribution to the solution of this problem. Indeed, I thought it would be more than just a contribution. For I was unable to see what any system amounted to over and above the argumentative fabric supporting it and distinguishing it from its rivals. To establish this fabric would be to establish the system.

But I probably went too far at the beginning in assuming that I needed to exhibit the validity of philosophical arguments as an objective property. It is sufficient, I now think, to characterize validity as a perennial concern of philosophers, a regulative ideal. The claim that philosophers are concerned with validity is probably sufficient to overcome the scepticism engendered by the Strife of Systems.

The rather long story I have just told of the origins of my concern with validity can be supplemented by a shorter one. I was, after all, using the phrase *argumentum ad hominem* to name my paradigm of philosophical argumentation. But the *argumentum ad hominem* has generally been regarded as an invalid argument. So I had to show how there could be valid cases of it. But of course I would not have been concerned to do this at all if I had not supposed that philosophical arguments can be valid in the first place.

To have made the claim that the validity of philosophical arguments is a regulative idea is one of two distinct ways in which I attempted to deal with the Consistency Problem. I have pointed out that this claim deals with the Consistency Problem by repudiating it altogether. I also attempted to solve the problem without repudiating it. A series of efforts of this kind eventuated in my theory of the self. I reasoned in the following way. The critic of an alien philosophical position is locked into his own view of the nature of inconsistency. But as a critic he must be able to take the view of his opponent. For it must be possible for him to foresee the effect of his own criticisms. This means that he must somehow be able to grasp his opponent's view of the nature of inconsistency. In other words he must occupy both his point of view and that of his opponent. This feat is itself inconsistent, for it entails that the critic both occupy his own point of view and not occupy it. The self emerges as the perspective from which the poles of this contradiction are seen as juxtaposed. From this perspective the adoption of two inconsistent views of the nature of inconsistency is no mere schizophrenic alternation of the views. It is a burden. The self takes up this burden.

In "Some Reflections on Argumentation," the concept of "risk," rather than "burden," is emphasized, and I am not wholly concerned there with *philosophical* argumentation. But the paper can easily be recognized as a precursor of later writings on the self.

I have talked so far about inconsistency of two kinds: the inconsistency of a philosophical position with its presuppositions, and the inconsistency of different views of the nature of the inconsistency of a philosophical position with its presuppositions. It is now necessary to bring up an inconsistency of a third sort. For I want to say that I am not sure that my attempt to grapple with the Consistency Problem via a theory of the self is consistent with my attempt to grapple with it via the thesis that validity is a regulative idea. For the former attempt is an attempt to solve the problem while the latter repudiates it.

But let me examine in greater detail this latter attempt. It has wider implications than I have so far suggested. Once we abandon the search for objective conditions under which a philosophical argument can be valid, we must listen to the claim that rhetoric has a legitimate role to play in philosophical argumentation. For it is only when validity satisfies objective conditions that we can clearly distinguish a valid argument from one having a primarily rhetorical function. We can argue, as in "The Relevance of Rhetoric to Philosophy and of Philosophy to Rhetoric," that the *point* of a philosophical argument is something entirely different from persuasion, even though the argument may happen also to be persuasive.

Yet that article, in fact, has already moved far beyond the position stated in "Persuasion and Validity in Philosophy" in the direction of seeing the legitimacy of rhetorical activity. In the earlier paper I presupposed that it is never necessary to use rhetoric. I regarded rhetoric as a particular set of techniques available for use when we wish to act unilaterally on people. But I thought that such unilateral action not only was in principle always avoidable but also that it ought to be avoided. In the spirit of my early rationalism, I was taking a Kantian view of the morality of argumentation. I saw the use of rhetorical techniques as the response to a hypothetical imperative: "If you want people to do or believe X, argue in such-and-such a way." But the categorical imperative, the only one dictating arguments of moral worth, was the universalization of the maxim to argue not persuasively but validly. Such argumentation is intrinsically bilateral.

"The Relevance of Rhetoric to Philosophy and of Philosophy to Rhetoric" has moved beyond the position taken in "Persuasion and Validity in Philosophy" in that it declares the necessity of rhetoric. Man, I here aver, is a persuading and persuaded animal. But I still distinguish sharply between rhetoric and philosophical argumentation; and it is the model of objective validity on which I base this distinction.

But I begin to feel that in excluding rhetorical activity from the philosophical enterprise I have somehow misrepresented the latter. (Is this feeling ultimately an appeal to facts? I would not in any event be able to enumerate the facts I appeal to.) Yet I do want to continue excluding unilateral persuasion — if such a phenomenon ever occurs — from the philosophical enterprise. So a shift occurs in my understanding of "rhetoric." My conception of it broadens to embrace what I call "Evocation," and in the paper "Rhetoric and Communication in Philosophy," I claim that philosophy properly has an evocative function. In "Truth, Communication, and Rhetoric in Philosophy," I say that the *argumentum ad hominem* in philosophy is precisely the exercise of that function. Philosophical argumentation evokes by addressing the man where he lives, not by hitting him over the head with facts.

What is it that philosophical argumentation evokes? In "Rhetoric and Communication in Philosophy" I began by taking the line that it evokes memory. It recalls to us our authentic language or mode of being. Such evocation is necessary, I claimed, when the one to whom it is addressed is confused. He may not at first admit his confusion, but he shows it in alienated attitudes that neglect or distort his linguistic or ontological roots.

When, at the end of this paper, I began referring to this confusion as "a loss of morale," I was probably generalizing it a little. I was thinking of morale as both perception and acceptance of one's place in the world and the purposes of one's life. To have morale is to be clear about the standards in terms of which one controls one's own thought and conduct. Loss of morale is either confusion about what standards to accept or else ignorance of the very possibility of living with assurance and clarity.

At this point I had recovered something of my own past. For I had first heard of the morale function of philosophy from those colleagues at Williams College who so long ago had launched me on my study of philosophical argumentation. They had characterized the great systems — Spiritualism, Naturalism, Idealism, Realism, Pragmatism, as *loci* of morale, as sources of the standards in terms of which a person can contol himself.

I have suggested that the sequence of ideas of which I am now describing one stage diverges fairly sharply from the sequence that eventuated in my theory of the self. That theory was an attempt to solve the Consistency Problem, while the developments I am now discussing presuppose the repudiation of that problem. And yet evocation is clearly concerned with the self in some sense of that word. It is an appeal to the true self, and an attempt to put a person in charge of himself. This sense of "self" emphasizes the reflexivity of the self. The self is seen here as a relation to itself — it arises as self-knowledge and self-control. But there is another emphasis in the sense of "self" I proposed in order to try to solve the Consistency Problem. That emphasis is on tension and sometimes opacity. The self arises to accept a burden; its genesis is a step back from the transparency of immediate experience.

But evocation and morale cannot be the final story. We need assurance that genuine morale cannot arise from an evil inspiration. Morale of a sort is, after all, what Faust bought from the devil. In searching for such assurance, furthermore, we must avoid appealing to the idea of validity; for that would plunge us back to the beginning of the path we have already trodden. In "Rationality and Rhetoric in Philosophy" I try to form such assurances in terms of a self-perpetuating rhetoric that criticizes *con amore*. Both of these conditions on the rhetoric of philosophical argumentation seem to me to guarantee the eventual elimination of morale based upon evil inspiration.

For those put off by "a self-perpetuating rhetoric that criticizes *con amore*," however, there is one other attempt that might be made to solve the Consistency Problem *ab initio*. This attempt assumes an organic view of society, perhaps a Platonic or Instrumentalist view, according to which the individual is an abstraction and what is concrete or real is the social tissue from which the individual is abstracted. According to this position, there is no "problem of other minds." Because you and I belong to the same social tissue, we have only to recover something of our primordial unity in order to have direct access to each other's mental content. Such recovery can take the form of what is called "empathy." But if I can empathetically insert myself into your mind, I can perceive directly what criterion of inconsistency will be operative for you if I am to attack you ad hominem.

What seems to foreclose this attempt to solve the Consistency Problem, however, is that it repudiates the very Strife of Systems which gave rise in the first place to the need for a distinction between valid and invalid arguments. For if people are not radically cut off from one another, then their philosophical positions cannot be in radical disagreement. Any apparent strife among systems can be overcome through a perspicacious use of empathy.

"Rationality and Rhetoric in Philosophy" is followed by "The Philosophical Basis of Rhetoric" which, although chronologically earlier, claims a position here because it can be taken to be a final statement regarding the nature of rhetoric in general (not just its role in philosophical argumentation). During the past ten years I have seen no reason to retract or revise my view that rhetoric is fundamentally a wedge between a percipient and an object of perception.

It remains to say a word about the papers in this volume that are primarily critical of the works of others. These are "Self-Refutation and Validity" (a criticism of Passmore) and the three reviews of Perelman, one including an account of a book by Crawshay-Williams. The Passmore review helps me to develop the early version of argumentum ad hominem, extending the range of this argument into the domain of the presuppositions of language. But it does not represent any basic change in my position, nor do the Perelman reviews. They serve as a bass continuo to the melodies that are weaving themselves in the upper registers. For here is a constant story which I have always been criticizing, even though my criticisms have taken many and sometimes inconsistent forms.

There is a final question which I cannot answer. One important use of a valid argumentum ad hominem is to demand that an account of the nature of philosophy be an example of itself — that it be consistent with its own presuppositions. I do not know, however, whether my claim that philosophy must be evocative is itself evocative. I am not sure that my insistence that philosophical criticism be carried out con amore is itself con amore. Nor am I even convinced that I ought to be held responsible for such self-instantiation.

Selected Bibliography

I. Books and Further Articles of Mine Relating to
Rhetoric and Philosophical Argument

A. Books

Philosophy and Argument. University Park: The Pennsylvania State
University Press, 1959.

The Problem of the Self. University Park: The Pennsylvania State
University Press, 1970.

Philosophy, Rhetoric, and Argumentation (with Maurice Natanson).
University Park: The Pennsylvania State University Press, 1965.

B. Articles

"The Methods of Philosophical Polemic." *Methodos* (Milan), 5
(1953): 131-140.

"Cause, Implication, and Dialectic." *Philosophy and Phenomenological Research,* 14 (1954): 400-404.

"The Nature of Philosophical Controversy." *The Journal of
Philosophy,* 51 (1954): 294-300.

"Some Aspects of Philosophical Disagreement." *Dialectica* (Zürich),
8 (1954): 245-257.

"The Logical Powerfulness of Philosophical Arguments." *Mind* (Oxford), 64 (1955): 539-541.

"Scepticism and Dialectic." *Entretiens Philosophiques d'Athènes,*
2-6 April, 1955 (no date of publication given), pp. 156-160.

"Hume's Arguments Concerning Causal Necessity." *Philosophy and
Phenomenological Research,* 16 (1956): 331-340.

"Argument and Truth in Philosophy." *Philosophy and
Phenomenological Research,* 18 (1957): 228-236.

"Systèmes Formels et Systèmes Ontologiques." *Logique et Analyse*
(Brussels), 1 (1958): 24-27.

"The Law of Non-Contradiction." *Logique et Analyse,* 3 (1960): 3-10.

"Theory of Argumentation." In *Contemporary Philosophy.* Florence:
La Nuova Italia Editrice, 1968, pp. 177-184.

"Some Trends in Rhetorical Theory." In *The Prospect in Rhetoric,*
Bitzer and Black, eds. Prentice-Hall Publishing Co., 1971, pp. 78-90.

"Reason Limited." In *Essays in Philosophy.* University Park: The
Pennsylvania State University Press, 1962, pp. 115-132.

"De la vérité en Métaphysique." *Actes du XIIᵉ Congrès des Sociétés
de Philosophie de Langue Française.* Louvain: Nauwelaerts,
1964, pp. 33-36.

"Controversy and Selfhood." *Journal of General Education,* 19
(1967): 48-56.

"The Categorio-Centric Predicament." *Southern Journal of
Philosophy,* 4 (1966): 207-220.

"From Philosophy to Rhetoric and Back." In *Rhetoric, Philosophy,
and Literature: An Exploration,* Don M. Burks, ed. West Lafayette:
Purdue University Press, 1978 (forthcoming).

"Rhetoric and Death." In *Rhetoric in Transition: Some Points of
Focus,* Eugene White, ed., University Park: The Pennsylvania State
University Press, 1978 (forthcoming).

II. **Writings Concerned Wholly or Partly with My Views**

Rorty, Richard. "Recent Metaphilosophy." *The Review of Metaphysics,* 15 (1961): 299-318.

Natanson, Maurice. "Rhetoric and Philosophical Argumentation." *The Quarterly Journal of Speech,* 48 (1962): 24-30.

Burkholder, Peter M. "*Petitio* in the Strife of Systems." *Tulane Studies in Philosophy,* 16 (1967): 19-31.

Zaner, Richard. "Philosophy and Rhetoric: A Critical Discussion." *Philosophy and Rhetoric,* 1 (1968): 61-77. (My reply, 165-167.)

Pieretti, Antonio. "Argomentazione e filosofia in Johnstone." *Proteus,* 1 (1970): 143-160.

Benfield, David W. "Johnstone on the Truth of Philosophical Statements." *Philosophy and Phenomenological Research,* 32 (1971): 96-102. (My reply, 103-104.)

Anderson, John R. "The Audience as a Concept in the Philosophic Rhetoric of Perelman, Johnstone, and Natanson." *The Southern Speech Communication Journal,* 38 (1972): 39-50.

Carleton, Walter M. "Theory Transformation in Communication: The Case of Henry Johnstone." *The Quarterly Journal of Speech,* 6 (1975): 76-88. (My reply, 89-91.)

Barth, E.M., and Martens, J.L. "Argumentum ad Hominem: From Chaos to Formal Dialectic." *Logique et Analyse,* 20 (1977): 76-96.

In addition, the following doctoral dissertations have been concerned in part with my views:

Hockenos, Warren J. "An Examination of *Reductio ad Absurdum* and *Argumentum ad Hominem* Arguments in the Philosophies of Gilbert Ryle and Henry W. Johnstone, Jr." Boston University, 1968.

Casey, John F. "Refutation and Argument in Philosophy: A Metaphilosophical Inquiry." Fordam University, 1975.

LeFevre, Joseph C. "Philosophical Commitment and the Given: A Study in Speculative Philosophy." Tulane University, 1976.

III. **Some Important Books and Articles on Rhetoric and Philosophical Argument by Other Recent Writers**

Rogge, Eberhard. *Axiomatik alles möglichen Philosophierens: Das grundsätzliche Sprechen der Logistik, der Sprachkritik und der Lebens-Metaphysik.* Meisenheim: Westkulturverlag, 1950.

Weil, Eric. *Logique de la Philosophie.* Paris: Vrin, 1950.

Waismann, Friedrich. "How I See Philosophy." In *Contemporary British Philosophy: Personal Statements.* H.D. Lewis, ed. London: George Allen and Unwin, 1956, pp. 447-490.

Crawshay-Williams, Rupert. *Methods and Criteria of Reasoning: An Inquiry Into the Structure of Controversy.* New York: Humanities Press, 1957.

Williams, B.A.O. "Metaphysical Arguments." In *The Nature of Metaphysics.* D.F. Pears, ed. London: Macmillan, 1957, pp. 39-60.

Toulmin, Stephen E. *The Uses of Argument.* Cambridge: At the University Press, 1958.

Ryle, Gilbert. "Philosophical Arguments." In *Logical Positivism*. A. J. Ayer, ed. Glencoe, Ill.: Free Press, 1959, pp. 327-344.

Hall, Everett W. *Philosophical Systems*. Chicago: University of Chicago Press, 1960.

Passmore, John. *Philosophical Reasoning*. New York: Charles Scribner's Sons, 1961.

Gallie, W.B. "Essentially Contested Concepts." In *The Importance of Language*. Max Black, ed. Englewood Cliffs, N.J.: Prentice-Hall, 1962, pp. 121-146.

Perelman, Ch., and Olbrechts-Tyteca, L. *The New Rhetoric, A Treatise on Argumentation*. Wilkinson and Weaver, trans. Notre Dame: University of Notre Dame Press, 1969.

Lange, John. *The Cognitivity Paradox, An Inquiry Concerning the Claims of Philosophy*. Princeton: The Princeton University Press, 1970.

Boyle, Joseph M., Jr. "Self-Referential Inconsistency, Inevitable Falsity and Metaphysical Argumentation." *Metaphilosophy*, 3 (1972): 25-42.

Rescher, Nicholas. *Dialectics, A Controversy-Oriented Approach to the Theory of Knowledge*. Albany: State University of New York Press, 1977.

In addition, the following articles in *Philosophy and Rhetoric* are directly relevant:

Bitzer, Lloyd. "The Rhetorical Situation." 1 (1968): 1-14.

Arnold, Carroll C. "Oral Rhetoric, Rhetoric, and Literature." 1 (1968): 191-210.

Bywater, William G., Jr. "Argumentation and Persuasion in Philosophy." 2 (1969): 167-177.

Schouls, Peter A. "Communication, Argumentation, and Presupposition in Philosophy." 2 (1969):185-199.

McNally, James R. "Toward a Definition of Rhetoric." 3 (1970): 71-81.

Wilkerson, K.E. "On Evaluating Theories of Rhetoric." 3 (1970): 82-96.

Campbell, Karlyn K. "The Ontological Foundations of Rhetorical Theory." 3 (1970): 97-108.

Burks, Don M. "Persuasion, Self-Persuasion, and Rhetorical Discourse." 3 (1970): 109-119.

Apostel, Leo. "Assertion Logic and Theory of Argumentation." 4 (1971): 92-110.

Schouls, Peter A. "Reason, Semantics, and Argumentation in Philosophy." 4 (1971): 124-131.

Rotenstreich, Nathan. "Argumentation and Philosophical Clarification." 5 (1972): 12-23.

Iseminger, Gary. "Successful Argument and Rational Belief." 7 (1974): 47-57.

Burke, Richard. "Rhetoric, Dialectic, and Force." 7 (1974): 154-165.

Kruger, Arthur N. "The Nature of Controversial Statements." 8 (1975): 137-158.

Grassi, Ernesto. "Rhetoric and Philosophy." 9 (1976): 200-216.

Kekes, John. "Essentially Contested Concepts: A Reconsideration." 10 (1977): 71-89.

Finocchiaro, Maurice A. "Logic and Rhetoric in Lavoisier's Sealed Note: Toward a Rhetoric of Science." 10 (1977): 111-122.

INDEX

DATE DUE

5 27 '82	
ret 8/12/85	
8 26 '86	

BRODART, INC.   Cat. No. 23-221